CONFRONTING THE CHAOS

sean m. maloney

CONFRONTING THE

a rogue
military historian
returns to
afghanistan

naval institute press
annapolis, maryland

Naval Institute Press
291 Wood Road
Annapolis, MD 21402

Library of Congress Cataloging-in-Publication Data
Maloney, Sean M., 1967-
  Confronting the chaos : a rogue military historian returns to Afghanistan / Sean M. Maloney.
    p. cm.
  Includes bibliographical references and index.
  ISBN 978-1-59114-508-0 (acid-free paper) 1. Afghan War, 2001- 2. Afghan War,
2001—Civilian relief. 3. Postwar reconstruction—Afghanistan. 4. Humanitarian assistance—
Afghanistan. I. Title.
  DS371.412.M34 2009
  958.104'7—dc22

                                                                    2009009078

Printed in the United States of America on acid-free paper

14 13 12 11 10 09   9 8 7 6 5 4 3 2
First printing

All photos were taken by the author except where otherwise credited.

Dr. Shawn Cafferky, friend, colleague, and fellow motorcyclist, died the day I submitted the final manuscript for publication. This one's for you, Shawn.

Four wheels move the body. Two wheels move the soul.

—AUTHOR UNKNOWN

contents

acknowledgments

I'll skip the usual and predictable intro to this section whereby the author humbly acknowledges debts both great and small and begs forgiveness for any potential misunderstandings. Of all the people who assisted, I would like to thank Lieutenant General Andy Leslie for the unstinting support he has given me over the past five years in my quest to document the latest war in Afghanistan and the role of coalition forces in it. He and his staff(s) overcame numerous bureaucratic and personality-based obstacles time and again on my behalf, and I thank them for their efforts, which led to this book and its sequel. They understood what I was trying to accomplish and accommodated how I do business—especially when it came to fieldwork. I would also like to acknowledge Major General Doug Dempster and Major General Mike Ward in this regard, who also assisted in numerous ways and means.

For the 2004 trip, some of those obstacles could not be overcome, particularly when a skittish LEGAD at Camp Julien insisted that civilians couldn't go on patrol with Canadians—even though I was a Department of National Defence employee and the Ombudsman and the Minister of National Defence, who are incidentally also civilians, accompanied Canadian troops in Kabul. There were other obstacles/ people at Camp Julien who aren't worth mentioning. As a result, I directed my efforts into examining the German PRT contribution instead of the Canadian ISAF contribution in Kabul. I would like to thank in particular Lieutenant General Johann-Georg Dora for approving of my trip to RC (North) and my *alt Kamarad* Oberst Uli Scholtz for facilitating that approval. Others who enthusiastically helped bypass the stupidity I encountered in Kabul (in many cases, with some relish) included Ambassador Chris Alexander; Colonel Dave Banks; Dr. Nipa Bannerjee; Colonel Randy Brooks; Lieutenant Colonel Scotty Macdougal; Major Jim Fitzgerald; Major Brian Hynes and his ETTs; Major Trevor MacCauley; Captain Eghtedar Manouchehri; Captain Brian Roach; Captain John Cochrane;

and last, but not least, our American driver/bodyguard, Cpl. Billy Groseclose. At ISAF HQ, I'd also like to thank Major P. Mireaux and Colonel Jacques Pierquin, both of the French army.

The German contingents in Konduz and Feyzabad were most hospitable, again in complete contrast to the staff at Camp Julien. *Vielen Danke* to Oberst Reinhardt Barz; Oberstleutnant Bokelman; Oberstabsfeldwebel Christian Kaiser; Thomas Shultze; Oberstleutnant Michael Meyer; Hauptmann Helmar Koch; and Oberstleutnant Rainer Stadelmann. It was a pleasure to encounter Oberstleutnant Matthias Reibold again, this time leading his men in the field.

I experienced no obstacles when visiting Task Force Kandahar and the Provincial Reconstruction Team in Kandahar in 2005. Lieutenant Colonel Dave Anderson and Colonel Steve Noonan at TFK and Colonel Steve Bowes and their staffs afforded me willing and open access into all activities "down south," and I remain duly impressed with their interest in my activities and their assistance.

The list of people at the PRT who need to be thanked is a long one and in no particular order: Captain Derek Gilchrist; Niki Palmer; Lieutenant Colonel Steve Borland; Warrant Officer Dan Hitchcock; Regimental Sergeant Major Ward Brown; Company Sergeant Major Billy Boland; Corporal Adam de Bartok; Corporal Tim Northcotte; Sergeant Sue Coupal; Corporal Loralai Corsiato; Glyn Berry; Erin Doregan; Phoenix from USAID; Matthijs Toot; Michael Callan; Major Sanchez King; Sergeant Chuck Cote; Sergeant Chris Thombs; Master Corporal Keith Smith; Private Dan Cote; Sergeant Reg Obas; Yusuf Zoi; Lieutenant Andy Bone; Master Corporal Keith Porteus; Private Sarah Keller; Private "Dutch" Vandermeulan; Sergeant Jamie Bradley; Captain A. J. Lutes; Sergeant Clayton Schoepp; Superintendent Wayne Martin and Corporal Bob Hart of the RCMP; Master Corporal Joe Dupuy; Sergeant Ken Lockie; and Warrant Officer Gavley.

I would especially like to thank all of our interpreters, including Habib, Niaz, Sammi, Aktar, and The Mullah. We couldn't do it without you.

Too many authors overuse the phrase "I would be remiss if . . . " Forget it. Colonel Mike Capstick: you had an awesomely talented and hospitable team at SAT-A during your tenure in Kabul, and it was an enlightening experience learning about the ins and outs of the Kabuli political scene from them. Thanks to all, particularly Lieutenant Colonel Christian Drouin; Major Duart Townshend; Lieutenant Commander Albert Wong; Commander Mark Chupik; Major James McKay; Dr. Elizabeth Speed; Andy Tamas; and Wu-Tan. I need to thank D.T. and J.M. once again for driving me to the doc in the dark of the night down Route Violence. Why *was* the road trafficless at that hour of the morning, exactly? And what *was* that car doing on its side in the middle of the road surrounded by what looked like police? They both deserve the Medal of Clueless Heroism (we found out about the IED THREATWARN much, much later . . .). I would also like to thank Ahmad for introducing me to the haunting music of Ahmad Zahir.

I would also like to thank a number of people from the Canadian OGDs who provided me with extremely frank commentary on their parent agencies' failings in Kabul and in Ottawa—they must remain anonymous to avoid bureaucratic retaliation and harassment by superior but lesser individuals.

Similarly there are numerous members of the intelligence and special operations communities that helped me from time to time by providing insights into the shadow world. They obviously cannot be named, but their labors have not been in vain.

As usual, all opinions I express herein are my own and don't necessarily represent the opinions of the Canadian government or the Department of National Defence. Blah, blah, blah. They *definitely* don't represent the opinions of any national government, other government department or agency of the Canadian government, or NATO, etc., etc.

introduction

Why are your governments, especially those of Britain, France, Italy,
Canada, Germany, and Australia, allying themselves with America
in its attacks against us in Afghanistan?
—Osama bin Laden

We're going to wish this was the Balkans.
—Condoleezza Rice

It was December 2005, and we were coming close to the fifth year of the war in Afghanistan. The U.S. Army CH-47 Chinook flared slightly and hovered as it came into Kandahar Airfield. The huge rotors beat the air with a sharp "whup-whup-whup" that sent mini shock waves through the air. An armored Mercedes jeep, called a "G-Wagon," or at least the tattered remains of it, was slung underneath. The vehicle had been recovered from the field in a remote district of Kandahar province in order to prevent its exploitation by the enemy. An improvised explosive device had detonated and completely shorn off the front of the vehicle. The wheels were gone. The blast's shock wave penetrated the crew compartment and shattered the legs of the driver and codriver, who both miraculously survived thanks to the efforts of the medics and the on-call medevac UH-60 Black Hawk crew.

The G-Wagon and its Canadian crew were members of the Provincial Reconstruction Team (PRT) operating from Kandahar City, the capital of Kandahar province. They were not part of an elite special operations forces "door-kicking" special missions unit, nor were they part of a traditional combat unit jumping out of helicopters in the hills to root out the elusive Taliban. The PRT is a wholly new weapon in the counterinsurgency war against the Taliban and its supporters. It is a unit that combines the vital tasks of rural area assessment, reconstruction aid delivery, security sector reform, and government capacity building. The coalition can fight the Taliban with combat forces all it likes: without a government and the services that a government delivers to its citizens, the whole effort becomes pointless over the long term. The question is, how, exactly, do you stabilize a country that has seen near-continuous war for twenty-plus years? It is not a matter of long-term "peacekeeping" or short-term "humanitarian aid." Stabilization operations sit on the conflict spectrum somewhere between those operations and counterinsurgency operations. Indeed, coalition operations in Afghanistan between 2003 and 2005 had attributes of both stabilization and counterinsurgency.

Overshadowed by the war in Iraq, forced to operate as a secondary theater of operations, and denied adequate resources, the forces of Operation Enduring Freedom (OEF) and the International Security Assistance Force (ISAF) labored, fought, and bled in near obscurity in Afghanistan from 2003 to 2005. The West's first victory over the Al Qaeda movement was smacked down in the backlash fury of left-wing critics of American policy in Iraq and called into question for domestic political purposes in the United States during a major federal election. Indeed, some people began to even conflate the two very different conflicts: Afghanistan was, it seemed, merely an eastern extension of Iraq. It was, after all, all dun-colored, full of violent, nasty people, and "over there, somewhere" near the Arabian Gulf.

This disinterest, this simplicity, is patently unfair to the Afghan people and particularly to those who have traveled to their country to assist them. The disinterest has obscured what is thus far the most important campaign in the larger war against the Al Qaeda movement, the lessons of which need to be understood as they are and will be applicable elsewhere. It is one thing to take down a country; it is quite another to bring it back up. These labors of Hercules are readily ignored by the media and assailed by the critics; they lack the "excitement" of terrorist decapitations broadcast on the Internet, the Paris Hilton sex video, or Madonna's African adoption. *Confronting the Chaos* is less concerned with combat and focuses on the incredibly important noncombative aspects of the counterinsurgency campaign. Indeed, it is these aspects that will determine whether we will succeed in Afghanistan. The enemy understands this and has directed significant amounts of violence against the aid and construction efforts. PRT operations, as *Confronting the Chaos* demonstrates, are not risk-free.

The war in Afghanistan has progressed through several discrete phases since 2001. Essentially, there was a proxy war whereby the United States supported the Northern Alliance to take down the Taliban shield, while another campaign superimposed on the proxy war hunted out Al Qaeda's leadership, destroyed its infrastructure, and killed or otherwise dispersed its personnel. These operations continued into 2002 as the last Taliban/Al Qaeda strongholds were reduced. The next phase, which lasted from mid-2002 to the end of 2003, consisted of the first stumbling steps of the initial stabilization efforts; the prequel to this book, *Enduring the Freedom,* describes events during that time.

Confronting the Chaos covers the subsequent 2004–5 phase. During this period, OEF and ISAF successfully prevented a civil war among the victorious anti-Taliban Afghan groups and continued to keep the emergent Al Qaeda–supported Taliban insurgency at bay, which led to countrywide democratic elections certified by the United Nations. Later on during this period, the slow stabilization efforts were starting to bear fruit in the outer provinces of the country, but this progress was accompanied by a sharp increase in insurgent activity as the Taliban and its allies started to recover from the shocks of 2001–2 .

Confronting the Chaos, like its prequel, is structured as a travelogue. Each trip, each meeting, is a piece of the puzzle necessary to understand the counterinsurgency effort, and the intent is for the reader to put those pieces together to discern the picture that emerges. It is not and cannot be a detailed treatment of each activity. At the same time, the reader can appreciate the atmospherics of the Afghanistan Zeitgeist in 2004–5.

During these trips, I observed ISAF and OEF stabilization efforts in Kabul and the Embedded Training Teams (ETTs) with the Afghan National Army (ANA); met with the Strategic Advisory Team–Afghanistan (SAT-A); watched the emergence of the German ISAF Provincial Reconstruction Teams located in Konduz and Feyzabad (northern Afghanistan); and participated in operations conducted by the Canadian-led Provincial Reconstruction Team that was supporting an American infantry brigade in Kandahar province (southern Afghanistan). *Confronting the Chaos* will take you into the Augean Stables of these efforts and introduce to you the courageous men and women who risk their lives day in and day out to help the Afghan people make their world a better place and at the same time deny the Taliban and Al Qaeda the victory they so crave. As one OEF officer said to me in a discussion of how long we would be in the country, "You want us to get out of Afghanistan? Go see what the PRTs do."

Note: *Confronting the Chaos* is the second book in a trilogy dealing with my experiences in Afghanistan. The third book in the series, *Fighting for Afghanistan: A Rogue Historian at War,* will relate the story of my journey to Afghanistan in 2006 to observe the operations of a combined American, British, Canadian, and Dutch brigade. During that journey, I came close to being killed or injured on numerous occasions, and circumstances put me in the position to be the first

Canadian military historian to go into combat with Canadian troops since at least the Korean War. *Confronting the Chaos*, however, is an important lead-in to that story, particularly the sections dealing with operations in Kandahar province and that province's political, cultural, and social context. Note also that the dialogue between me and other people in this book is approximate, so apologies in advance to all if it isn't exact. I'd say it's 80 to 90 percent there, but time does have a way of tampering with fidelity.

the war in afghanistan, 2003–4

The president won't want to use troops to rebuild Afghanistan.
—ANDREW H. CARD JR., WHITE HOUSE CHIEF OF STAFF, 2001

the strategic context

Coalition military operations in Afghanistan are part of a global effort to confront the Al Qaeda movement and any group that chooses to affiliate with it. Operation Enduring Freedom was the first of these operations: this mission removed the Taliban regime shielding Al Qaeda in Afghanistan and then destroyed the Al Qaeda terrorist infrastructure in the country, forcing its leadership to flee and reconstitute its efforts elsewhere. Subsequently Operation Enduring Freedom–Philippines assisted the Filipino government in combating radical Islamist guerrillas on the southern islands of their archipelago. Joint Task Force Horn of Africa, based in Djibouti, conducted operations in Yemen, Ethiopia, Eritrea, Kenya, and Somalia in an effort to deny Al Qaeda sanctuary in that region. A low-profile American mission in Mali called the Trans-Sahara Counterterrorism Initiative (also known as OEF-Trans-Sahara, or OEF-TS) and Operation Enduring Freedom–Chad were also part of the effort to counter the spread of Al Qaeda influence in Africa in 2004–5.

Though originally designed to take down the Hussein regime, Operation Iraqi Freedom became part of the anti–Al Qaeda effort after 2003. The discovery of Al Qaeda cells working amid the chaos of post-Hussein Iraq and the prominently brutal tactics employed by Abu Musab al-Zarqawi quickly became the centerpiece for American efforts owing to the sheer number of forces involved and the dramatic upsurge in violence in Iraq, which had the potential to affect the region. The influx of foreign jihadists only confirms the fact that OIF is now a primary theater of operations in the Al Qaeda war.[1]

Al Qaeda did evolve to meet the challenge posed by the United States and its allies after 2001–2. More emphasis was placed on conducting terrorist "spectaculars" in London and Madrid and then linking them to coalition operations in Iraq and Afghanistan. There was also increased Al Qaeda global recruitment in order to pin down and bleed coalition forces in Iraq. Keep in mind that the war against Al Qaeda is as psychological as it is physical. Terrain and geography aren't the only battlegrounds. Cyberspace, demographics, the will to fight, and perceptions of the threat are all just as important. Western countries fighting in Afghanistan and Iraq, especially Spain, quickly learned that there was linkage between these factors. It wasn't all "over there somewhere."

The main American effort in the global conflict, therefore, is in Iraq, while the U.S.-led African and Asian operations are designed to preempt enemy attempts to influence those regions. So where does Afghanistan fit? Afghanistan is the first victory over Al Qaeda, and the military operations conducted there in 2004–5 were designed to consolidate that victory. The indecision in the American and European policy worlds as to what international organization would handle the consolidation is the background to *Confronting the Chaos*. The Taliban and Gulbiddin Hekmatyar's HiG (Hezb-e-Islami Gulbiddin) organization made common cause with Al Qaeda: their objective is the ejection of the international community from Afghanistan. In effect, Afghanistan became the forgotten war, but one that has equal importance to the war in Iraq because of the large-scale psychological consequences of losing it and its linkages to Osama bin Laden's insistence that anti-Islamist forces cannot win in Afghanistan because nobody ever has. Allegedly.

the situation in 2003

In 2003 international forces in Afghanistan were part of one of two organizations. The American-led Operation Enduring Freedom deployed 18,000 personnel from some twenty-one countries. Its task was to hunt and destroy the remnants of the Taliban regime and ensure that Al Qaeda was incapable of using Afghanistan as a base for international terrorism. The International Security Assistance Force (ISAF) was a UN-mandated but European-led force that had about 4,500 personnel. Initially confined to Kabul, its mission was limited to assisting the Afghan Transitional Administration achieve some level of security in the capital. Both organizations would change dramatically throughout 2003–4, and it is that process that is the context to the first part of *Confronting the Chaos*. Both military organizations had to evolve to handle the rapidly changing political environment in Afghanistan. Enemy activity—Taliban, Al Qaeda, and HiG—came to be more and more associated with attempts to alter that political environment, much more so than it had in 2002–3. Indeed, this was a period of transition for the enemy, in that its activity shifted from mere survival in the face of OEF's onslaught to a steadily building and sophisticated insurgency.

The groundwork for that insurgency was established back in 2002, but OEF operations in 2002 and 2003 kept the Taliban and its allies off balance. In February 2002 propaganda leaflets extolling resistance were posted by the Taliban and Al Qaeda in public places throughout Helmand and Kandahar provinces while Mullah Omar directed that weapons be dispersed for future use against coalition forces. In March Mullah Omar and Mullah Osmani started to broadcast propaganda from a mobile transmitter, while weapons were distributed in Oruzgan and northern Kandahar. Recruiting in the Pakistani madrassas was dramatically stepped up in Pakistan by the end of 2003 and training camps reopened in early 2003. At this time, Mullah Omar directed the infiltration of small groups into interior provinces to serve as cadres for the projected insurgency effort. Limited attacks, mostly in the border areas, were conducted in 2003, but in practically every case they resulted in the destruction of the attacking forces by OEF. Major terrorist attacks in urban areas were initiated in 2003 but their numbers were small and the effect was marginal. This would all change over the course of the next two years.[2]

operation enduring freedom: 2003–4

OEF in 2003 was commanded by Combined Joint Task Force 180 (CJTF-180), a corps-level headquarters commanding an enlarged infantry brigade, a smaller mini brigade, a Combined Joint Special Operations Task Force, and all the helicopters and tactical airlift elements associated with supporting the OEF mission inside Afghanistan. In the fall of 2003, Combined Task Force DEVIL, the brigade headquarters located in Kandahar,[3] transferred command authority to CTF WARRIOR, a brigade headquarters from the 10th Mountain Division. At this time, command of CJTF-180 was taken over by an organization based on the divisional headquarters from the 10th Mountain. The aviation elements were grouped in Task Force FALCON, and there was a multinational engineer brigade called TF GRYPHON.

CTF WARRIOR consisted of five infantry battalions. The 151st Romanian Infantry Battalion (Black Wolves) was situated at the Kandahar Airfield (KAF) and handled its security in association with the 3-62 Air Defence Artillery Regiment, plus the local Afghan forces and the Special Forces teams working with them. The 1-87th Infantry Regiment was located at a series of firebases in Gardez and Paktika, 2-22 Infantry Regiment at Kandahar Airfield, and 2-87 Infantry Regiment at Bagram Airfield. Task Force GERONIMO, the 1st Battalion from the 501st Parachute Infantry Regiment, was based at FOB SALERNO in Khost, which replaced Task Force NIBBIO, an Italian infantry battalion, in late 2003. 3-6 Field Artillery Regiment supported the whole CTF. Task Force DRAGON, based at Bagram Airfield, included the 2nd Battalion, 8th Marine Regiment; two artillery batteries; and 3-62 Air Defense Artillery. There were a small number of firebases in the northeastern provinces that were occupied on a rotating basis.

CTF WARRIOR's concept of operations and deployment pattern was an evolution of CTF DEVIL's. Some units were deployed in a relatively small number of forward operating bases along the border with Pakistan, with an airmobile reserve located at Bagram Airfield and Kandahar Airfield. OEF units reacted to intelligence sent in by special operations forces (SOF), civil affairs units, SIGINT (signal intelligence), and HUMINT (human intelligence) and pursued any enemy unit that could be tracked. Sweep operations into remote areas suspected of harboring the remnants of the Taliban regime and operations designed to locate and destroy weapons caches were the order of the day in late 2003.

Enemy activity in 2003 was extremely limited in RC (Regional Command) North and RC West. RC East's main problem area was Khowst, followed by Paktia and Paktika, and to a lesser extent Kunar and Nangarhar. Most of these incidents occurred along the border, where the Taliban, Al Qaeda, and HiG operated from Pakistan with near impunity. RC South had comparatively high levels of violence in Kandahar, particularly at the border near Spin Boldak, and moderate levels in Oruzgan and Zabol. Helmand had a significant increase in violence, but it was unclear how much was drug related and how much was Taliban.

During this period, OEF established and deployed Provincial Reconstruction Teams (PRTs) throughout Afghanistan. Though the details of how and why this was done are handled in a later section, it is important to understand that the PRTs were designed, initially, to provide a coordination point between the Afghan Militia Forces (what the media called the "warlords" but in fact were the anti-Taliban groups working with OEF), OEF, and the Afghan Interim Administration and Afghan Transitional Administration. Their purposes included the development of information on the provinces: demographics, the security situation, economy and so on. In time, the PRTs would be involved with national development organizations, nongovernmental aid organizations, and national development program coordination, but in 2003 this role was embryonic. PRT deployment was slow in early 2003 but by 2004 there were PRTs in nearly every province in Afghanistan.

the NATO-ization of ISAF: spring 2003

The other international military organization in Afghanistan was ISAF. In 2003 ISAF had a divisional headquarters that commanded the Kabul Multinational Brigade (KMNB) and a multinational protective and control unit that maintained the Kabul International Airport. ISAF was mandated by the UN but was led by European countries. Initially ISAF was a "fig leaf" to assuage the UN, and it was kept small on the insistence of Fahim Khan, who commanded the Northern Alliance and didn't want too much outside interference in his attempts to exert influence on the new Afghanistan. ISAF, essentially, protected the Afghan Interim and Transitional Administration in Kabul.

The German/Netherlands Corps, which handled ISAF at this time, requested NATO assistance back in 2002 in some critical areas, particularly in intelligence capacities and command, control, and communications equipment. This was NATO's first involvement in ISAF, though it remained a non-NATO organization. More important, however, the Germans and Dutch couldn't get another country to take ISAF lead. The only options were to fold ISAF; develop a closer relationship to OEF; or transition ISAF to a NATO command and get all NATO partners to contribute.[4]

The diplomatic maneuvering on this issue was intense. Those discussions took place from November 2002 to April 2003, a period that coincided with extreme distancing between the United States and "the old Europe" over the mounting war against the Hussein regime in Iraq. Broadly put, some nations didn't want to commit to fight in Iraq but at the same time didn't want to overly antagonize the Americans.[5] Committing to ISAF, which many, many commentators started to erroneously call a "peacekeeping mission," was a viable alternative, but nobody wanted to lead it. Some observers pointed out that the UN wanted ISAF to expand and take over from OEF because the UN didn't want to be associated with OEF's counterinsurgency campaign and it would be easier for the United Nations Assistance Mission in Afghanistan (UNAMA) to operate with ISAF in charge. But nobody wanted to take charge.

The mistaken idea that ISAF expansion was designed to somehow free up significant American forces for operations elsewhere floated around the policy world at this time. ISAF expansion was in fact discouraged in certain American quarters in early 2003, specifically at the Secretary of Defense level.[6] Though there were numerous reasons, one revolved around the matter of potential interference in the high-value target (HVT) hunt. In Bosnia, it was believed by some that the American-led Stabilisation Force's attempts to capture HVTs had been thwarted by elements in the NATO command structure and by lackadaisical HVT policies from countries that didn't want "American Justice." In Bosnia and Kosovo, for example, American-led military operations were compromised by French officers. There was no way that the Americans would permit the hunt for Al Qaeda leadership to be compromised in a similar fashion.[7]

Somebody had to take over ISAF, regardless of what it would do in the future. The Constitutional Loya Jirga was set for the fall of 2003. Afghanistan desperately needed a constitution; then it needed national elections. Afghanistan needed a legitimate government. There were too many players who could interfere with Afghanistan's political development, and those players were not all Taliban or Al Qaeda. A strong ISAF was crucial for security in the capital if Afghanistan was going to avoid a slide back to the bad old days of 1992–93, but who would lead it?

canada and NATO ISAF: 2003–4[8]

In February 2003 Canada informed NATO that it would accept ISAF lead after the German/Netherlands Corps term was finished. This was the result of intense discussions between the three nations. Nobody else would step up to the plate. But what motivated Canada to make this offer? In the summer of 2002, Canada examined how best to contribute to ongoing global operations against Al Qaeda. The war in Afghanistan appeared to be winding down, and U.S. Central Command (CENTCOM) was now focusing on going into Iraq. The Horn of Africa operations were limited because there were no Al Qaeda targets identified. There was some discussion by American military commanders and the coalition staffs at CENTCOM about the future direction in Afghanistan after the Canadians, British, and Australians pointed out that CENTCOM needed a formal plan to transition from combat to stabilization—and that plan didn't exist in part because of how quickly the Taliban regime collapsed, because of the staffing requirements for Iraq, and because the Europeans were reluctant to really commit to ISAF. The possibility that ISAF might expand into areas where there was chieftain rivalry and extend government authority was explored, but nothing in detail came of it at the time.

Canada considered military commitments to both Iraq and Afghanistan at the same time. The Afghanistan options included leading ISAF and sending a battalion, sending a battalion only, training the Afghan National Army (ANA), or sending a battalion with OEF. There were arguments against committing to ISAF; most of them revolved around the uncertain future of the mission and its incoherent mandate. At this point, it wasn't a question of Iraq or Afghanistan. Canada was considering both. NATO was told in February that Canada would send a battalion and a brigade headquarters in the summer of 2003. NATO was also told that Canada favored ISAF expansion. It wasn't until March that Canada decided not to commit forces to Iraq.

The Canadian decision to commit was a catalyst for the NATO decision to take over ISAF. NATO Secretary General Lord Robertson, an advocate of a NATO ISAF, had the leverage he needed, and in April 2003 the North Atlantic Council agreed to do so. This was ratified in at the June 2003 Madrid conference. Canada agreed to take the ISAF lead if NATO found a way to make the ISAF HQ a permanent headquarters instead of rotating it between a limited number of countries that possessed and could send a deployable headquarters.

The Canadian contribution to NATO ISAF was called Operation Athena. There were four rotations of Op Athena from 2003 to 2004. The first two involved a Canadian brigade headquarters taking over the Kabul Multinational Brigade and the deployment of a Canadian infantry battalion, with an ISTAR squadron[9] and artillery support as part of that brigade. The last two rotations involved a surveillance squadron and an infantry company, plus support elements.

The first iteration of Op Athena was based on 3rd Battalion, the Royal Canadian Regiment, and the Royal Canadian Dragoons recce squadron. KMNB HQ was based on 2 Brigade HQ, led by Brigadier General Peter Devlin. Kabul was divided into three battle group areas: BG-1, 2, and 3. 3 RCR was deployed to western Kabul, while German- and French-led composite battalion groups operated north and east. Additional force protection was deemed essential so Canada sent a battery of 105-mm guns, SPERWER unmanned aerial vehicles (UAVs), and special operations forces. ISAF HQ was now a NATO headquarters under a German general, but the deputy ISAF commander who really ran operations on a day-to-day basis was a Canadian, Major General Andy Leslie.

In the second rotation, which took place in February 2004, Canada sent Lieutenant General Rick Hillier to lead ISAF. KMNB was led by Brigadier General Jocelyn Lacroix and his headquarters from the French-speaking 5e Brigade, and the French-speaking 3rd Battalion, Royal 22nd Regiment replaced 1 RCR.

The most important achievement from the Canadian-led ISAF period was the Constitutional Loya Jirga held from December 2003 to January 2004. The Afghan Interim Administration and the Afghan Transitional Administration were only way points to the formation of a legitimate Afghan government. The Constutitional Loya Jirga was designed to bring together five hundred or more power brokers in Afghanistan and hammer out how the electoral system would work, what type of government the country would have, what kind of the judiciary, the role of Islam, and a host of other contentious issues. The most important part was compromising ethnic power sharing with all of them. Indeed, this six-week process was possibly the most important event in Afghan history.[10]

Of secondary but critical importance was the information operations benefit from the event. Collecting this disparate, suspicious, and disgruntled group of people together in one place without weapons and private armies and having them achieve a consensus was possibly the strongest weapon that could be wielded by the Afghan people, ISAF, and OEF against the Taliban, HiG, and Al Qaeda—and the chieftains who thought they could intimidate the Karzai government. This message was "We can do this, and we can do this with security. You can't interfere with it." The security arrangements were massive. The site of the loya jirga was inside the Canadian area of operations. An Afghan National Army battalion and the Canadian battle group handled the inner-cordon security, while the rest of ISAF with OEF support manned and patrolled three outer cordons. The star of the show was President Hamid Karzai, who through sheer force of personality and political skill forged the consensus that is the basis for the new political dynamics of Afghanistan, specifically the 2004 national elections and the 2005 provincial elections. Enemy forces were dissuaded by the massive security operation and were unable to have any effect on the proceedings.[11]

Second, the Disarmament, Demobilization and Registration (DDR) program, but more particularly the Heavy Weapons Cantonment program that was established in the fall of 2003, were also significant contributors to security in Kabul during and after the Constitutional Loya Jirga and were major factors in undermining chieftain violence in Afghanistan well into 2004. These programs "defanged" the Afghan Militia Forces so that private armies could not be used to either actively or passively intimidate the electoral and constitutional processes. This ultimately had important implications for the credibility and legitimacy of those processes.

special operations forces, 2003–4

There were many different types of special operations forces active in Afghanistan in 2003 and 2004. The specialized high-value target hunters were designated Task Force 5, which replaced the 2001–2 TF-11 organization. TF-5 was a combination of Joint Special Operations Command subunits (mostly the Combat Application Group/Delta and SEAL Team 6/Development Group), the CIA's Special Activities Division, the Grey Fox intelligence collectors (e.g., the Intelligence Support Activity), and elements from the 1st and 2nd battalions of the 160th SOAR, in this case Company D, 1-160th SOAR. TF-5 also had Rangers from 2/75 and 3/75 Rangers to act as the "green box" protection organization for the "black" operators from JSOC and SAD.[12]

TF-5's purpose was to hunt the senior Al Qaeda and Taliban leadership. After the war in Iraq was under way, a similar organization, TF-20, was established to hunt senior Iraqi leaders. By the fall of 2003, TF-5 and TF-20 were merged into a CENTCOM-wide command called TF-121. Elements of TF-121 were located in Afghanistan, but the lack of actionable intelligence on HVTs limited their employment; in some cases, TF-121 personnel were involved in regular SOF activity. The bulk of TF-121 was deployed to Iraq in 2003, leaving a steadily decreasing skeleton crew in Afghanistan.[13]

The original SOF structure established in 2001 to persecute the war in Afghanistan was long gone: TF DAGGER and TF K-BAR, two separate CJSOTFs, evolved into the Combined Joint Special Operations Task Force–Afghanistan (CJSOTF-A). CJSOTF-A included the 3rd Special Forces Group (Airborne) and the 20th Special Forces Group (Airborne). The 19th Special Forces Group was engaged in training the Afghan National Army and then mentoring it in the field during operations. It was located at Forward Operating Base 191, located in Kabul, but for the most part was in the field with the new ANA battalions as they deployed.[14]

3 SFGA had three battalions on a rotating basis in 2003 and 2004, with one battalion deployed at any one time in a six-month period. FOB 33, located at KAF, supported fifteen Operational Detachment As (twelve-man A-Teams) and three ODBs deployed across southern and eastern Afghanistan. CJSOTF-A also had U.S. Navy SEALs from Naval Special Warfare Group 2 (NAVSOF).

Coalition SOF partners in 2003–4 included the German Kommando Spezial-kräfte (KSK), the new Czech 601st unit, a Lithuanian SOF detachment, a Norwegian detachment, and some Italian SOF, which redeployed by the end of 2003. The United Arab Emirates also had a small SOF element deployed as part of OEF in 2003. The British had a combination of Special Air Service (SAS) and Special Boat Service (SBS) personnel, but they tended to work directly for the British contingents at Mazar-e Sharif and in Kabul and not the CJSTOF-A at this time.

In 2003–4 OEF's SOF was "used as a general purpose force for most of that rotation . . . there were a lot of long-range mounted vehicle patrols, numerous air assault operations against medium value targets and high value targets, and we shared in training the ANA. . . . It was hard to stay mission-focused on any particular thing during that rotation because we were never given a defined area to operate in." Indeed, FOB 33 units captured "low-level leaders or people associated with the Taliban. . . . We [never] caught anybody who was a confirmed Al Qaeda member."[15] A major coalition SOF operation in Kabul province did, however, net a medium-value leadership target in August 2004.[16] French SOF were not part of the CJSOTF at this time. The French units, mostly drawn from the 1st RPIMa (essentially the French SAS), worked alongside CTF WARRIOR in southern Afghanistan on the Pakistan border.

operation enduring freedom reorganizes: 2004

OEF underwent a complete reorganization in the spring and summer of 2004. CJTF-180 ceased to be the corps-level headquarters in Afghanistan. A new command, Combined Forces Command–Afghanistan, or CFC-A, took over. The Coalition Joint Civil-Military Operations Task Force (CJCMOTF) was gone and its responsibilities transferred to the new Office of Military Cooperation. Task Force PHOENIX, the ANA training organization, reported to it.

CJTF-180 reverted to a division-level organization. The 25th Infantry Division took over from the 10th Mountain and renamed it CJTF-76. Afghanistan was divided up into four Regional Commands (RCs): North, South, East, West. As the Afghan National Army slowly expanded, an ANA corps was associated with each Regional Command: 201 Corps was in Kabul; 203 Corps was in RC East; 205 Corps was in RC South; 207 Corps was in RC West; and 209 Corps was in RC North. CJTF-76 assigned a task force to each Regional Command; these were essentially brigade-level organizations.

The two largest were CTF THUNDER in RC East and CTF BRONCO in RC South. CTF THUNDER had its headquarters in Khost at FOB SALERNO. THUNDER had a Marine battalion (3rd Battalion, 6th Marines, also called TF STONEWALL); TF WOLFHOUNDS, based on 2-27th Infantry; 1-505th Parachute Infantry Regiment; and 3-116th Infantry, a National Guard unit. CTF THUNDER had PRTs in eight locations.

In RC South and situated at KAF, CTF BRONCO had a Romanian battalion, the 281st Bold Eagles, and three U.S. battalions: TF BOBCAT (2-5 Infantry Regiment); 2-35th Infantry; and 3-7th Field Artillery Regiment, reroled as an infantry battalion and called TF STEEL. BRONCO had four PRTs: Kandahar, Qalat, Lashkar Gah, and Tarin Kot.

RC North was a collection of Provincial Reconstruction Teams that were in the process of transitioning to ISAF. RC West was commanded by CTF SABER; it consisted of a reconnaissance battalion, the 3-4th Cavalry Regiment, an aviation maintenance company (B-193rd), and the PRTs at Herat and Farah.

Corps-level units included JTF WINGS, a large organization incorporating aviation elements from the U.S. Army, U.S. Air Force, and U.S. Marine Corps: Apaches, Black Hawks, Chinooks, Super Stallions, and Cobras. CTF COYOTE was multinational engineer brigade.

CJTF-76 altered the existing deployment pattern. The number of forward operating bases was expanded (taking over some established by the Special Forces, while others were newly built),[17] and platoon houses were also employed to disperse the infantry battalions in their assigned provinces.

In 2004 RC North had limited enemy activity, while both RC North and RC West were plagued with inter-Afghan militia forces disputes that had the potential to seriously escalate. RC East had lower levels of enemy activity compared with 2003, with the exception of the Khost-Paktika border region, which still suffered the effects of the ongoing border campaign. Kunar and Nangarhar experienced some limited contact. In RC South the level of violence dropped off somewhat in Helmand and Kandahar, but climbed steadily in Oruzgan and Zabol.

The CJTF-76 concept of operations in 2004 revolved around three large countrywide operations, as opposed to a plethora of smaller ones. Operation Mountain Storm was still in progress when the transfer of authority from the 10th Mountain Division took place, so the 25th Infantry Division units on arrival were immediately tasked with defeating the enemy's anticipated spring offensive by preempting enemy deployment in May and June. Operation Lightning Resolve was conducted from July to October; its task was to establish and support the conditions for the fall national elections by moving into population centers and assisting with voter registration security. Operation Lightning Freedom, set for November, was meant to provide direct support and security for the elections.[18]

The emphasis in 2004, therefore, was on the elections and the legitimacy to be conferred by them. The bulk of the OEF effort was focused on this task, not on long-term development or ANA training, as CJTF-76 believed that it needed every warm body on the streets for election security. PRTs remained small and tactical in nature, and were unengaged in tasks that did not directly support the primary CJTF-76 operations. At the same time, there were competing visions of how long-term development should be carried out, and these remained unresolved in 2003–4.

the war in pakistan

The problem of Taliban and Al Qaeda sanctuaries in Pakistan had not been seriously addressed in 2002, and even in 2003 it was a sensitive topic. The Pakistani government was cajoled into taking more aggressive action against the networks in the border regions between Afghanistan and Pakistan by the United States. It is important to understand that these border areas have a unique relationship to the Pakistan government in that they are, for the most part, self-governing and have significant autonomy. Using large-scale military force in these areas was potentially destabilizing to the Pakistani polity and could lead to not one but several antigovernment insurgencies, some of which had been dormant since the 1970s.

By the end of 2003, Pakistan had deployed its new Special Operations Task Force (a battalion-sized unit from the Special Security Group) on a significant operation in October 2003 to Waziristan, a tribal area opposite Khost. This mission stumbled across significant Al Qaeda activity and confirmed that there were sanctuary areas. In March 2004 a larger operation was mounted in the Wana valley; it destroyed or disrupted a large Al Qaeda communications and command network. Pursuing the fleeing operatives to the Shakai valley, the SOTF and the tribal Lashkars (militia) encountered several hundred foreign fighters who along with local fighters, engaged Pakistani forces. A ten-thousand-man cordon was put in and the valley cleared. Shakai was an intelligence bonanza, with laptops, communications equipment, and "facilitators" seized. These operations produced intelligence that led to urban cells and networks, including ties to financial organizations and nongovernmental aid groups. These operations received significant American intelligence support from U-2s, MQ-1 Predators, and a twelve-man CIA team.[19] As part of the 2004 campaign, Pakistan closed Afghan refugee camps in the border areas, suspecting that they were being used as recruiting centers by the Taliban. This generated a significant refugee flow problem for both Pakistan and Afghanistan.[20]

The 2004 operations in South Waziristan did coincide with Operation Mountain Storm.[21] There was increased hope for better cooperation between the Pakistan Army and OEF. OEF commanders wanted to conduct "hammer-and-anvil" operations all along the border from Kunar to Khost and Zabol. In effect, a series of "squeeze plays" would force the enemy away from one force to the other side of the border, where the other force would be waiting to kill or capture them. Unfortunately the mechanisms needed to coordinate these actions were embryonic at best in 2004.

NATO ISAF expansion: 2003–4

There was, back in 2002, some American interest in using ISAF as a successor organization to OEF, but there were mixed signals from Washington, specifically the Secretary of Defense, who doubted NATO's ability to independently mount and sustain such an effort. Pentagon planners suggested that it could be done, but Donald Rumsfeld wanted proof. Could NATO do so without relying on American "enablers" like strategic lift, command and control, and intelligence systems?[22] Rumsfeld was tired of having the United States bail out NATO, as he believed it had in the Balkans. The SECDEF's attitude was modified somewhat by 2004. The Iraq burden was starting to tell on the United States, and the possibility of having NATO back fill in Afghanistan looked more attractive. The idea of a phased OEF transfer to NATO ISAF was developed further by late 2004. There were four OEF regional commands. The most secure was RC North. NATO ISAF would, after it had proved it could handle RC North, move counterclockwise to RC West, then South, and finally East over the course of three to five years.[23]

The first real step in this process was the transfer of RC North to NATO ISAF command. And this is where the Germans came in. Germany wanted to find ways to bridge the gap with the United States on the Iraq War issue. At the same time, there was a German general in command of Joint Force Command Brunssum and there was subtle pressure from within German military circles to have Germany take a wider role in overseas operations. Consequently Germany agreed to take the lead of the first NATO Provincial Reconstruction Team in Konduz. This acceptance was the catalyst for expanded NATO involvement in RC North, and then the region was transferred to ISAF command in the fall of 2004.[24]

the 2004 national elections

The importance of the 2004 elections cannot be understated. The Constitutional Loya Jirga of December 2003–January 2004 was a critical step in establishing the type of government Afghanistan wanted, but Karzai needed to downplay the perception raised by his opponents that he wanted to remain in control of an interim administration that was increasingly perceived to be an American device. At the same time, there was concern that ethnic tensions would evolve if adequate power-sharing mechanisms were not put in place quickly.[25]

In mid-2003 Afghanistan established, with UNAMA's help, the Joint Electoral Management Body. The JEMB's task was "the issuance and publication of regulations, procedures, instructions, notifications, and guidelines for the registration process." Its mandate was expanded in 2004 to include "preparing, managing, convening, and overseeing the 2004 general elections."[26] The date for the election was originally established for June 2004.

The problem was the Taliban and its supporters. In early 2004 the JEMB had personnel canvassing the entire country in order to determine how many voters could be registered. Significant violence was directed against the JEMB registration staff in Kandahar, Jalalabad, and Zabol even after Karzai called on the Taliban to form a legitimate political party and join the process. Security concerns delayed the elections until 9 October 2004.[27]

Oruzgan province remained a tough nut to crack in 2004. There were simply not enough OEF forces to establish a presence everywhere, and Oruzgan lay outside the area controlled by TF BRONCO. Special forces had a presence but no influence in Oruzgan, so the decision was made to surge Task Force LINEBACKER into the region before the national elections. TF LINEBACKER, better known as the 22nd Marine Expeditionary Unit (Special Operations Capable), consisted of a Marine battalion (1-6 Marines), plus a helicopter battalion (CH-53 and AH-1W

Cobra gunships), AV-8B Harriers, and a logistics unit. 22 MEU (SOC) deployed to Kanadahr in April directly from the assault ships USS *Wasp*, USS *Whidbey Island*, USS *Shreveport*, and USS *Iwo Jima* and then to a FOB established near Tarin Kot.[28] The Marines mounted twelve major operations over a four-month period, ranging all over the province. All operations were accompanied by civil affairs missions' follow-up with the express purpose of securing population areas for the voter registration process prior to the elections.[29] TF LINEBACKER's deployment caught the Taliban completely off guard; they were expecting a series of sporadic SOF/ANA presence operations and instead got a flood of Marines for a protracted period.

NATO ISAF established the Election Support Forces in Kabul, which, according to the head of the CJTF-76 Joint Intelligence Support Element, "locked that city down pretty tight. . . . The attempts that were made [to disrupt the elections] were largely ineffective and were caught well outside the city."[30] The ESF included several surge forces from outside of Afghanistan: a Spanish battalion was deployed to Mazar-e Sharif, while an Italian battalion and an American infantry company went to Kabul. The Netherlands deployed six F-16s.[31]

When the registration process was completed in September 2004, there were 10.5 million Afghans registered to vote, of which 42 percent were women.[32] On election day, over 80 percent of the registered population voted, or about 8 million people, a number that exceeded the expectations of the JEMB, UNAMA, and the rest of the international comunity. Four hundred international monitors were deployed throughout the country to ensure that the process was not tampered with. Despite the usual "sour grapes" complaints from the losers (these were duly investigated), Hamid Karzai won with 55.4 percent of the vote.[33] The success of the elections was a major defeat for the Taliban, which only demonstrated that it was a marginalized group interested in violence and not in adopting legitimate, political means to accomplish its objectives. The Afghan people had spoken, and Hamid Karzai was free to form a government that had their support.[34]

NATO ISAF: kabul, 2004

In the last Afghan War, Kabul was occupied early in the campaign, after the overthrow of the troops of Yakoub Khan. But its capture by no means brought about the downfall of the Afghans as a fighting power, on the contrary it proved to be merely the commencement of the campaign.

—C. E. CALLWELL, *SMALL WARS* (1906)

back to afghanistan, but this time well escorted

It always seems to start with an Airbus . . .

I arrived at a Canadian Forces Base, prepared to take the usual monotonous trip to Camp Mirage, our secure undisclosed location in the Gulf, and stage to Kabul. It was pouring rain when I pulled up in my car to off-load my rucksack and equipment. There was a young and new clerk at the Air Movements Units—and she was friendly! This was a change from the old days (i.e., last year).

"Sir, you're not on the list."

"What? I should be . . . "

"Oh, you're one of the . . . what do they call them? Secret Squirrels!"

There had been some screwup with J-3 and J-4 in Ottawa. I played along. As usual, I was wearing jeans, polar fleece, Columbia jacket, and a ball cap. Oh, yeah: I kept the beard from my last trip to Afghanistan.

"Maybe." I smiled. "What or who are they?"

The older, more experienced clerk moved in.

"Sir, everything is set. Just bring your kit over here."

I had been told that a Strategy and Defence Forum (SDF) group from Alberta was going to Kabul. Usually the SDF consist of academics, students, and reserve military personnel in university who are getting a tour of an overseas operation. Just then a bus pulled up and a group of ten people got off: nine men and a woman, dressed more or less like me, all more or less my age. I turned back to the clerk.

"*Secret Squirrel* was an old spy cartoon on TV."

"Oh. I've never seen it. That must have been before I was born."

I sat down and pulled out Michael Crichton's *Prey*. The others who came in after me dispersed through the terminal. One more mature gent of short stature sat down and pulled out . . . *Prey*.

"Hey, what do you think of it?" I gestured to the book. He ignored me. I moved to his field of vision and repeated the question. He looked up at me, gathered his things, and without saying a word moved to another part of the terminal.

I didn't realize I had the plague. . . .

I took a closer look at the newcomers. Nah, can't be. Just an antisocial asshole.

The flight was delayed twenty-four hours, so I decamped to a local hotel. The next day, we were all boarding the Airbus. My neighbor in the same seat row was unable to find another seat that was isolated, so he sighed and sat down next to me and uncommunicated. Another antisocial asshole? Two on one CF flight? Hmmmm . . . must check my underarm deodorant. I inspected my face for hideous burn scars and pus: nope. No buboes in my armpits either.

We landed at an eastern European airport where we had an hour in the terminal while the Airbus changed crews. Two of the guys who looked like mature students were at the bar. Now, SDF did a lot of trips to visit SFOR, and in a spirit of in-transit solidarity, I asked, "Have you guys been here before?" Averted eyes. Then averted body. No response.

OK, was it something in my GI tract? Some pestilence, perhaps?

After another long haul, we landed at Mirage. It was dark, and, as usual, the off-load was controlled chaos. A group of uniformed personnel were proceeding under direction of the loadies to a low-slung building. I went to follow them when a loadie said, "No, you go that way." The other bearded un-uniformed people were proceeding to a pile of pallets. Being tired from the trip, I just followed orders. It wasn't a Nuremberg situation, after all.

A wild, bearded guy started a briefing about Kabul, where I was going. Just then a short guy with a beard like Genghis Khan turned around and glowered at me. I glowered back.

"Hey, you don't belong here!"

"I was told to be here!" I started to get my Irish up. Don't tell me what to do, you little shit, oozed out of my pores and I suppose my body language. I noticed that my six-foot-two-inch frame was head and shoulders above the group.

"This is for Kabul only!" he said.

"Well, that's where I'm going!" I was starting to get steamed.

"You're going to Kabul?" he asked with some incredulity.

"Yeah! And it's not the first time either!"

"Who are you?"

"Who are *you?*" I retorted.

It was only when I noticed that the other members were uncrating a variety of exotically and obviously personally modified small arms did I fully realize that I was in the middle of a special operations forces detachment from Joint Task Force Two (JTF-2).

Oops. They were my favorite bunch of special operators, whose continued existence and expansion I championed in my writings on Canadian defense policy.

Of course, I wasn't just going to slink away, even with ten heavily armed commandos staring at me . . .

"Get out of here!"

"OK, where exactly the fuck am I supposed to go? The loadie sent me over here. I'm not wandering all over an unfamiliar base with armed people and propeller aircraft everywhere at night!"

They have assault rifles with laser sights. But I'm taller.

Genghis Khan was fulminating inside. I could tell. He wasn't used to defiance from unarmed people; he was used to double-tapping them with a Sig Sauer pistol after bursting in through a window after rappelling down the side of a building. I leaned against a crate and crossed my arms. Then a somewhat-chastened loadie appeared, and I was off for some prime rib and a bed at Camp Mirage.

I figured, like the situation with Geraldo Rivera in Afghanistan the last time, that I wouldn't see these cats again. Wrong. You always meet everybody again some day.

We had only three hours to get ready for the Herc flight to Kabul. I changed into desert combat kit; the last time I was in Afghanistan I had been warned not to dress like special operations personnel (i.e., jeans, ball cap, and body armor). So this time I had tan pants, tan shirt with a "Non-Combatant Civilian" brassard, desert CADPAT (Canadian Disruptive Pattern) helmet, and desert CADPAT load-bearing vest for my body armor. No weapon, of course: Canadians are funny about allowing civilian personnel to carry weapons. They don't trust us, or this is some sort of subliminal discouragement aligned with the antigun ownership laws in the Canadian Nanny State.

The four uniformed people heading for Kabul and me were instructed to meet at the weapons lockup where they would get weapons and a safety briefing, then a ROE (rules of engagement) briefing. I almost scored a C-8 assault rifle from the armorer, but she declined, saying that the only one she had was malfunctioning. One of the clerks who were going to Kabul was Navy. And she was nervous about weapons carriage. "I haven't used a rifle since basic," she told me. One of the defense platoon sergeants, an ex-Airborne guy, noticed this and gave her extra instruction.

The ROE brief was even scarier:

"What are ROEs?" she asked.

I mean, here we were, getting ready to go into *Afghanistan,* into *Kabul,* and she doesn't know what ROEs are? Her home unit, which should have prepared her for this and did not. Lieutenant Jim Davis, the commander of the composite defense and security platoon drawn from the reserve personnel of 38 Canadian Brigade Group, took her aside.

We trooped out to the Herc after getting the safety briefings—that is, avoid the spinning propellers. Oh, and we will be tactical going into Kabul; wear your body armor for takeoff and landing. Don't scream when the surface-to-air missile hits the plane. Die as quietly as possible so as not to distract the crew. That sort of thing.

I strapped in. The JTF-2 guys trooped on after us; they had to wear their kit too. One had a tan-painted helmet with no cover, another had a CADPAT cover. All had personalized body armor chest rigs with ballistic plates, some tan, other green-colored, plus black gloves. The weapons included what looked like M-4s with several types of rail attachments. Some weapons were attached via clip systems to the load-bearing vests. Their kit was designed for maximum flexibility for the arms; the arms were not constrained like they are with the Gen II and Gen III armor I was familiar with. (I was wearing the old Gen II, the same stuff used at Oka* and Bosnia, with chest and back plates inside a CADPAT vest slung over the whole thing: heavy and turtlelike. I don't recommend it.) There was an empty place beside me. One JTF-2 trooper reluctantly strapped in. I guess it was the plague again. So I decided to have some fun.

"Been to Afghanistan before?" I inquired pleasantly.

A shake of the head.

"Oh, well, you'll love it. Hopefully nobody takes a shot at us with a MANPADS [a shoulder-launched surface-to-air missile] on the way in."

A grunt.

"It's a neat country. The last time I was there with the warlords they cut this guy's throat . . . "

The engines started up. We were off.

---

* The Oka insurrection in 1990 blockaded Southern Montreal, Quebec. Several Mohawk bands were involved, prompting the deployment of a mechanized brigade group.

It was a boring and uneventful flight: Hercs are slow. Fortunately the crew cranked the heat up, which made the interior of the plane rather womblike, which increased drowsiness. I chatted with the crew, who were all in their late twenties.

"What model of Herc is this?"

"We don't know any more! E, H, so many mods. The plane was built in 1968 . . . "

I was one year older than this particular aircraft.

There was a RWR (radar warning receiver) mounted among the cockpit avionics. Essentially the RWR is a "fuzzbuster." A really scary fuzzbuster. The nav has another. Cryptic symbols flashed on . . . and disappeared. These were radars, mostly air traffic control radars, but some were Pakistani air force and, I assumed, friendly AWACS systems. This Herc had flares to divert surface-to-air missiles but no chaff.

"Déjà vu," the pilots told me. The only fun they get was preparing to approach Kabul—the plane dropped like an elevator onto the deck. I could see rolling terrain and dunes through the portal as I twisted around in my seat. We were instructed to put on helmets and body armor thirty minutes out. Lots of hand motions as we all had earplugs in. The JTF-2 guys, who immediately on takeoff abandoned the canvas benches to scramble onto the cargo pallets and lounge among them looking for any horizontal space to lie down, returned to their seats. On approach to Kabul International Airport (reacromymed "KAIA" instead of the old "KIA," which implied "killed in action" in the American lexicon) the Herc dropped like an elevator again and fired flares from its defensive suite to discourage infrared-equipped antiaircraft missiles.

My later conversations with NATO flight crews while sipping espresso in the KAIA waiting area presented me with a slightly more detailed picture. Over the course of 2004, there had been 10 firings of MANPADS at ISAF and OEF aircraft (this was a decrease from 250 over the 2001–3 period). Three were launched at aircraft on approach to or taking off from KAIA. The enemy's record was 0 for 10. The pilots wanted to keep it that way, so they were understandably reticent in discussing specific defensive measures. As usual, however, the enemy had access to vast amounts of open-source information on the mechanical and electronic means of how to defeat defensive measures. Did they possess the technical means in-theater to modify their systems in a mini arms race with the coalition forces? That was unclear. A learning curve, however, might produce the deployment—or "migration," as the intelligence community called it—of techniques and equipment from the Iraq theater of operations, particularly French-augmented Soviet or Chinese systems provided to Saddam Hussein's forces. Or from elsewhere, maybe Iran, whose representatives in Lebanon learned a lot from fighting Israeli forces. The political implications of having, say, a French-supplied system shooting down a Canadian Forces aircraft would be too great to contemplate.

KAIA was just as frenetic as it was on previous trips. Two IL-76 CANDIDs, an Antonov An-124, a clutch of Hercs (Portuguese and Swedish, plus an RAF "J" model). An unmarked, unregistered 737 with modified winglets, most likely from the updated version of Air America, was struggling into the air. The Dutch AH-64 force committed to ISAF had a swarm of mechs sweating over one machine.

The CANSOF filed off to their four-wheel drive vehicles. The bearded, heavily armed men made a semicircle around an "old hand" who had an even longer beard. Nondescript ball caps (no "CNN" this time—or any other form of national indicator) proliferated as much as individually modified M-4s painted in mottled brown cam patterns. Sigs were strapped into thigh holsters as the customized web gear was untangled and checked. Black streamlined "hockey helmets" with attachments for a variety of night observation systems bobbed up and down.

KAIA had been significantly cleaned up since my last trip. A new monument was next to the Turkish eagle, the BMP hulks were all gone, as was the BTR-60U wreck. No AMF (Afghan Militia Forces) guards; all NATO-member nations with Belgian APCs (armored personnel carriers) patrolling. Aircraft wreckage and spares had been bulldozed together into a rotting rusted mess; Turkish UH-60s took off and clawed their way into the sky.

I heard my name from the direction of two G-Wagon armored jeeps parked on the road.

"Dr. Maloney, welcome to Kabul." I was greeted by Captain Brian Roach and Captain John Cochrane, both from the Lord Strathcona's Horse (Royal Canadians) armored regiment.

The trip from KAIA to Camp Julien was very different from the last time: instead of a "soft" minivan with two drivers, we had two armored jeeps, and at least seven drivers, gunners, and others. The Canadians weren't wearing berets with regimental cap badges; they wore CADPAT soft hats. There were no name tapes. The vehicles had their registration numbers covered. National markings had the country name in Dari and Pashto written underneath, a significant change from 2003. There was a convoy briefing, action on contact and so on. Constant radio communication was maintained from KAIA to Camp Julien. I made the comparison to 2003. Why the changes? The German bus attack?

"Yeah, that was the big one. Thirty wounded and six dead. We don't move personnel en masse like that any more. Then the suicide attack on our patrol: they were in an Iltis jeep, no armor. Two dead, more wounded. When we rotate troops we use armed Bison eight-wheeled APCs so they're not concentrated and are armored."

And I could see why: To get from KAIA to Camp Julien, one had to drive through the most congested parts of Kabul, including the market area known as "Holy Fuck Circle," or HFC, cross a bridge, go through a gap between two mountains, and then proceed along an arrow-straight boulevard before passing the huge, decrepit King's Palace. There were unlimited vantage points from which to mount ambushes. The crews were very professional, alert, and well aware of all of them. For example, one traffic circle forces the vehicles to slow down and even stop to turn right. There is a high-walled graveyard adjacent to it. My escort pointed out that an insurgent could lob an explosive over the wall and escape with near impunity in the confusion. They gave this area and others like it special attention.

The G-Wagon ballet through the congested streets was effective and we made good time. The codriver read off pogo-points to let control at Camp Julien know our progress. It was a bit like air traffic control with no radar.

It had been more than a year and a half, and I noticed significant change as we drove through Kabul. There was lots of construction: even giant cranes. The American embassy compound was doubling or even tripling in size. DynCorp hirelings were everywhere alongside Afghan security police, especially in the embassy/government district; these guys looked like SOF personnel, which could get a bit confusing (I'll return to this later). Street shopping had exploded. There were kiosks, fence markets, hawkers of every type selling everything imaginable: counterfeit North Face clothing, fake Calvin Klein belts, bogus Tommy Hilfiger T-shirts. Plastic everything from the Pacific Rim. Ahmad Shah Massoud's portrait was everywhere, with a judicious sprinkling of Karzai. Two gray-painted Russian-made jeeps passed us: NDS (Afghanistan's National Directorate of Security) on a raid. The streets teemed with masses of people. Color was starting to return: cement gray was starting, just starting, to give way to yellows, reds, greens. Advertising was next. It wasn't New York, but it no longer was a ruined battleground.

camp julien

There was a full moon, with mist and haze. The mountains were silhouetted. It was cold. I heard the call to prayer, but it was drowned out temporarily as I walked past the line of generators. I heard it again and moved away from the freezer containers. I was fatigued—broken sleep from four flights, three Airbus and one Hercules, plus a 9.5-hour time change and a serious altitude change. My heart worked harder to keep up, my lower back and right knee ached. Body armor plus contorted maneuvers on canvas benches on the plane plus g-forces.

The Nepalese camp staff served breakfast and a curried lunch—just like the 1800s, sahib! I sat at a white faux-marble table in a large Weatherhaven tent building, observing six Gurkhas sweep and clean the floor. They wore masks as music was played softly—was it Pakistani? Afghani? Indian? I was unsure. A DJ/announcer broke in, crying *"Alaikum!"* and then adamantly said something in either Dari or Pashto. The Canadian provincial and territorial flags were suspended horizontally; the first thing I see is Nunavut, with its red pile of stones shaped as a man—the inuksuk! A good omen. The dance of the masked mops continued to the tunes of someone who must be an Afghan Frank Sinatra, crooning into the mike. Some form of stringed instrument riffed in the scene, and the crooner broke in with bongo drums and a wind instrument.

Camp Julien is located in the shadow of the wrecked King's Palace and the Queen's Palace in southern Kabul. Bunkered OPs in both palaces overwatch the camp, which is surrounded with enough HESCO Bastion to resemble a fort from the 1800s, including loopholes and gun slits. If future archaeologists uncovered it, it would not compare favorably with the constructions of Vauban, but for our purposes, Camp Julien was adequate.

I walked past the monuments to the Canadians that had been killed in Afghanistan. My friend Chris Wattie, a reporter, had been in-theater when Sergeant Robert Short and Corporal Robbie Beerenfenger from 3rd Battalion PPCLI (Princess Patricia's Canadian Light Infantry) had been killed back in 2003. Chris, who is a former soldier himself, had been on patrol with these men on numerous occasions. There had been some controversy about the incident: some wanted to downplay it as an explosion of a UXO (unexploded ordnance) left over from the war because they were worried about waning public support for the mission, but Chris and others knew differently and made sure the facts were known. Our men had been targeted and killed by terrorists. This was a war. There will be casualties. Dishonoring them by pretending otherwise was something that happened in Bosnia during the bad old days of UN peacekeeping, not now. Not when the stakes were so high. Not when Canada's soldiers were putting it on the line day after day.

The "Alternate Service Delivery" contractors, the Canadian equivalents to Kellogg, Brown and Root, hired about three hundred Nepalese to maintain the camp. I liked this touch: we have our own Gurkhas. I wondered, however, what impact this might have on the locals. Usually we employed local people, which augmented the local economy and contributed to the stabilization effort. It may have been for security: infiltrating the camp staff to gather intelligence was an assumed part of the game. And what of defense? What would happen to the contractors if we had to pull out? Would there be a priority for evacuation? Better not to ask such questions . . .

The Nepalese were extremely friendly, smiles all the time. I chatted with one who told me he had been in a Gurkha recce platoon. A couple of guys had even been in Kosovo back in 1999, serving with British forces. I was informed later that defense plans for the camp included Nepalese with military training.

The relationship between the Canadians (uniformed and civilian) and the Nepalese was more than amicable. Some Canadians greeted the Nepalese in their native language. The Nepalese gave lectures on Nepal, and in fact many Canadians serving at Camp Julien took some of their leave vacationing in Nepal.

There was an irony to all of this, however.

A number of Canadians called Camp Julien "Stalag Julien." Movement outside the camp was forbidden. Interaction with Afghans by Canadians on the camp not assigned to outside duties like patrolling was extremely limited. The irony was that many Canadians had more contact with Nepalese than with Afghans and knew more about Nepalese culture than the culture of the country they were living and operating in. There is always a balance between security and interaction, but what were we trying to accomplish? This was a theme that ran through this trip.

Camp Julien was built originally for the first two six-month rotations of the Canadian ISAF contribution in 2003–4. Roto 0 and 1 were based on a 700-man infantry battalion plus a recce squadron and support elements. In the summer of 2004, ISAF requested that Canada remain in Kabul, specifically the Coyote-equipped surveillance squadron. When the infantry battle group redeployed this essentially left a 1,500-man support base supporting a 120-man reconnaissance and surveillance squadron. A number of other NATO members contributing to ISAF were canvassed and Julien became the base for several other ISAF subunits operating in the southeastern districts of the city, which were isolated by a mountain chain from KAIA and the main part of the city.

Hygiene was heavily emphasized; there was some stomach bug going around. No hand washing, no eat. We were instructed to keep food out of the quarters; the logic was that spiders and scorpions appeared in the Weatherhavens only if there were smaller bugs, and that smaller bugs would show up only if there was some-thing to feed on. There were plenty of cats; this kept the rodent population down.

Around this time there was a suicide attack on an American mess hall at a camp in Iraq. The large number of casualties was in part the result of concentrating people in one vulnerable area at predictable times. Camp Julien, as originally designed, was structured to prevent this. The camp had three messes, and each mess was divided into a cook area and three eating areas; each area was partially revetted. If the enemy dropped mortars or rockets into the camp, the chance of casualties was dramatically reduced.

In my daily acclimatization walks, I came across a large square pit in the east end of the camp, out where the previous Canadian contingents had constructed 105-mm artillery positions. It was crammed with about one hundred Iltis jeep carcasses. I was quite familiar with this vehicle type, as it was used in the light recce role when I was training an age ago. Was one of my old jeeps here? Had it been transported all this way to wind up rusting in a hole after being found to be operationally useless after a suicide attack on it? In typical Canadian fashion, the spin doctors at NDHQ got upset when a public declaration was made about the limitations of the Iltis in Kabul. The Belgian contingent still used them and plans had been made to give the Afghan National Army a batch of these now-surplus machines.

I met and got to know Omer, the chief Afghan interpreter at Camp Julien. "We have about sixty interpreters here," Omer explained. "About fifteen support the Canadians, the rest the other ISAF units here."

"How are things for you in Kabul?" I inquired.

"I'm from Kabul originally. I live an apartment complex built during the Soviet time. Things are significantly better here in Kabul. There is a lot of construction, a lot of jobs."

Omer assured me that Kabulis were finally starting to understand that ISAF was here to help. It had taken time, given what had gone on in the past. People understood we are not the Soviets.

"We are having serious problems with the education system. The Taliban let all of the professors go at the university. Anybody who was Soviet-trained was let go. All of our engineers were trained by the Soviets." He chuckled. "It has been difficult to reconstitute the university. Those professors are not interested in returning to Afghanistan. I can understand that. I was present when the suicide attack killed the Canadians. I saw severed fingers in the street, and it took everything I had to control myself."

kabul: the situation in late 2004

After picking up some sugar-laced liquid mud at the "Stand Too" CANEX shop, I chatted with those who professed to know what was going on. There had been an incident the day I arrived: Camp Phoenix, an American camp on the other side of the mountains near ISAF Kabul Multinational Brigade HQ's Camp Warehouse, had come under attack. Details were, as usual, sketchy, but as time wore on, it emerged that an Afghan individual passing by hauled out a firearm and started shooting at the gate guards. A passing French patrol stopped and wasted the gunman. It was unclear as to the gunman's motives; at the time it was billed as a suicide attack. In this environment, however, motives were hard to determine. It could have as easily been a suicide by a guy suffering from PTSD after twenty-five years of war.

For Camp Julien, the threat state was "Medium-low" for insurgents, "High" for terrorism, and "High" for espionage. In the main, and I'll return to this later on, the priority targets for the enemy included NGOs (nongovernmental organizations) and contractors, with kidnapping and assassination the main weapons. There were, as usual, still rocket attacks up and down the Pak border: two American OEF troops had been killed. An isolated rocket attack against Bagram Airfield had hit nothing. I noticed that new terminology had been coined: the enemy was collectively referred to as the "OMF," or Opposing Militia Force. I thought this might have been a corruption of the Canadian nonterminology "Opposing Manoeuvre Force," which had been employed recently since it was believed in the Canadian bureaucracy that we had no enemies. We had OMF, but no enemies. Orwell strikes again.*

Over the course of the past few months, there had been significant incidents. The fallout from the October kidnapping of three JEMB civilian staff by six enemy personnel wearing military uniforms was still in the air; nobody wanted to discuss this one, which meant there was more to it than met the eye. There was a thwarted attack against a German communications site on TV Hill; the Afghan Militia Forces shot up the vehicle carrying the attacker. Another German patrol on Route Green was attacked with a grenade: one wounded. An American patrol was engaged (yes, the United States had joined ISAF by this time). My favorite carpet sales district, Chicken Street, was hit by a suicide bomber. This guy attacked with a vest full of grenades; when he detonated himself, the explosion blew him into about four or six pieces (it was hard to tell from the photo), not the sort of gray-red plasma I'd seen in the Middle East. Wounded ISAF personnel included members of the Icelandic contingent, who I didn't even realize had sent a contingent to Afghanistan. Nobody was killed except for the bomber. Another shooting on Chicken Street: an American soldier from Task Force APACHE was wounded. The widely reported attack against the DynCorp safe house was another highlight: six dead, three wounded. Canadians in Camp Julien, on the other side of the mountains, felt the concussion wave from the explosion.

The MANPADS threat was still out there, though I had to dig out the details from the air force community: SA-7 Strela and some Stinger constituted the main threats to ISAF and OEF aircraft in late 2004. Indirect rocket attacks had ramped up over the past three months, probably in response to preparations for the election. Five rockets hit ISAF facilities, with one civilian killed. Most attacks against fixed ISAF positions occurred along Route Violet: this was the main east-west axis leading from the city center to Jalalabad and the Khyber Pass. Camp Warehouse, ISAF HQ, Camp Phoenix, KMTC, and so on: everybody called it

---

* This all changed in 2005 with a change of leadership in the Canadian Forces.

Route "Violence." An emplaced IED (improvised explosive device) on Blue Route was spotted and defused using UXO engineers. A rocket was fired at Camp Julien but dropped eight hundred meters short.

At this point in time, there was substantial hostile intelligence gathering against the Canadian contingent and ISAF. Distinct patterns of behavior were noted. Canadian personnel driving around frequently noted surveillance: cameras that no Afghan could afford, for example, or males wearing blue burkas with click counters and cell phones. When I asked who the main players were from outside of Afghanistan and not necessarily in the OMF camp, I was told that China was conducting massive intelligence-gathering operations in the city. Not surprising: people forget that China has its own Islamist insurgency to deal with in the western provinces, one of which abuts the thin, long Badakhshan province of Afghanistan. When I went back to Afghanistan, it was in the wake of the daily breathless reports in the Western media about every ambush or attack against American forces in Iraq. The term "VBIED" (vehicle-borne improvised explosive device) entered the public vocabulary. The North American public was treated to a nightly (actually minutely) blow-by-blow of how these things worked, and their effects. In effect, a year of IED and VBIED terrorism played out in the public domain, Internet, and chat rooms had produced, if one drilled into it deeply enough, a database on how, where, and the optimum time to attack an armed convoy. Anybody with access to the Internet could compile this data, add it to what was known about how Hezbollah and Hamas and other Palestinian extremists attacked Israeli vehicles and installations, and you had a nascent training manual for budding terrorists. At a more intimate level, Al Qaeda was active in Iraq, and Al Qaeda was active in Pakistan and Afghanistan. The term that was used was "migration." There was massive concern that tactics would "migrate" to Afghanistan and be employed against ISAF in the city and elsewhere. Convoy briefs contained up-to-the-minute changes to conform to what was being experienced in Iraq. The ever-practical Canadians were experimenting with new actions on contact and procedures, which I will not elaborate on here. It was a constant cat-and-mouse game, an arms race in micro.

What did the Taliban and its allies want in 2004? That wasn't totally clear. The predominant theories suggested that Al Qaeda was interested in supporting any Islamist group that was around; it provided equipment, advice, and suicide bombers. Hekmatyar's HiG was starting to fragment, with some pieces aligning themselves ideologically more and with Al Qaeda. As for the Taliban, there were three possibilities. First, analysts thought they wanted to provoke and ethnic war between the Pashtuns and everybody else. Second, they wanted to amalgamate the

Pashtun areas in Pakistan and those in Afghanistan into "Pashtunistan." A third possibility was that Taliban leaders wanted to leverage violence so that they could be part of the political process. This theory was losing credibility day by day in late 2004.

operation athena: task force kabul

The Canadian ISAF contingent by this time was referred to as TFK, or Task Force Kabul. I had to be careful: to me TFK meant Task Force Kosovo (what we called Operation Kinetic), an operation that I had worked on. In Afghanistan I reflexively kept referring to Kosovo instead of Kabul, which produced some hilarity at times: "There's really no difference!" one officer chortled.

Operation Athena was the Canadian code name. This was Rotation 2, or Roto 2. Roto 2 was very different in scope and capability from Rotos 0 and 1. Roto 2 was in many ways a "caretaker" roto, maintaining Camp Julien until the Canadian government could figure out what it wanted to accomplish in Afghanistan and in NATO forums. In terms of structure, Roto 2 had an engineer squadron with EOD (explosive ordnance disposal) capacity (11 Field Squadron); a mechanized infantry company (B Company, 1 PPCLI) equipped with LAV III; and a reconnaissance and surveillance squadron from the Lord Strathcona's Horse equipped with Coyote vehicles, plus an infantry platoon from 3 PPCLI pretending to be an assault troop.[1] The Coyote vehicles are eight-wheeled armored cars equipped with a 25-mm gun and a surveillance system mounted on a hydraulic mast. The surveillance package includes thermal imagery cameras, a ground search radar, and other devices that provide an unprecedented capability unavailable to NATO at the time.

Camp Julien was also the home for Operation Archer, the Canadians working with OEF intelligence personnel and the component training the Afghan National Army, a twelve-man team called the ETT, or Embedded Training Team. Op Archer and Op Athena were separate missions but were housed in the same facility. Together, the missions included 724 Canadians in Kabul. Contractor staff consisted of 405 civilians, who supported the camp only, not the Canadian units in the camp. Roto 2 had its own mechanics and logistics support staff. Camp Julien and TFK to a certain extent supported the other Canadian Forces personnel in Kabul. This included Canadian officers and men who were part of the various multinational commands in Kabul: ISAF HQ, Kabul Multinational Brigade HQ, Combined Forces Command Afghanistan, Operation Accaus (the Canadian representative to the United Nations Mission in Afghanistan), and Operation Altair (the Canadian representative to Central Command in Qatar).

Camp Julien also boasted the ASIC, or All-Source Intelligence Centre. ASIC was in many ways a grand experiment in intelligence fusion. Data provided from the whole spectrum of sources, including the recce and surveillance squadron's Coyote vehicles, was brought together, Black magic was performed by the High Priests of Intelligence, and a product presented to those with an alleged need to know.

TFK's mission at this time was to "assist ISAF and Afghanistan security institutions in ensuring a secure environment within the Kabul Area of Operations with a view to facilitating Afghan national development." TFK units conducted a series of standing operations and a number of directed operations. The infantry company protected Camp Julien, which at this point housed a Belgian company, a Hungarian company, a Slovenian recce platoon, and an American infantry company that was surged in for the elections. Operation Horseshoe was a standing operation to disrupt attacks against the camp through random patrols, checkpoints, and monitoring possible rocket-launching sites. Related to Horseshoe was Op Lurker, which involved mounted and dismounted patrols designed to provide a random presence and deter attacks. There were also a series of operations involving the engineer squadron that were established to collect and destroy any ammo found in the Canadian area of operation to prevent their misuse as IEDs.

The recce squadron was engaged in a number of overwatch and surveillance tasks. Op Bighorn, for example, provided surveillance overwatch for the patrol company when it was involved in a Lurker operation in the eastern districts; suspicious people trying to move away from a Lurker patrol would be observed using the Coyote's surveillance gear and apprehended or tracked as necessary. Octopus and Hunter were operations designed to disrupt rocket attacks on the city or vital points in it like ISAF HQ.

Op Raccoon and Op Fox were examples of directed operations. A Coyote troop provided overwatch for the British Patrol Company as it conducted a series of cordon and searches to apprehend a HiG cell. Drumheller did the same on the main route to Jalalabad when intelligence was tracking a large explosives shipment coming in from Pakistan. Recce Squadron also deployed en masse whenever an important political event occurred in Kabul: this included surge operations for the 2004 elections, the presidential inauguration, and senior VIP visits of all kinds.

On another operation just before the 2004 election, recce squadron tracked a suspected suicide bomber with Coyote cameras. He had the signature of a jihadist: white robe, clean shaven. He was spotted on a street and tracked by Coyotes all the way across Kabul—on and off buses and taxis, and so on. Special operations forces did a takedown and apprehended him.

Recce squadron was one of several layers of ISAF surveillance over the city. The Dutch AH-64 helicopter unit was another, as was the German LUNA UAV (unmanned aerial vehicle) unit. The French operated a C-160 Transall equipped with signals intercept equipment, while the Germans were conducting experiments in Kabul with a Coyote-like vehicle. Any combination of these resources could be used to feed the intelligence fusion centers at KMNB or ISAF. Of course, there were other "special intelligence" capabilities available to ISAF and KMNB. There were, however, significant problems in tasking all of these resources, which increased the frustration level among the Canadians.

First, there were major multinational rivalries that generated a certain amount of "static" at the brigade level (as discussed later). And then there was Ottawa. At this time, TFK had to refer each "directed operation" all the way to Ottawa for approval. I understand from talking to people that sometimes this had to go all the way from Kabul to the Deputy Chief of the Defence Staff to the Minister of National Defence and/or the Chief of Defence Staff. The staffs in Kabul and Ottawa tried to reduce the approval time and were successful in getting it done in less than an hour. This kind of overcontrol clearly reduced reaction time, especially if there was a fleeting target like an enemy leader or a package of explosives that was on the move.

There were additional complications relating to the extent that Canadian ISAF units could support OEF operations in Kabul area of operations. This related to the emergent issue of detainee policy, which reached a high-pitched screech after the Abu Ghraib "fraternity prank."[2] If OEF mounted a mission to apprehend terrorist leaders and those people were sent to Gitmo, was it OK for Canada to provide surveillance and/or the outer cordon of the operation? This was the sort of question that legal advisers and bureaucrats got wound up about regularly. Like the air campaign in Kosovo back in 1999, lawyers had now successfully inserted themselves into the targeting process. Each directed operation, if it focused on an individual, had to be approved by a targeting board. How do we *know* this guy's a terrorist? Is your plan based on the use of minimal force? How much collateral damage *may* result? If there is too much potential for damage, change the plan. Or don't mount the operation. And so on. It all seemed to be about reducing *potential* liability and being able to provide answers/excuses for the politicians in case anything went wrong rather than fighting a war. It all seemed overly legalistic and *American Justice* like. I could just envision a *Law and Order* episode in Afghanistan involving ROE and a directed operation. Or Bill Curtis on A&E yakking on about "the raid gone wrong." Of course, the bureaucrats and politicians watched those shows too.

On the surface, recce squadron seemed to be the perfect bureaucrat's tool for Afghanistan—watch and let somebody else do the dirty work—but I understand the lawyers assigned to SOF were really, really busy in Afghanistan. To paraphrase *Apocalypse Now:* "The Taliban didn't have much use for JAGs and LEGADS: he was dug in too deep or moving too fast. His idea of great justice was beheading teachers or burning down schools. He had only two ways home: death or victory."

the chessgame

When you disarm the people, you commence to offend them and show that you distrust them either through cowardice or lack of confidence, and both of these opinions generate hatred.

—NICCOLO MACHIAVELLI

I waited for my escort in the mess. There was a Canadian patrol going out; they were going to drop me at the embassy, then pick me up later. Two American senior NCOs were grousing. "I don't get it. What is this 'metrosexual' stuff all about? I have guys that want manicures and skin care now! In the field! It's not like the old days, goddamnit." The other one nodded into his beer. The big screen TV had a feed from Al Jazeera, something not available in North America. It was all in Arabic, of course, but it wasn't hard to figure out what was going on. The current affairs program had a documentary about Islamic guerrillas in the Philippines, with footage shot from the perspective of MILF, the Moro Islamic Liberation Front (never, ever try to Google MILF . . . put the whole thing into the search engine, please). There was an ad for an upcoming documentary on the French use of torture in Algeria in the 1950s and its connection to Chile and Argentina security services excesses. Then the start-up montage was on: a British soldier with a skull and crossbones flag flying from his APC, an American soldier trying cover the camera lens with his hand, an Apache flyover, and an IED explosion, all set to dramatic music. What has our media wrought?

Everybody in the Foreign Affairs Canada should love Chris Alexander. Foreign Affairs Canada should preen itself because of Chris Alexander. Foreign Affairs, if it could as an institution, should be ecstatic over the presence of Chris Alexander in Kabul. Why? Because Chris Alexander is the epitome of what a Canadian ambassador should be and what most of them are not. That aside, and more important, he understands "the Chessgame." And Ottawa doesn't.

What I do care about is that Chris not only understands the Chessgame, he is a player in it, and he can explain his part in it to me. He recognizes that the game exists, even though "Chessgame" is a term I have applied to it merely to give it a shorthand. Chris, unlike his myopic counterparts in the Canadian International Development Agency (CIDA) and his somewhat arrogant contemporaries in

Foreign Affairs, realizes that a synergy of efforts is necessary for success in Afghanistan, and he has worked tirelessly to achieve that synergy: "The situation is stable, but fragile," he told me. I agree. But was he referring to the relationship between the Department of National Defence (DND), DFAIT, and CIDA, or the competing Afghan factions? I pressed on . . . Few appreciate how delicate a mechanism like the Chessgame is. Chris does, and it cannot be easy to explain to his masters in Ottawa, where domestically expedient "big hand–small map" thinking prevails, where there is lip service paid to *Auftragstaktik* but communications technology permits unprecedented levels of interference. One of the significant factors in the success of the ISAF mission in Kabul thus far was the Vulcan mind meld that existed between Chris Alexander and Major General Andy Leslie, when he was deputy ISAF commander. The two of them were the prime movers behind Heavy Weapons Cantonment and the use of DDR as a coercive tool, converting it from the limp weapons turn-in program that others advocated.

Let us consider the "chessboard." It is more than the territorial confines of what we call Afghanistan, and it is more than just the region of the world in which Afghanistan is a neighbor. It is the matrix of personalities and the forces they control, and the balances that exist between all of this and the international community. The chessboard operates on several planes.

One of the main problems that confronted the stabilization effort while the Taliban was being destroyed was the possibility of a return to the 1992–96 period, when victorious mujahideen from more than twelve factions fought among the ruins; defeat was truly pulled from the jaws of victory. This was one major factor that led to the rise of the Taliban in the first place, and why there was initially popular support for the Pakistani-created and supported movement. In 2001–2 it was one thing to strip away the Taliban, the layer protecting Al Qaeda. It was another to build a functioning government.

The situation in 2003 was precarious. The Taliban was, for all intents and purposes, destroyed and discredited among most of the population. Power lay in the hands of several OEF-backed "warlords" who were really tribal chieftains with tanks, APCs, and artillery. Most of these chieftains were part of the anti-Taliban effort. In the past, some fought for the Soviet-backed regime, while others fought with the mujahideen groups. They were the victors in 2002; and as victors have throughout history, they set themselves up in the provinces of Afghanistan. In Kabul, the leader of the Northern Alliance, Fahim Khan, dominated the city, established a security service, and, like his colleagues, maintained a mobilized military force.

The Afghan Interim Administration, later the Afghan Transitional Administration, was the nascent national government installed by the international community. Led by Hamid Karzai, the AIA/ATA had little coercive power. Even if it had been augmented by American firepower to compete with the chieftain's forces, it would have been unable to make headway. It would have been viewed as an American imposition on the country, and Karzai, a Pashtun, would have drawn as much ire as Mohammed Najibullah back in 1992. There was no national army. It was under construction, but the pre-NATO ISAF dropped the ball in 2002, and it took over a year to get a program established to build up the ANA. It was slow going.

By the end of 2003, the factions included OEF; ISAF in Kabul; the ATA and its slowly building Afghan National Army; plus at least eight chieftain armies collectively referred to as the Afghan Militia Forces, or AMF. The AMF units were grouped for identification purposes as "corps" in their geographical areas of operations. The AMF units were not exactly the "private warlord armies" that the press called them, but their loyalty lay with the main chieftain and, of course, money and security. Oh, by the way, the Taliban remnants in the southeast, Al Qaeda, and Hekmatyar's forces (HiG) were all still active.

Weak central government in a country that had never known a strong central government. A defeated enemy that won't quit. At least eight major local players with forces under their own control, fueled in some capacity with profits from the narcotics production industry. Two international military forces that at times worked at cross-purposes. A UN that was not trusted by the people, let alone the chieftains. This was not a prescription for success. And the stakes were high: American prestige, let alone the upcoming American presidential elections with the high level of invective we have come to expect from the opposition, were factors not to be underestimated. "Afghanistan as Vietnam" was the motif, then "Iraq is Vietnam." Two Vietnams at once?

U.S. forces could not occupy Afghanistan; that had been tried before. Afghanistan could not be allowed, by dint of the outright removal of Western coalition forces, to lapse back into Lebanon-like multifactional fighting: the Taliban and Al Qaeda would just come back. The United States and the West could not be seen to run Afghanistan like an 1800s-era colonial outpost; that had been tried before too. Chris and his American, British, Afghan, and Japanese counterparts understood this. The Chessgame slowly emerged in late 2003 as the solution to these interconnected problems.

In effect, the Chessgame is a combination of games. First, there is the OEF game: the United States is the dominant Western player, with a global and regional agenda. Then there is the ISAF game: generally this is a European-dominated game with European stakes, though Canada plays a significant role. Then there is the Afghan game: the Karzai government, and not the chieftains, is the dominant domestic player. The pieces are the chieftains, the AMF, the ANA, and the UN. The spoilers are the triple-barreled threat of the Taliban, Al Qaeda, and HiG and whichever chieftain decides to fight the tide of change.

Within each game are a series of moving parts; some of these moving parts mesh with the moving parts of the overlapping games of adjacent players. For example, ISAF and OEF cooperate in provincial stabilization operations; this has a synergistic effect in that region where the gears mesh.

The OEF game moving parts include the high-value target hunt and SOF operations; Provincial Reconstruction Team (PRT) development; border operations; and Afghan National Army development and training. The ISAF game includes Kabul stabilization operations; expansion of ISAF to the provinces and PRT development; security sector training; and the Heavy Weapons Cantonment and DDR programs. These last overlap with other games. The Afghan game revolves around personalities: who controls what provinces, what do they control, and how are they supported.

House of cards is an imperfect analogy; a shift in one move of the Chessgame, however, produces sometimes measurable effects in other areas of the matrix. At other times, effects are unpredictable. The goal of the Chessgame remains the same, however: ensuring that there is a stable central government, that the outlying and remote regions of Afghanistan are responsive to it and safe from attack from both internal and external enemies. Only then can long-term reconstruction and therefore economic security be achieved. And that is the basis for "Al Qaeda-proofing" Afghanistan: so it can never again be used as a transnational terrorist base area.

Chris explained how the Chessgame swung into action in the summer of 2004. "Shindand, Farah, Ghor: that's what we called the 'arc of instability' out in the west," he said. "Ismael Khan had been in control in Herat even during the Taliban period. His followers were displeased with the new government, and particularly the ANA. The AMF out there were starting to assert influence and not all of them were loyal to Ismael Khan. Why? Fahim Khan was starting to influence them. There were standoffs, violence, particularly around Shindand, where there is an important air base. The media started to portray what was going on as cataclysmic, while the Northern Alliance claimed that the Taliban was coming back. Neither were accurate, of course.

"Ismael Khan, who styled himself as 'the emir of the west,' was allowed to be the commander of IV AMF Corps until last year. He wanted to remain a political leader, but under the rules he can't be both military and political leader. Then this summer he claimed that he was under attack and had to respond. With his own forces. Which he wasn't supposed to have. The attacker, Aminullah Khan, was into power; he's a power warlord, not interested in the 'cover' of office like Ismael Khan understands. Essentially both Khans are to blame. But what was Karzai to do? He has a potential civil war on his hands and he isn't the elected leader of Afghanistan yet.

"The situation was aggravated by the March 2004 killing of Ismael Khan's son, who was a minister in Kabul. There was an accident: a situation had escalated and it appears as though a personal dispute was to blame. Karzai had a dilemma: does he add insult to injury by removing Ismael Khan so soon after that? It's a real Hobson's choice. The Americans relied on Ismael Khan a lot; they weren't keen on his removal. Karzai consulted with the American embassy, OEF, ISAF, and us. Everybody except the Americans agreed that Ismael Khan had to go before the election. We were able to convince the Americans this was best." He smiled.

"In August there was a riot in Herat, UN buildings were torched, but there were scant details coming out of there. A security plan was put together between OEF, the Afghan National Army, and the Afghan National Police. A Special Forces team and an OEF Provincial Reconstruction Team, and some other units, about a thousand personnel, were formed into Task Force LONGHORN and deployed to Herat, and then the Afghan National Army brought along about five battalions. The plan was to interpose this force between both Khans. I tried to get the Canadian Embedded Training Team, who trained one of the battalions, to go, but we were blocked by Ottawa." (Chris, of course, is much more diplomatic than I am: I discuss this situation in more detail in the ETT section.)

I learned elsewhere that there was another dimension to the Herat-Shindand operations. The Americans had concerns about Iranian meddling in western Afghanistan and wanted a "foot on the ground" from Kabul to influence any future Iranian behavior. The fact that Shindand is the only large air base in the west was not inconsequential. There were some split opinions; Ismael Khan was known to have close contacts with Iraq. Some Americans thought he would become a liability even though he helped oust the Taliban. Other Americans wanted to keep working with him, but the decision was made by Karzai.

"Once the force was on the ground, they initiated the Disarmament, Demobilization and Reintegration process with both Afghan militia force groups there. By the time of the election, 50 percent of the heavy weapons had been cantoned and 50 percent of the AMFs were demobilized. Once the DDR of Ismael Khan was accomplished, we could then move on to the smaller AMF groups in the west using Herat as a precedent. The Old Guard learned that if they wanted to play in politics, they couldn't have private armies. [Abdul Rashid] Dostum, [Burhanuddin] Rabbani, [Abdul Rasul] Sayyaf: they all got the message. There was limited media coverage, so everybody saved face."

Indeed, Rashid Dostum's AMF were gone by early 2005, and Rabbani and Sayyaf were well on their way. There was the problem of Fahim Khan, but that was being worked on. Karzai created an associate minister of national defense and slowly, carefully moved responsibilities over to him and away from Fahim Khan. With Khan's AMF demobilized, and with decreased power in the defense establishment, Fahim Khan was marginalized over time. He was eventually offered a cabinet post. Except for his buddy, the chief of police in Kabul, who was corrupt and had his own police forces . . .

I asked Chris what the main success stories were.

"There are three. The first is the Heavy Weapons Cantonment program. The second is the removal and consolidation of the massive ammunition stockpiles. This is a huge challenge, but we have a grip on it now we didn't have before. This is a Canadian-led effort. The third main success is the reduction of the AMF, though we now have a problem with 'irregular militias': these are the remnants of some AMF formations. There are about a hundred of these groups, numbering between ten and the low hundreds in strength. They cross over into the drug trade. There is no regulation of them."

"How are the Americans handling the fact that Canada is taking a leadership role in Afghanistan?" I asked.

"The U.S. is in listening mode: it's not a one-way street here like is it elsewhere. The Americans came up with the PRT concept; they understand that this is a stabilization and counterinsurgency mission." Chris, being diplomatic, let me fill in the blanks. Others didn't see Afghanistan as a stabilization or counterinsurgency mission; they thought it was peacekeeping. And it wasn't. We were there in support of a legitimate government, and we were not impartial, we were not interposed between the Taliban and the "warlords."

the american game: CFC-alpha

I met up with Colonel Dave Banks and Colonel Randy Brooks while they were visiting Camp Julien. Dave and Randy were Canadian exchange officers who were part of Combined Forces Command Afghanistan, or CFC-Alpha, the American command for Afghanistan. Along with Major Jim Fitzgerald, Canada had a significant presence and role to play in the American staff that was generating current and future plans for the stabilization of Afghanistan and building the institutions necessary for an exit strategy.

I spent some time with CFC-A to get a grip on the unfolding strategy, but first I had to get there. As I mentioned earlier, moving around Kabul with the Canadian contingent was a production: I think the requirements involved two armored vehicles, at least eight armed personnel, and constant radio contact with point-to-point movement. When I inquired why this policy was still in place over a year after the suicide bomb attack against the Iltis, I was informed that the probability of attacking a hard target was less than a soft one. I had a number of observations, however. If Kabul was progressing to a safe, secure environment, then how did the presence of armored vehicles in clogged city streets contribute to or detract from that assertion or perception? Similarly it was extremely difficult to interact with the population from a vehicle that had windows that could not open, or from the high perch of a LAV III turret. When I was in Kosovo, Canadians derided the American contingent for traveling in two-vehicle armed convoys; now the Canadians were doing the same thing. The choices were closed and uncommunicative, less risk; and open and communicative, some risk. A decision was made either in Ottawa or at the Task Force Kabul level for the former.

Colonel Brooks understood my exasperation with moving around Kabul under armor. That is when I met Corporal Billy Groseclose and his civilian-pattern jeep. Corporal Groseclose, a former U.S. Marine helicopter crewman, now U.S. Army, provided transport, protection, and color commentary as we wove our way through Kabul's traffic nightmare (actually Cairo is worse). Corporal Groseclose was in his mid-twenties and was the epitome of a switched-on soldier, undaunted by the completely alien environment he was operating in. With his easygoing, friendly southern/western accent, Corporal Groseclose could deal with the most self-contained Afghan. He had learned enough to deal with the CFC-A Afghan security staff in their own language. He knew more about Afghan history than Canadian history, so I provided him with some key tidbits from out violent past.

The laid-back, easygoing nature, the Cuban cigars (thank God, I was running low again), and so on completely belied Corporal Groseclose's hardened, professional edge that came out instantly when a threat presented itself. We were driving from CFC-A to Camp Julien: the unmarked jeep was right-hand drive, I was in the passenger seat, and there was a Special Forces major with an M-4 behind me. Billy drove with a cocked pistol between his legs and an assault rifle in the backseat. I expected high speeds, weaving in and out. Nope. The Kabul Police laid colored bricks along all of the center lines to prevent this, so we were blocked in and forced to travel at the same rate as the traffic flow. We entered a traffic circle and got caught in a jam. Instinctively I watched the area to my left, since it was open road and a drive-by could get us and get away. There was this young guy standing next to a parked motorcycle staring at us. Just then the Lada in front of us stopped abruptly and the driver hopped out and put the hood up. We were stuck.

"Is this a setup?" I wondered aloud as my "spidy sense" was tingling. Billy immediately, if not faster, placed his hand on the pistol and scanned right and forward. Adrenaline surged as the guy in the vehicle in front came at us waving his arms. Billy stepped on the gas, hitting the horn, and pushed the stalled Lada forward to give us room to get out. The guy freaked out, placing both hands on his head, wailing. I heard the SF Major click off the safety on his M-4, keeping one eye on the Lada driver, and one on the motorcyclist. The Lada moved forward of its own volition, hood still up, empty. Another man walking toward us calmly slammed the hood down and kept walking while the driver ran after his Lada. We passed him with upraised shoulders—"Sorry, man!"—and plunged into the maw of Holy Fuck Circle, where a German machine gunner with a headset, face mask, and goggles overwatched the action from a Fuchs APC. False alarm, this time.

We had a good laugh about it later, especially over the helpful guy who slammed the hood of the empty, moving vehicle. Not in LA! Not in New York! It was easier, in certain cases, to blend in as much as possible, in a more mobile vehicle without a lot of hoopla.

This was in complete contrast to a similar situation where I was with Major Jim Fitzgerald and two Canadian G-Wagons clearly marked with ISAF insignia. We bumped or were bumped by a local guy, a common scam to extort money from the international community playing on guilt and lots of gesticulation. We were stuck for nearly twenty minutes, immobile on a crowded Kabul street, dealing with this scam artist. We presented a greater target (two vehicles, eight guys) for a longer period to deal with the paperwork and emotions. I liked Jim's wit, however. When confronted with people demanding money, he told them that "Allah is keeping *you* poor to test *our* compassion." There could be no argument after that . . .

CFC-Alpha was established between February and April 2004 to replace a con-voluted command structure set up in early 2002. Like the more familiar and traditional staffing positions, CFC-A had principals grouped from CJ-1 to CJ-6 (CJ stands for Combined Joint), but the old designators had a new twist. The "1" was still personnel, the "2" was still intelligence, "3" was still operations, and "4" was still logistics. The "5," however, was plans. The "3," operations, handled immediate ops; "5" planned for the future and dealt with policy, and strategy. There was also the relatively new "Effects" staff, which grouped public affairs, information operations, and PSYOPS together. Essentially this was an EBO (effects-based operations) cell. The most straightforward definition is that EBO "are coordinated sets of actions directed at shaping the behavior of friends, foes and neutrals in peace crisis, and war."[3] The EBO proponents argue that in the past military operations were viewed as being directed against other militaries, whereas EBO supposedly takes into account all military and nonmilitary means to achieve an objective, which is defined as the effect that a protagonist wants to produce on the target audience.

For me, as a military historian, EBO is not new. In many ways it is just another expensive buzzword applied to what commanders have done since war was invented: prevail using all means fair and foul to intimidate an opponent. Clausewitz was all about EBO: force the enemy to do our will. When Julius Caesar cut off the hands of several thousand Gauls to deter them from taking up arms against Rome a second time, this was also an "effects-based operation." The difference now was that the commander had a cell to model the third- and fourth-order effects of his decisions in the psychological and sociological domain and didn't have to keep it all in his head.

The "2" was organized differently from a traditional intelligence staff. CJ-2 handled threat projections with the "2" staff, but there was also a "2X" staff, another innovation, which was responsible for real-time, immediate, tactical intelligence linked to the high-value target hunt.

The high-value target hunt, as usual, was highly sensitive because of the political ramifications of cross-border coordination and ops, internal Afghan politics, the fragility of intelligence that could activate a response by the JSOC units, and the secrecy needed to protect information sources, let alone the misperceptions that the media and interest groups could rapidly generate to support their objectives, which were not in consonance with stabilizing Afghanistan. Obviously nobody wanted a JSOC team ambushed, like in Mogadishu.

There were further complications in the HVT hunt. President Karzai initiated a Taliban/HiG reconciliation program as part of the DDR program. The American HVT list, I was told, had some thirty-five names on it who were not "reconcilable," that is, they were to be captured or eliminated. However, there were some 150 names on the Afghan list, for which there could be no "reconciliation." Deconfliction was, of course, critical. At the same time, the Americans had to very careful to make sure they were not manipulated into eliminating legitimate political opponents. It was all a balancing act.

HVTs were not always grabbed when spotted. In some cases they led observers back to other cells and supporters. In some cases they were permitted to go about their business to "put them to sleep" and get them to drop their guard before a snatch. It was all very, very calculated. The levels of coordination belie the assertions in the media that the intelligence community is broken and useless. This was all part of the Chessgame: DDR, reconciliation, and HVT operations. JSOC spent a lot of time in the eastern provinces, like Kunar and Nangarhar.

Commanded by Lieutenant General David Barno, CFC-Alpha had three primary organizations under its command. The Office of Military Cooperation

(OMC) was funded by the U.S. State Department and was responsible for Task Force PHOENIX, the Afghan National Army Embedded Training Teams. The "Other Coalition Forces" (OCF) was in charge of unconventional forces and Tier I targeting ("black" SOF ops). CJTF-76 was essentially a division-sized HQ commanded by Major General Eric T. Olson. CJTF-76 had several task forces situated around the country based on a brigade from the 25th Infantry Division from Hawaii, plus a Combined Joint Special Operations Task Force (CJSOTF) that handled "white" SOF ops.

The relations between CFC-A, ISAF, and various commands were strained during this time, a serious decline from the period when Lieutenant General Rick Hillier, a Canadian, commanded ISAF. Hillier got along with everybody and served as great "connective tissue" between OEF and ISAF, primarily because of his experience commanding a multinational division in Bosnia and his previous job as the deputy corps commander to III (U.S.) Corps in the United States. The perception when I was on the ground at the time was that Barno and Olson did not get on well, so relations between CFC-A and CJTF-76 were defined by some as "not good." ISAF commander French General Jean-Louis Py and Barno "sort of" got along, but Olson and Py were actively hostile toward each other. I understood that this was nearly totally driven by French versus American problems as much as personality-based issues. One possible culprit was, according to some officers, the lack of coalition operation experience within the 25th Infantry Division. Isolated in Hawaii, the division had little or no experience dealing with NATO or other allied forces.[4] The hope by some officers was that the situation would improve with the deployment of the 173rd Airborne Brigade, which was based in Europe and had a repository of coalition experience. American internal problems aside, the real issues revolved around the French-American interface, which was in turn linked to the Iraq War problems. This had a direct impact on OEF-ISAF operations, which was played out within the Kabul Multinational Brigade HQ (as described later on) and in other forums in Kabul.

three wars at once

The CFC-A depiction of what was going on in Afghanistan circa late 2004 suggested that there were three overlapping conflicts. The first was the HVT hunt, as described above. Second, there were the Al Qaeda, Taliban, and HiG networks operating inside Afghanistan. Finally, the planners used the phrase "the centrifugal forces of Afghanistan" to describe the spinoffs: warlords, narcotics, and factionalism. The identified centers of gravity, to give it a Clausewitzian spin, varied. For the HVT hunt, the planners knew that the enemy leadership knew that CFC-A penetration into the frontier areas of Pakistan was problematic, so the center of gravity here was targetable intelligence. In essence this appears to have been based on national technical means because of the problems in developing HUMINT (human intelligence). For the terrorist networks, CFC-A planners understood that they could survive only with the assistance of the Afghan peoples. Therefore, the peoples of Afghanistan became the center of gravity in the fight against the networks. To deal with the centrifugal forces effectively meant that there had to be a strong Afghan government, so that was the third center of gravity.

Keeping the same strategic objectives that were established back in 2002–3, CFC-A was to conduct "full spectrum operations in order to establish enduring security, defeat Al Qaeda and the Taliban, and deter the re-emergence of terrorism in Afghanistan." The briefers explained that Afghanistan was a "chicken-and-egg" problem: security was dependent on reconstruction, while reconstruction was dependent on security. At the same time, CFC-A knew that there had to be some relationship to ISAF and what it was doing. The broader CFC-A objectives therefore included the statement that CFC-A had to "set the conditions for NATO assumption of the combined ISAF/OEF mission and coalition drawdown." And to do that, CFC-A and ISAF had to "enable good governance and democracy; and enable socio-economic development and reconstruction." A defined strategic end state for the international community mission in Afghanistan was, in the planners' words, an Afghanistan that is:

- Moderate, stable, and democratic, though it is understood that Afghans will not copy U.S.-style institutions
- Representative of all responsible elements in Afghanistan and formed through the political participation of the Afghan people
- Capable of effectively controlling and governing its territory
- Capable of implementing policies to stimulate economic development to the point of self-sufficiency and export
- Willing to contribute to a continuing partnership with the U.S.-led coalition in the global war on terror

Taking all of this together, the effects that CFC-A wanted to generate included the defeat of Al Qaeda; the defeat and reconciliation of the Taliban and the HiG; the defeat of narcotics networks; and the reintegration of the warlords and their militias. That was the best application of military force at this time for this region.

CFC-A's strategy for Afghanistan, therefore, looked to influence the Afghan peoples. The base of that strategy was information operations to ensure that the Afghan peoples remained convinced that the coalition effort was effective so that they would support it. The five lines of operations that were distilled from the appreciation of the situation included "Defeat Terrorism and Deny Sanctuary; Enable Afghan Security Structures; Sustain Area Ownership; Enable Reconstruction and Good Governance; and Engage Regional States." "Sustain Area Ownership" really meant explaining to the Afghans that they were not fragmented entities, that they owned Afghanistan. "Engage Regional States" meant that isolation and isolated operations inside Afghanistan were not conducive to success; only a cooperative effort would be successful.

CFC-A's counterinsurgency strategy was a significant change from what was going on in 2002–3. At that time the enemy forces were less of terrorist threat and more of a guerrilla force. There was no strong central authority in Kabul. The entire country could have plunged back into the violence of the 1993–96 civil war period. OEF forces were raiding Taliban and Al Qaeda base areas in nearly inaccessible regions, while special operations forces raided training camps and WMD (weapons of mass destruction) labs. OEF had a small number of large air bases from which they sallied forth as necessary, based on intelligence "hits." By 2004–5, however, this had changed. The stress now was on Provincial Reconstruction Teams.

CFC-A planners understood what the deficiencies of the Afghanistan program were in 2004. Information operations was the weakest area: the enemy ran rings around the coalition in Information Operation (I/O). Any attack against an NGO or aid agency should have been be considered enemy I/O, but it wasn't: it was just another attack. There was no counter other than hunt the perpetrators. There was no post-attack "messaging" by the coalition to the Afghan population, that is, "look at the effects of this attack on you, the people." Nobody aggressively countered the Taliban's inflated claims that they were able to get into mainstream Western media. "Night letters" and other intimidation tactics were being used against people who worked for OEF, but there was no counter to them. The enemy used tribal connections and communications systems to get their message across, yet there was no coalition program to address those messages. The one success that CFC-A could point to was in response to a Taliban kidnap operation. The I/O specialists were able to rock the Taliban back on their heels by slagging them when they kidnapped women, by subtly insulting their manhood: "See how tough they are? They kidnap *women!*" The more politically correct Westerners in the PSYOPS policy world were uncomfortable with that kind of response. Information developed later indicated this approach caused a division within the Taliban as they debated the merits of kidnapping women versus the potential backfire from such operations.

The biggest area of concern was the Afghan National Police. There was an authority problem both in Kabul and in the provinces. Who was in charge? The

Germans were the lead nation, but they weren't leading in the field. They provided good training, but it was, according to CFC-A, taking too long. There were regional training centers, but there were connectivity problems with the Kabul police training system because the German police trainers couldn't leave Kabul by German ministerial order. CFC-A wanted to overhaul the police completely, but it wasn't in charge.

the american game II: provincial reconstruction teams

Throughout 2004, the buzzword in the analytical communities and among NGOs was "PRTs." Papers emerged extolling the possibilities, how they could be expanded, what they could be mutated into to fit the objectives of a variety of interest groups. Other papers were published decrying the PRTs as an expansion of American military influence and a corruption of the humanitarian mission in Afghanistan. Lost in all of this so-called analysis were the origins of the PRT and how the concept evolved over time. In addition, the differences between "coalition"—that is, OEF-controlled—PRTS and NATO ISAF PRTs were not adequately explained in the public domain.

By October 2002 there was recognition within CJTF-180 that the gears in Afghanistan were shifting from war fighting to stabilization. Planners were increasingly concerned about, in their words, "removing the causes of instability" and enabling Afghan government institutions to take control of the country. Many OEF planners had extensive experience in Bosnia and Kosovo, and there were some who thought these cases might provide a model for Afghanistan. A more detailed analysis conducted within CJTF-180 dissuaded the "Balkans" school of thought. First, the planners noted that the situations in the Balkans "were settled by agreements that established international responsibilities and process that all parties agreed to and which enabled the international community to establish secure environments in conjunction with the parties." There was no such equivalent to the GFAP (General Framework Agreement for Peace in Bosnia–Herzegovina) in Afghanistan. The Bonn Agreement of 2001 was not structured to be like the GFAP in any way. More important, OEF briefers were quick to point out that Afghanistan had a population eight times that of Bosnia, and that thirteen Bosnias and thirty-nine Kosovos would fit inside the territorial confines of the country.

In contrast to Bosnia and Kosovo, the primary challenge in Afghanistan was not at the microethnic level. The wars had not been fought on strictly ethnic lines, though ethnicity was a factor at the regional level. One primary issue was how to develop a strong relationship between the regions and the new central government. In Bosnia and Kosovo, the primary issue was the reweaving of the ethnic matrix and forcing that matrix to work together at the street, village, canton, and federal level.

In the initial concepts, the Coalition Interagency Regional Team, or CIRT, which was changed to Joint Regional Team by late 2002, was to be structured as a small-scale, understated presence backed up with a dedicated rapid reaction force that was kept in the wings. The JRT was to influence and coordinate, and not control events at the provincial level. As for specific tasks, the original planners believed that the JRTs would "create the conditions for the United Nations Mission in Afghanistan to conduct Disarmament, Demobilization and Reintegration with the focus on organized militias and heavy weapons." The JRTs would monitor said militias and provide professionalization training to them while keeping an eye on their activities. JRTs were also to coordinate NGO and UN aid activity with the provincial governor's administration, while at the same time serving as an information broker between all parties involved in stabilization and recons-truction activities. Indeed, CJTF-180 planners believed that the JRTs could replace the U.S. Special Forces activities in some locations. Finally, the initial conception of the JRT included provisions for coordinating agencies involved in law enforce-ment, particularly those involved in counternarcotics.

As early as October 2002, CJTF-180 planners were already conceptualizing a situation whereby coalition operations in Afghanistan were split between a large number of JRTs throughout the country and a separate Combined Task Force (CTF) for handling counterinsurgency operations along the Pakistan border. This separate CTF was to consist of a light infantry brigade, a Special Forces ODB with a number of ODAs, plus a forward support base and two or three JRTs. An operational reserve with aviation support rounded this out. For the rest of the country, there would be several JRTs operating at the provincial level, and a smaller number of forward Support Bases to assist them in emergencies. In effect, the CTF would go after Taliban, Al Qaeda, and HiG elements in the east and southeast, while the other JRTs would handle reconstruction and suppress those opposed to the extension of central governmental authority. The CTF JRTs would have augmented intelligence capabilities and greater force protection. All JRTs would rely to a certain extent on Afghan National Army protection.

Throughout 2002, there were shrill calls from the NGO and aid communities to have ISAF (recall that ISAF was not yet a NATO organization) replace OEF throughout Afghanistan. Boiled down, this debate reflected the problems of Europe versus the United States in the run-up to the next phase of the decade-long Iraq War. Some commentators preferred a multinational organization that was not American dominated so that the world could see that operations in Afghanistan did not constitute "American imperialism." Many commentators weighing in on the side of ISAF, however, did not appreciate the realities on the ground. ISAF at that time was not even a hollow shell: It was a near-token European presence in Kabul that was unable to carry out the bulk of the limited missions that the Bonn Agreement assigned to it. Indeed, ISAF spent more time protecting itself than supporting the emergent transitional government. ISAF was outgunned by the Northern Alliance. Demands by the noncognoscenti to instantaneously increase the forty-five-hundred-man ISAF (of which three thousand were support personnel) to a command numbering in the tens of thousands to "replace the drug warlords supported by the CIA" was completely unrealistic.

CJTF-180 planners knew this but had to respond to the continual carping from those who thought they knew better. As one briefer pointed out to me, "simply 'expanding ISAF' isn't a guarantee to solving the problem—its current structure and military capability isn't appropriate for all regions in Afghanistan."

The JRT concept was continuously refined in the fall of 2002. A formal mission statement emerged. The JRTs were to "conduct activities and operations to strengthen the Interim Transitional Government of Afghanistan's influence through effective interaction with regional political, military, and religious leaders, UNAMA, Security Sector coordinating bodies and NGOs within the regions." JRTs will "encourage peace and stability within provinces and regions through the monitoring and supervision of the reorganization process of militias, in order to stimulate developmental activity and reconstruction." At the same time, certain JRTs were to be responsible for "cuing the employment of operational fires, reserves, and security forces when the situation demands it," as one planner explained.

The planners also acknowledged that JRTs might, in fact, become multinational in structure, through at this point no thought was given to having JRTs under something other than CJTF-180 command. JRTs would also be interagency in nature and not strictly a military subunit. There would be "assessment patrols" and information coordinators, but there would also be UN DDR reps, a police expert, and liaison staff for the embryonic judicial system. The numbers were still small: an early estimate suggested that each JRT would be around twenty personnel, excluding rapid reaction forces and special forces working with the AMF and ANA. Other ideas included engineer and medical "surge" capabilities, public health teams and the like that would move into an area as needed, and redeploy as necessary. CJTF-180 planners also recognized that some kind of higher command and coordination structure would be needed at the CJTF-180 level and even higher when the JRTs had to coordinate with the Afghan government. The initial name for this planned structure was the Regional Team Directorate.

As with every plan, the JRT plan had to be washed through the bureaucratic bowels of CJTF-180's higher headquarters, CENTCOM. There were other policy implications, so the State Department was increasingly involved. And so on and so forth. CENTCOM, concerned about future operations in Iraq, decided that if CJTF-180 was to implement the JRT plan, it had to find manpower from within CJTF-180 for the "test bed" JRTs that were planned for Gardez, Bamiyan, and Konduz. Oh, and the JRTs were to be renamed Provincial Reconstruction Teams.

And there was more refinement. PRTs, expanded from about thirty to approximately one hundred personnel, were to "extend the Authority of the Central Government; assist in establishing stability and security; and enable reconstruction." How? PRTs were to establish "good relations with regional political, military, community, and religious leaders; engage and influence those leaders; promote the policies and priorities of the central government; promote Security Sector Reform [i.e., DDR]." The method? PRTs were to "help defuse tensions through mediation, based on the trust and confidence established with leaders and communities; help develop the Afghan National Army, the police and border police in the region; and monitor and assess the local and regional situation."

It is extremely important to note that the planners realized that the PRTs had to maintain "an understated presence that is non-threatening to the Afghan people, that the PRT achieves its effects through non-violent means but retains a robust capability to project force." Combat operations, "should they be necessary," would be handled by other CJTF-180 forces and not the PRT. This thinking reflected the need to avoid the conditions that helped bring about the demise of the Soviet presence in Afghanistan in the 1980s.

Indeed, by late December 2002, the prototype PRT was established at Gardez. In the spring of 2003, OEF started to look for coalition partners willing to take over PRTs. Allied PRT leadership responded to two problems: the manpower ceiling and the demands by critics for multinational participation. In March 2003 the Konduz PRT stood up. The CJTF-180 assessment on the PRT concept was extremely positive, though there was no ability to measure success established yet. The mere presence of the PRTs at this point was considered a success to be built on for the long term.

CENTCOM then instructed CJTF-180 to accelerate the PRT deployment schedule and even increased CJTF-180 manning to meet the demands for eight planned PRTs. By July 2003 New Zealand and the United Kingdom agreed to take on PRT leadership at Bamiyan and Mazar-e Sharif respectively. CJTF-180 hoped that Canada would provide the problematic Jalalabad PRT. Canada's reputation for being able to handle critical missions at a low level, the aggressiveness of its soldiers in both fighting, stabilization, and reconstruction, plus the unique surveillance capabilities Canada brought to bear were valued by the American planners. Ultimately risk-adverse elements in the Foreign Affairs and DND policy bureaucracy blocked Canadian acceptance of the Jalalabad PRT.

CJTF-180 was able to get dribs and drabs from other NATO members. Denmark, for example, committed six personnel, while Italy sent two to the Gardez PRT to gain an appreciation of the mission. Romania and South Korea also sent small numbers of staff. France remained aloof, as did Canada, though Germany, Turkey, and Norway expressed serious interest.

There were, however, big changes in the offing in the summer of 2003. On 11 August 2003, NATO took over ISAF, which in turn altered the military objectives and structure of that mission vis-à-vis the provinces.

NATO's long-term strategy for Afghanistan was formulated with clear recognition of CFC-A's already-established strategy. Indeed, both recognized that the overall objectives included a united and sovereign Afghanistan with a broad-based multiethnic government integrated with the international community. Support for the Afghan Transitional Administration was the key, and this could be done only through coordination with other international institutions like the UN, and that would happen only if NATO took on PRT tasks. NATO, however, was caught in a complex circular argument. If ISAF was to expand outside of Kabul, the mandate had to be changed and NATO members had to be willing to step up to the plate with force commitments. NATO members, however, were not encouraged by the existing lack of coordination between ISAF and the other entities, the shaky status of the central Afghan government in 2003, and were unwilling to commit. They wanted to see the establishment of a constitution that all ethnic groups accepted, and they wanted elections to prove it. None of that could proceed, however, unless there was a relatively secure environment and the chieftains and governors incorporated their military forces into something that had legitimacy in Kabul.

Within some NATO corridors, PRTs were seen to be the key, but someone had to commit to take over ISAF and get the ball rolling. Securing Kabul and propping up the interim government remained a priority. Canada agreed to take the lead in ISAF, and by August 2003 had deployed resources to do so, even though a German general was at the top of the command pyramid: a Canadian brigade HQ took over Kabul Multinational Brigade, and a Canadian recce and surveillance squadron and a mechanized infantry battle group took up station at Camp Julien. Some Canadian policy makers mistakenly believed that ISAF was a peacekeeping mission, and, rather than contribute troops to the OEF "warfighting" mission, they viewed Canadian command of ISAF as morally preferable for their consciousness. Little did they understand that ISAF was a stabilization mission, not a peacekeeping mission, and that it was under constant terrorist attack by Al Qaeda and HiG forces.

In time the ISAF area of operations expanded beyond the city limits to encompass Kabul province. By 14 October 2003, ISAF was authorized by NATO and the Afghan government to plan to move beyond Kabul. By the end of 2003, the United States had seven PRTs—Gardez, Konduz, Parwan, Kandahar, Herat, Khost, and Jalalabad—while Britain had Mazar-e Sharif and the New Zealanders Bamiyan for a total of nine CFC-A-controlled PRTs. Three more followed in early 2004: Ghazni, Asadabad, and Qalat, all American. NATO's ISAF still had to determine where PRTs would fit within its emerging concept of operations.

significant incident

My arrival also coincided with a "significant incident," one which had the potential for massive political damage at the time (no longer: by the time this book is published, it won't matter). A vehicle patrol from 3 PPCLI, working as part of the Recce Squadron, was working an area north of Kabul. The G-Wagon patrol was minding its own business when it came under fire from an American helicopter. The versions I heard were contradictory; this always happens, and the first reports are usually wrong. It appeared as though this helicopter fired in front of the lead vehicle. The implication was that it was coercing the patrol to stop. The problem lay in that members of the patrol were part of 3 PPCLI; they had been shot at by Americans before at Tarnak Farms near Kandahar back in 2002, and four of their friends had been killed and eight wounded. The patrol came close to engaging the helicopter; one member told me that if he had been in a LAV III with the 25-mm gun, he would have. The helicopter withdrew.

Several things fell out of this. First, President George Bush was visiting Halifax, Canada, that day. The implications, according to the PAFFO (public affairs officer), were staggering. If there had been casualties, it would have disrupted Canadian-American relations at a very delicate time. The Chrétien government originally was going to join Operation Iraqi Freedom but succumbed to a caucus revolt led by the anti-American elements. The conspiracy theorists would have had a field day.

The other problem was the owner of the helicopter. There were conflicting versions of what type it was. Initially it was a CH-47 Chinook. Then it was a CH-53. The French staff at ISAF KMNB tried to humiliate the American liaison officer by smugly telling an assembled briefing (I was present) that it was a "CIA" helicopter, and then proceeded to interrogate the Canadian liaison officer, implying that Canada and the CIA were in cahoots on a special operation not coordinated with ISAF. I was then told later that it was a Defense Intelligence Agency (DIA) helicopter, not a CIA helicopter. I didn't realize DIA had its own helicopters . . .

The incident highlighted an ongoing hazard of coalition military operations in the new century: the coordination of special operations forces with conventional forces. The high level of operational security deemed necessary for elements of SOF to go after high-value targets was paramount. Obviously nobody wants HVTs slipping away because they have been tipped off. The movements of Tier I SOF units conducting black ops was an indicator to any watchful enemy. Recall the scene from *Black Hawk Down* in which the child holding the cell phone near the airport lets his superiors know about the deployment of Task Force RANGER and you understand the problem.

Another issue is that units conducting this sort of work have looser rules of engagement than regular units. Combine the two and you could get a situation like this one.

As to the owner of the helicopter, there were several candidates. If it was a CH-47, both regular U.S. Army units and the Night Stalkers (160th Special Operations Aviation Regiment) used them. The SOAR operated heavily modified CH-47s that to the casual observer are indistinguishable from regular CH-47s. If the bird was a CH-53, it would have belonged to the U.S. Air Force or the U.S. Marine Corps. The U.S. Air Force operates the CH-53 in a number of capacities, but there is a special operations variant. CH-53s and CH-47s were therefore both used by the Tier I special operations force, Joint Special Operations Command (JSOC), which combined army, navy, and air force Tier I units. In addition, JSOC has an intelligence unit. The media uses various names for it, Gray Fox most of the time. The JSOC intelligence unit conducts full-spectrum intelligence operations in support of Tier I operations. As for the CIA, the only helicopters it owned in Afghanistan at this point were a number of Mi-17s, many of which were not serviceable by late 2004. As far as I know, DIA does not operate helicopters, unless some new black unit was formed and placed under DIA to conceal it. Black within black? Entirely possible. With their own CH-53s? Unlikely.

I favored the Occam's razor solution to this mystery. When I have flown with American CH-47s in Afghanistan, the three gunners check their machine guns after they have taken off. It is possible that this was an inadvertent "blue on blue" by someone who was not paying attention to what was on the ground.

The French, however, blew this out of proportion for their own purposes. They had reason to. They strongly suspected that Canada, the United Kingdom, and the United States were colluding and conducting operations in and around Kabul, that the national, "undeclared" elements embedded in the national ISAF contingents were cooperating outside of the ISAF and NATO command chain. As usual, the French were left out of such things because of their obstreperous behavior over Iraq (and in Bosnia and Kosovo). They were just whining and being disruptive. They were just being French. Oh, and by the way, they do exactly the same thing, so if the foo shits . . .

In any event, the spin control started more or less immediately. Only one small story showed up in the press and no damage was done. The guys from 3 PPCLI were pissed off, but that was, as they say, easily contained.

I found out later that the bird was a Hughes 500D variant, a MH-6, a small special ops helicopter that I didn't realize could operate at Kabul-level altitudes. The PPCLI patrol, operating apparently without IFF (Identification Friend or Foe equipment), entered a training area outside Bagram Airfield that also served as a security buffer zone for the base. The Little Bird variant had, apparently, been modified so that the entire cockpit is virtually one big screen (since it operates mostly at night) and is dependent on inputs like IFF for locating and targeting. All the more reason to have an integrated command for Afghanistan, some might argue (like the French), but the special ops people will always work inside a compartment no matter who is in command. In this case, the incident had political ramifications far beyond Afghanistan.

the european game: kabul multinational brigade HQ

My escort and guide to things KMNB was Captain FEZ, whose real name was Eghtedar Manouchehri. A Canadian of Iranian descent, he was dubbed "Captain FEZ" by his squadron mates based on their inability to pronounce his last name, like the foreign exchange student character in *That '70s Show*.

"I have to use a LAV III vehicle every time I go anywhere," he pointed out as the crew loaded kit into the eight-wheeled vehicle. "I'd rather have a G-Wagon." I shared his sentiments: climbing up and down the sides of armored vehicles all the time slowed things down and didn't allow you contact with locals. Moving through the crowded streets of Kabul was a feat for the Strathcona drivers, who were, of course, excellent. I climbed in; the American LO (liaison officer) and I stood in the rear hatches, keeping an eye on the rear arc of the vehicle to make sure nobody tried to lob a grenade in or attach a sticky bomb.

"KMNB is weird," Eghtedar told me over the i/c. "It gets to be a real pain in the ass," as we weaved through the vehicular detritus of Holy Fuck Circle.

When I last visited the Kabul Multinational Brigade HQ in early 2003 it was a non-NATO headquarters led by a headquarters derived from the German/

Netherlands Corps. Now, at the end of 2004, KMNB was based on the Franco-German Brigade HQ, which mirrored how the Franco-German-dominated Eurocorps HQ was the basis for ISAF HQ. The Franco-German Brigade was tasked only two months prior to deployment with taking over the KMNB in Kabul. My visit revealed incredible fissures that couldn't be papered over. The British G-5 was unhelpful: he revealed to me that he was going to use the problems with the KMNB as a case study when he went to staff college, and I suspect that was his motivation behind frustrating my research as opposed to the ostensible security reasons he deployed. Using the same alternative methods I had to employ to get around the same sort of problems with the Canadians, it was not hard to see what was going on.

KMNB HQ was a train wreck.

My first clue was when I questioned the Canadian recce squadron about the KMNB concept of operations. They were the brigade recce and surveillance squadron, so in theory they were governed by the KMNB concept of operations. My question was met with the most incredibly impolite cynical laughter on many occasions; the attitude was "You're an idiot. Can't you see there is no concept?" But when pressed nobody would provide details. I had to piece this one together from scratch. And it wasn't a pretty picture at all.

KMNB had twenty-eight countries but only 3,800 personnel, of which 1,500 were "bayonets." There were 100 soldiers for every 260,000 inhabitants. KMNB consisted of three multinational battalions, with the French, Norwegians, and Germans in the lead. There was an independent British company, the Canadian recce squadron equipped with Coyotes, Italian engineers, and Turkish UH-60 helicopters. The Germans had a LUNA UAV unit. In time the Dutch brought in AH-64 Apaches. Countries were deploying subunits and even sub-subunits to create an incredible Tower of Babel. Each contingent had its own "caveats," or limitation on the types of operations that could be conducted with their forces, so KMNB had to keep a matrix so they could select what unit or subunit would be permitted to do what under certain circumstances. This was a problem with the multinational battalions: a battalion-level operation would have to be approved by three or more *countries*, sometimes at the national level!

More telling were the official statements of purpose. In one briefing, I was told that KMNB "assisted in safeguarding a perception of security in our area of operations." That was frightening. That reminded me of UNPROFOR in Bosnia when UNPROFOR decided that its forces were to "deter" Serb attacks against safe areas, but not defend them. KMNB forces spent a lot of time doing force protection tasks in and around Kabul, framework patrolling on the streets, and counter-rocket operations, such as Hunter and Rattlesnake. KMNB was a major participant in major events security, like the loya jirga and the national elections. In other words, there was some evolution from the pre-NATO ISAF of 2003, but not a lot.

It was evident from attending briefings that the Germans and the French officers did not get along at all. It wasn't just one or two bad apples; it was almost all of them. They actively "pinged" off each other to the detriment of the meeting subjects. They attempted to humiliate each other. I was absolutely shocked when a French officer attempted to humiliate the German ops officer, and then turned on the American liaison officer, and then the Canadian liaison officer, possibly because I was present. But I'll come back to this.

I discovered that there were separate and informal French and German national "stovepipes" from ISAF HQ to KMNB HQ. In some cases, competing plans were issued to KMNB HQ via these stovepipes to KMNB units. In one case, the Canadian Recce Squadron received one plan to deploy its Coyotes on high features to cover the western routes to Kabul. While the deployment was in progress, orders were received from a KMNB ops officer who ordered the Coyote observation posts to a whole set of adjacent but completely different high features. The confused Canadians queried this through its liaison people and found out that a German had issued the first plan and a Frenchman the second one, but both worked in the same plans shop! Either they were not coordinating their actions or they were competing with each other.

I also learned that the UK Patrol Company had better intelligence than the KMNB and even resisted KMNB HQ's attempts to direct it within the city. Clearly the British were plugged in to the ABCA (armies of America, Britain, Canada, and Australia) intelligence network, didn't trust KMNB HQ, and didn't share intelligence with the feuding French and Germans. This may or may not have had something to do with the split over the Iraq war, but I got the impression this was local and personal. Indeed, when Joint Electoral Management Body employees were taken hostage in November 2004, the information that they had been seized was passed to the British G-5 by the NGO community. ISAF HQ and KMNB HQ were not called in part because elements in the NGO community knew that the G-5 was reliable, and other entities were not.

The national caveat issue was so bad in the KMNB that it was apparent to me that numerous national force contributions were for show, not use. I saw incredible numbers of shiny new kits and vehicles at Camp Warehouse: Estonian route-proofing vehicles, German armored ambulances, and so on and so forth. Most of it was not in use. I saw a lot of clean uniforms at Camp Warehouse (unlike my last trip, when I visited the German *Gebirgsjäger*). The restriction parameters must have been very high. This, of course, made life difficult for the KMNB HQ: it had to rely on personalities, informal alliances, back channels to national representatives in the headquarters, and "flexibility" to get anything done. I came away with the impression that it was one big nightmare.

I was able to glean that the KMNB had informal tasks in addition to election security, counter-rocket operations, and framework patrol operations. These "directed operations," or what I would call direct action, operated nearly independently by units assigned to the KMNB. The "useful" units in the KMNB appeared to be the Canadian Coyote squadron, the Dutch AH-64 detachment, the British Patrol Company, and little else. These kinds of operations were all driven by intelligence and information collection, which provided a "hit," and then forces responded as required. But that was the theory. There were, for example, electronic warfare/SIGINT assets from a particular country in ISAF that were being directed against other ISAF contributors more than against enemy forces. This was somewhat mysterious and unnerving. There were some embarrassing incidents involving UAVs. I visited an ISAF contributor that showed me a clip of a film taken from a German LUNA UAV. It showed the engine cowling of an Ariana airliner growing closer . . . and closer . . . and closer . . . until the camera showed the ground rushing up *verrry* quickly. Of course ISAF didn't corner the market on UAV accidents. The U.S. security contractor, DynCorp, had its own UAVs. One crashed into a house next to the presidential residence and had to be covertly recovered.

The significant incident involving the American helicopter and the Canadian patrol was used for political purposes in the KMNB environment. The French briefing officer sneered and made snide remarks during a briefing to put the American liaison officer on the spot: "So tell us about the CIA helicopter. Why was this not cleared with ISAF? Why did you shoot at the Canadians?"

The American LO, a captain from the American Embedded Training Team, had little or no knowledge of the event. His inability to answer questions was capitalized on by the French officer, who used it in an attempt to convince the others in the meeting that the Americans were "holding back." He then turned on the Canadian LO and virtually accused Canada being complicit in American "black operations" without informing the KMNB and ISAF. It was clear that he believed that there was collusion between the OEF Americans and the ISAF Canadians and that this blue on blue was related to some joint black operation. The Canadian and American LOs were unable to respond effectively. I was fuming. I turned around, and a Dutch colonel behind me rolled his eyes. A minor incident was thus magnified into a breach of "trust" between Canada, the United States, and the KMNB. The French colonel was fishing for more. The Canadian KMNB HQ air ops officer, perhaps not realizing the minefield that had just been sown, then asked the American LO if anybody had seen a missing two-man USAF FAC (forward air control) team. Bagram Airfield was asking if anybody had seen the two men in Kabul (it turned out they were safe and sound at TF PHOENIX across the road). The French briefing officer had a field day with that one.

The helicopter incident was a legitimate accident. The more time I spent in Kabul, however, the more I developed the impression that there was something going on, something behind the scenes. That was normal; as I discussed in *Enduring the Freedom*, there was significant overlap when it came to OEF special operations and ISAF operations in the capital city. Up was down, right was left, and so on. Normal shadow world stuff. Given the dysfunctionality inside KMNB HQ and the shenanigans I witnessed, however, it would not surprise me in the least if the ABCA powers and the Dutch were cooperating on an informal basis and not cutting the French and German KMNB HQ in on the action. This, of course, was an extremely sensitive topic and probably remains so. I believe that the Iraq War split was only part of it. The OEF versus ISAF versus integrated command issue was part of it, and French insecurity is always part of it (vis-à-vis ABCA intelligence sharing; this goes back to the late 1940s and is not new, nor is it secret). Personalities were clearly part of it here. But there were several cases that pointed in the direction of functional informal cooperation.

One of these was a peculiar incident that involved the British Patrol Company, the Canadian Recce Squadron, and the Afghan NDS. I was prohibited, during a briefing, from looking at Coyote footage taken of the takedown of enemy terrorists. I developed information from other sources that painted a picture of HUMINT developed by British Patrol Company sources, and from other sources, that an Al Qaeda–trained cell was inserted into Kabul just before the national election in the fall of 2004. It was a big cell; there may have been as many as twelve triggermen split in teams of three or four. Apparently Canadian observation assets were directed onto the enemy teams while they were practicing. The terrorists were seized by the British Patrol Company and then turned over to the NDS. In hours, the NDS uncovered, via interrogation, all of the support cells assisting the Pakistan-based "shooters"—that is, safe house operators, communicators, procurers, and so on. In effect, an entire terrorist network was ripped out of Kabul before it could do anything.

There was little or no coverage in the media of this at all. Nor did ISAF take credit for it. It was deemed to be an NDS operation and billed as an Afghan success story. I understood that the French were very pissed off because they had not been informed about the operation. *C'est la guerre.* Was this an ISAF victory? An ABCA victory? An Afghan victory? Or did it really matter, since there was no violence during the election or, for that matter, the inauguration? Experience in Bosnia and Kosovo has demonstrated to some in ABCA circles that the French cannot be trusted, that they will blow operations if their politicians deem it necessary to embarrass the Americans and British. What is more important—a safe and secure Kabul, or French pride? You be the judge.

The French KMNB staff kept trying to tell the Canadian liaison officer that the Coyotes worked for their French-dominated ISTAR cell; the Canadians resisted and insisted that they worked for the (German) Brigade Commander. This was no mere spat over tactical control; it was in part over the product provided by the Coyote vehicles, who got to look at it, and when. Information is power, and it will always be so. Recce squadron personnel believed that KMNB HQ didn't exploit the vehicle and its capabilities and that this was related to national, not exclusively French agendas. There were personal agendas in play too. The astonishing clarity of Coyote imagery, particularly at night, meant that a regiment of the vehicles could have been usefully employed in this environment.

It was clear after numerous discussions that the French were trying to use ISAF resources for their own national purposes without the Germans knowing. The exact purposes remained obscure. Word on the street was that the French recontributed special operations forces to OEF, that this commitment was designed to compete with the TF-121 units in a bid to grab Osama bin Laden. The Tier I HVT hunt was jealously protected by the Americans in OEF, which blocked the integration of ISAF and OEF at this time.

The Germans, on the other hand, were playing their own game. Germany brought its own signals intelligence assets to Kabul, but these were ostensibly for German force protection tasks and were not integrated into ISAF. Neither was the German SIGINT station located somewhere in the Pamir Mountains. Similarly the LUNA UAVs were "undeclared" and used for force protection missions. Apparently informal mechanisms were used to have information flow from these resources to KMNB. The French have similar mechanisms.[5]

Early in December 2004, there were a series of explosions east of Camp Julien, off Green Route. A Canadian quick-reaction force (QRF) mounted in LAV III, and Coyotes rolled out the gate to investigate. They were held up at a roadblock that consisted of a mix of NDS personnel, what appeared to be American contract personnel, and special operations forces, including a sniper. The Canadian QRF was politely told "the situation was under control" and to go away. Within twenty-four to forty-eight hours, the Afghan government was announcing the release of the kidnapped JEMB employees. There was a lot of disinfo on this one; some still argue that a deal was cut between the Afghan government and the kidnappers for money. If so, what was this NDS-OEF SOF operation all about in such close proximity to the "release" date? Again, this is an example of the ambiguity of the complex political situation in Kabul and the role agendas play in the conduct of operations.

the canadian game: DDR-ing and HWC-ing

A government must not waiver once it has chosen its course. It must not look to the left or right but go forward.

—OTTO VON BISMARCK

One of the larger pieces in the Chessgame was DDR, which stands for Disarmament, Demobilization and Reintegration. How, exactly, do you convince the AMF to stop playing at war? DDR, at least in theory. The man who was going to explain the reality of DDR to me, Major P. Mireaux of the French army and currently working at ISAF HQ, had few illusions left about what was and what was not possible: he had been around the world a few times in the 1990s.

"OK, you are familiar with DDR-type programs from your time in the Balkans? Good. We did the same thing in Côte D'Ivoire. The first thing you must understand is that the DDR program and the HWC programs in Afghanistan are separate but related. HWC stands for Heavy Weapons Cantonment. It is an independent program for a variety of financial and political purposes."

DDR deals with individual soldiers and personal and crew-served weapons under 12.7 mm, while HWC is reserved for tanks, APCs, artillery, mortars, anti-aircraft guns, and other systems. HWC, actually, is a subset of the UN's Afghan New Beginnings Programme, which has the cunningly simplistic acronym ANBP. However, most of the money for HWC comes from the United States. DDR, on the other hand, is primarily funded by Japan, Canada, the United Kingdom, and the United States.

Canada, however, played a major role in establishing the HWC process. Lieutenant General Andy Leslie, the deputy ISAF commander in 2003, and his planning staff looked at the problem before they deployed and determined that the main threats in Kabul were the various armed militias. These had to be disarmed so that the political process could not be intimidated. Looking back to their experiences with IFOR (Implementation Force) and SFOR in the Balkans, when the factions in Bosnia were progressively disarmed by the international force, the Canadian staff developed the prototype weapons cantonment plan.

ISAF, as such, doesn't disarm the AMF. ISAF, apparently, plays an indirect role: it handles "negotiation" with the Afghan MOD (Ministry of Defense) and with the AMF units. We can, of course, speculate what constitutes "negotiation," but we'll come back to that later. Major Mireaux is the primary point of contact at ISAF, while the PRTs handle local negotiations. For example, the Mazar-e Sharif PRT protected the ANBP team while it was disarming the AMF independent units operating in that area. ISAF does, however, handle direct action for HWC in Kabul. In a sense, ISAF is pseudo-ly TACOM'd from the UN for it in Kabul province. Why? Kabul is the *Schwerpunkt* for the HWC program, and the objective is to have a psychological impact. If Kabul disarms, why should the other regional commands not disarm?

The situation is further confused, at least for some analysts who crave order, by the fact that the British PRT at Maz started to "DDR" the AMF there before it became the ISAF PRT. The situation vis-à-vis Rashid Dostum was considered serious enough and critical enough to mount DDR before the program was fully in place.

The broader objectives of DDR and HWC are straightforward: disarm and disband the AMF, which, for planning purposes, consists of 100,000 personnel. The pilot phase (March–May 2004) was to do the first 6,000, while subsequent phases throughout 2004 were to handle 25,000, 27,000, and so on, at a rate of 800 a day. The realities were that the numbers came to 8,000 for phase II and 7,500 for phase III, or around 100 a day. By December 2004 an estimated 30 percent of the task was completed, with phase III under way while I was there.

In essence, the "Reintegration" component of DDR for a typical AMF soldier amounted to turning over his personal weapon to the ANBP representatives. He then went to the regional office and was given US$10.00, plus an additional US$200.00 worth of food, clothes, and tools. He also received a "Good Soldier" certificate, a medal, and an ID card. He then signed up for a new job training scheme.

Note that he was fingerprinted and photographed for his new ID card . . . Oh, and there could be no political registration, that is, forming a political party, without DDR certification. This applied to the chieftains and all of their subordinates.

One of the problems was that the DDR staff didn't have the tools to measure what happened to these guys after they signed up for job training. Did they take the training? Where did they go? What did they do? It was this sort of seam where the military-civilian linkages broke down.

As Major Mireaux explained, "Even our working numbers as to how many AMF there are is unclear. One hundred thousand is only an estimate. Under the Soviet Union, there were 400,000 Afghan militia fighters under arms, for comparative purposes. Where are those weapons? Let us also look at the 'AMF' commanders. These are feudal barons backed up with force. They have protection rackets, they own the taxis. They don't pass on taxes to the central government. They need small weapons and men, not tanks and artillery, to keep operating. Do we DDR people or weapons?"

Mireaux explained their predicament: "We expected to find a structured army, but the bulk of the AMF consisted of a postapocalyptic feudal army. The local 'nobles' levied small armies from the people, who are already armed. But they bore the unit designation of some old Soviet-Afghan militia unit! We really believe that there is a lot more to it here. In effect, there may well be 100,000 AMF, but then there are these others who can or could be called up if the nobles are prepared to pay. They retain their civilian jobs and form up when needed. In effect, then, there is a three-tiered system we are dealing with, like the Soviets, or what we used to call Category A, B, and C. The numbers are artificial, but better than nothing. We have focused on the heavy weapons, since they pose a direct threat to ISAF operations."

"So the statistics could be misleading?"

"Oh yes. We can count tanks and APCs and we can claim success here. But is that indicative of overall success or just success in securing heavy weapons?"

I was impressed with Mireaux's frankness. I expected the public split between the French and the Americans over Iraq to color most of my dealings with French officers. This was an incorrect assumption. Mireaux understood that the compromise that existed was better than nothing; and, in fact, it provided a window for future analysis once these phases were completed and new information came in.

Mireaux also pointed out that HWC wasn't merely a matter of deploying observation personnel. There were serious issues involved, including the need for cranes, tank transporters, POL (petroleum, oil, lubricants), and security over the HWC storage sites. Ammunition needed special handling by professionals. And that money had to come from somewhere. In the main, Japan had taken over as the prime donor here. The British only paid for the process in their PRT area. Mireaux said the Americans claimed to give money, but actually didn't give as much while making numerous proposals and then not backing them up. "Canada, led by Chris Alexander, is the only good player in this game," he said. ISAF gave gas to the tank transporter units, and some ISAF members gave money to pay for those vehicles. ISAF HQ was able to make the case to NATO that HWC in Kabul stabilizes Kabul indirectly. Canada had a number of Camp Julien outstations for weapons collection, while Germany provided cranes, France deployed inspectors, and the Afghan MOD scraped up every tank transporter it could. Overlap with the Embedded Training Team's logistical training group at TF PHOENIX was under exploration, yet another area of OEF-ISAF cooperation.

Mireaux believed that ISAF was successful in the HWC program because of the close contact ISAF had with the Afghan people at all levels of engagement. He noted that there were numerous proposals from the Afghans, including the AMF, on what to do with ammunition and heavy weapons. That said, however, AMF commanders had tried to hide equipment using the "Oops, I forgot!" excuse. They would not always tell the whole truth but would cave in when asked. It was a game, where face-saving is an important aspect. In many ways, it reminded me of the same situation that was played out in Kosovo between NATO and the Kosovar Albanian UCK, something Mireaux noted when I remarked on the similarities.

It all fed into the Chessgame, when the AMF "generals" got involved. The chieftains and their primary military leaders had to be handled individually. Commanding generals, if they accepted DDR, were paid for the next two years at US$300 to US$600 a month. The international community paid for the first year, and the Afghan MOD the second. Then there was "job placement." I had a flash of an AMF general on the street with a cup and a sign reading "Will lead a postapocalyptic army for food." But I digress.

Job placement, which we will examine when we deal with the case of Herat, had interesting side effects. General Daoud, the chieftain in Konduz, was made a deputy minister in the Ministry of the Interior with a portfolio for counternarcotics. In another case a Herat AMF corps commander transitioned to the ANA after some screening. AMF commanders of a certain rank were, in fact, encouraged to become part of the civil components of the government, in Kabul or elsewhere. The problem, I learned, was not necessarily the "general" level: it was the "colonel" and "major" levels of the AMF. They received US$200, which was not enough for them, and they were always looking for more money after being DDR'd. There were still discussions as to what to do: Encourage them to join the ANA? The police forces? I felt that this was a critical question that was not being addressed, one which would have long-term repercussions.

And then there was the special problem of the AMF in the Panjshir Valley. As Afghanistan aficionados know, the Panjshir was Ahmad Shah Massoud's stronghold during the Soviet era, the site of numerous offensives that failed to destroy Massoud's forces. As part of the Northern Alliance, the Panjshiri forces never succumbed to the Taliban. The Panjshiri "1st Division," and AMF formation, was currently led by a General Gaddar; intelligence estimates suggested that there were massive amounts of equipment in the valley. None of it had been subjected to HWC, nor had the 1st Division been subjected to DDR. There were, apparently, good reasons. First, when Fahim Khan was the main power broker in Kabul in the concluding round of the anti-Taliban war, he was a stabilizing force in the region. He was the primary military power. The Chessgame took care of Fahim Khan eventually, but it was an incremental process. ISAF, in its pre-NATO incarnation, lacked the forces to coerce the Northern Alliance in Kabul, let alone the Panjshir Valley. It was better to leave well enough alone back in 2002–3 and focus on Kabul.

With Fahim Khan sidelined, Gaddar declared that Khan was no longer the legit leader in the Panjshir; he was. He declared that the Taliban threat was not over, that 1st Division was providing a stabilizing influence and a critical bulwark against the Taliban (and Al Qaeda, to his American audience). He therefore needed troops, which amounted to six thousand fighters, to fight, and they needed their heavy equipment, including SCUDs. He further claimed that OEF couldn't operate everywhere, and he could help stop infiltration from Pakistan through the Panjshir Valley.

When not taken at face value, the 1st Division was a potentially destabilizing factor in the fragile ISAF and OEF stabilization campaign. It had to be handled delicately. After a significant amount of pressure placed by COMISAF (Commander, ISAF) on President Karzai, the Afghan leader met with Gaddar and convinced him to accept Afghan MOD command and control. COMISAF was also able to get the Deputy Minister of Defence to write a letter to Gaddar; General Abdul Rahim Wardak, an *alter kamfer* from way back, agreed. COMISAF was then able to convince Bismullah Khan and Fahim Khan to go up to the Panjshir and convince Gaddar to accept an initial DDR process. At this point in time, ISAF was awaiting a reply from Gaddar. All of the usual excuses—e.g., lack of tank transporters, lack of gas, and so on—were countered with specific offers from ISAF, and particularly Canada and Germany as individual donors. The matter was pending while I was in Kabul.

Major Mireaux confirmed that the main problem areas for DDR and HWC were the Panjshir and Kabul, for the most part. On the whole, the relationship between the programs and the PRTs was good. There were friction areas: the Germans, he claimed, had a "bunker" mentality, while the British were perhaps too open when dealing with the AMF. OEF, he thought, had not progressed with the programs to the same extent as ISAF, but he suggested this was because of the need to achieve equilibrium between the forces loyal to Bismullah Khan and Fahim Khan, and within the Northern Alliance leaders. ISAF's leaders understood that this could not be disrupted, even if it meant improved HWC statistics. Dostum, however, was caught out playing games with DDR/HWC, and Chris Alexander who led those who wanted to get tough with him. Chris used the threat of DDR to force Dostum to the table, apparently in the face of more conciliatory British arguments. This was a change: the Canadians getting tough and the British getting conciliatory? Perhaps it related to the vulnerability of the British PRT in Mazar-e Sharif. Canada, with no forces in that region, could be tough. (I saw the reverse in Bosnia in 1995 when the Americans wanted to bomb the Bosnian Serbs, but Canada had lightly armed troops on the ground who would take the heat.) Dostum then said he would go with DDR. Then one of Dostum's "problem units," 053 Division, started to act up. Was this sanctioned by Dostum as part of the game, or was it spontaneous? In any event, it highlighted the need to get ANA forces into the area as soon as possible to fill the security gap. Chris Alexander and others were also able to use political party registration as a lever to get Dostum to start playing ball again. The Afghan MOD was supportive, the Japanese ambassador was skeptical, but Chris Alexander was blunt: if Dostum was in fact controlling 053's behavior, his political registration was now invalid. If he wasn't in control, he needed to exert control and DDR 053. Caught between a rock and a hard place, Dostum caved in and complied. The division was DDR'd, to Britain's delight. This was yet another example of the Chessgame in action. DDR and HWC were tools, as was the use of selective Afghan National Army deployments to regions where recalcitrant behavior still lurked.

ISAF PRT development

The man who was going to explain NATO PRT development was Colonel Jacques Pierquin. Unlike obstructionist French staff officers I encountered in other head-quarters, I was impressed by Jacques, a Foreign Legionnaire who sported the famous winged dagger badge in his beret.

"So, are you a Pied-Noir?" I asked, referring to the French *colons* in Algeria who were forced to leave after de Gaulle pulled France out of their former colony.

"As a matter of fact, yes. My father served in Algeria. I grew up there," he replied with some surprise.

"So, I guess counterinsurgency ops here in Afghanistan are no different, then?"

He laughed. "Yes, some of us have some experience in this sort of thing. It's almost genetic."

The ISAF PRT issue was, by late 2004 to early 2005, really heating up, Jacques explained. "You are here at an interesting time."

There was, I found out, a number of significant differences between CFC-A PRTs and ISAF PRTs—not only in structure, but in terms of funding, and especially command and control. I recalled from my briefings with Colonel Randy Brooks at CFC-A that CFC-A PRTs were originally designed as part of the counterinsurgency effort in the east and southeast and that the concept evolved to help the Afghan government collect information and establish coordination and presence in the far-flung provinces. The complexities of "aid delivery" and "reconstruction delivery" and their relationship to what the Afghan government wanted to achieve were more and more important now that the Karzai government had received the blessings of the people during the fall 2004 election. In addition, the move toward a single command for Afghanistan, a merger of CFC-A and ISAF, was under discussion as well.

The CFC-A PRTs had, by late 2004, evolved to the point where there were now measurements of effectiveness, including a PRT Steering Committee to coordinate PRT efforts with CFC-A and the Afghan government and all of the trappings of a mature organization. CFC-A PRTs now numbered fourteen. There were forward support bases for them, manned by troops from a composite brigade of the 25th Infantry Division. All CFC-A PRTs were funded using CFC-A funds.

The ISAF PRT effort was very different. NATO expansion in Afghanistan, coordinated with CFC-A, created a northern command in Afghanistan. The British PRT at Mazar-e Sharif, formerly a CFC-A PRT, had transferred to ISAF. The Germans took over the American pilot PRT at Konduz, while the Dutch moved into Baghlan. The British expanded to take another PRT at Maimana, while the Germans also expanded to Feyzabad and Taloqan. These PRTs, however, received their funding not from CFC-A but from the "donor nations," that is, the countries that agreed to take on the respective PRTs. For example, the Germans funded Konduz. Not NATO ISAF, not CFC-A. In terms of sheer amounts of money, however, the available CFC-A funds dwarfed those of the donor nations in the ISAF schema.

The implications for this were significant. Essentially each donor nation created a fiefdom with its own area of operations, transport, medical support, and so on. Each donor nation solicited reconstruction aid from "back home" and coordinated its delivery in its area of operation. Smaller NATO nations, unwilling or unable to take on a whole PRT, were lobbied by the larger donor nations to send token numbers of troops to augment the donor nation forces. The danger in all of this, especially once donor nations sent civilian leadership from the ambassadorial level to manage the PRTs, was determining exactly who was in command: the military component or the civilian component? CFC-A PRTs subordinated civilian aid personnel to the military commander and the military commander controlled the funds, while ISAF PRTs had a split command and the civilian component controlled the funds.

And this is where it really got interesting: CFC-A, working with the U.S. State Department and USAID, created "Regional Development Zones," or RDZs, to correspond to the CFC-A PRT areas of operations. This was a test project designed to assist with connectivity to the Afghan government. Both Jacques Pierquin at ISAF and Randy Brooks at CFC-A explained to me that the Karzai government formed a National Priority Programme (NPP). The NPP was designed to establish reconstruction priorities so that the appropriate funds could be apportioned. There was a national NPP, but there were also provincial and regional equivalents. In effect, NPP money was allocated to a province with broad advice on how it should be used: road construction and, say, police infrastructure construction. The provincial governors, in theory, would determine their priorities and then take the NPP money plus donor aid and NGO money and allocate it regionally.

In theory. Nobody wanted a corrupt governor greasing the palms of his buddies with so much cash. At the same time, noncorrupt governors who were adept at killing Taliban and not necessarily adept at civil administration needed advice. The American RDZ concept as played out through the CFC-A PRTs was supposed to provide this coordination and advice. ISAF came up with a similar but more refined model, called the Provincial Development Committee (PDC). The PDC included the governor, the head of the PRT, a representative of the central government Ministry of Finance, another central government representative from the Ministry of the Interior, and in some cases a UN or NGO representative. There were plenty of checks and balances; it forced the provincial level to coordinate with the central government, and it ensured that the military component provided by ISAF or CFC-A was able to keep "eyes on" the whole thing.

Jacques also informed me that significant problems existed with the NGOs. They wanted to dictate how the money was dispersed, especially their own money. Many did not want to submit to coordinated dispersal of reconstruction and aid funds through the provincial government. They wanted to go off on their own and do it. We had all seen this problem before in Bosnia and particularly Kosovo. When NGOs ran off and did things on their own, they ran the risk of being labeled "partial" by some faction that wasn't getting any of what the NGO had to offer. If an NGO operated in areas of one ethnicity, it could be portrayed as siding with that group, which could and did lead to violence. In their emotional rush to help, NGOs generally did not respect the fine balance of power at these levels of political and social action. Military forces with experience in these kinds of situations were, paradoxically, better at it than many NGOs. And the NGOs had to be reminded, from time to time, that there was still a war on. No security, no aid delivery. Both ISAF and CFC-A planners realized, however, that NGOs were more likely to go with a PRT that was not completely military-controlled, so in some ways donor-nation-controlled PRTs could be more attractive.

The Karzai government also had to contend with this kind of problem at the provincial/regional level. Not all provinces were eligible for big-ticket reconstruction aid. For example, provinces with existing road nets were more likely to be funded over provinces that had few. Consequently the NPP created compensation projects so that regional and provincial leaders didn't get pissed off. Again the PRTs, with their information collection and coordination capacities, were ideal for providing feedback on all aspects of aid and reconstruction funding dispersal and activity. PRTs, Jacques said, provided a "channel of evaluation." Oh, and all sorts of other interesting information about what the bad guys were doing could be passed on as well to the right people.

In late 2004–early 2005, ISAF was preparing to expand yet again. CFC-A and ISAF had divided the country into four parts and planned to incrementally hand off each section from CFC-A command to ISAF command in a counterclockwise fashion. Phase I, which included Mazar-e Sharif and Konduz and the other northern areas, was already under ISAF command. The next to go was the western part of the country. NATO originally wanted Canada to take the PRT at Herat. A debate inside the Canadian policy-making community on whether Canada should go with Herat or Kandahar, however, delayed a timely decision, and the Italians put in a recce to Herat. Then the Spanish got interested, and a Spanish recce team showed up. Canada then was outbid for Herat (the Italians wanted to gather intelligence on the drug trade as a collateral activity, apparently) and eventually accepted the Kandahar PRT, which was an OEF PRT on the front lines of the continuing Taliban insurgency.

bagram run

I had some spare time and some of the CFC-A personnel were doing a personnel drop off to Bagram Airfield. I wanted to see the sights and any changes since my last trip, so I tagged along. We took two civilian-pattern 4x4s; this American light colonel was headed home, and we were the transport. During the convoy brief, he was adamant that *he* was the convoy commander and all action on contact would be under his direction. One of the guys rolled his eyes as he checked his weapons; he knew that any action on contact would have to be completely spontaneous without waiting for centralized orders.

What struck me most about this drive was the huge amount of construction along the MSR (main supply route) to Bagram. It was as if suburbs were being built north of Kabul. Ground was leveled and cleared, new (and painted!) gates were on all the compounds along the route. All of the tank and APC wrecks that littered both sides of the road were gone now. The fighting positions had been filled in with earthmoving equipment. There were the odd checkpoints along the way, but they were manned only by a couple of people instead of a platoon or section. There was still UXO about, and the nomads and camels were wandering through.

The town of Bagram was still a mess; traffic was backed up for security checks. BAF's PX had expanded dramatically: it even had a Burger King and a pizza place, plus Thai food. Throngs of OEF and ISAF troops queued up for something better than T-rations. Lots of construction: BAF was nearly unrecognizable from the BAF I visited in 2003. This was a permanent facility, not a ramshackle FOB.

We dropped off the colonel and proceeded on a vital CFC-A mission. The objective was to locate the Tobyhanna Army Depot Forward Repair Facility, Bagram. We drove around and around. I thought a forward repair facility would have cranes, a workshop, trucks, spare part shipping containers. We finally pulled over and asked somebody, who directed us through a maze of sea containers to an old Soviet-era building. Sure enough, there was the sign: TOBYHANNA ARMY DEPOT FORWARD REPAIR FACILITY, BAGRAM. No cranes, no containers. We went inside.

Tobyhanna Army Depot Forward Repair Facility, Bagram, was a computer and electronics boneyard. Instead of cannibalized armored vehicles, there were cannibalized ink-jet printers. Instead of spare barrels for 105-mm guns, there were spare photocopiers. Instead of a team of wrench benders, there were two overworked, burned-out civilian DoD techs with five-day growths of beards, the shakes from too much coffee, and dingy desert combat clothing.

The guys went back to the jeep and brought in some broken computer gear. It was totally surreal. Warfare in the information age was impossible without photocopiers, printers, hard drives, and modems. These two guys handled the maintenance and replacement of all of these vital weapons here at Bagram. The environment gave a beating to the delicate equipment originally destined and built for an insurance company in Ohio or a lawyer's office in Maine. These machines were war-weary, their silicon hearts pushed to the limits by the war in Afghanistan. In World War II, it would have been some forward repair depot in France or Italy servicing Sherman tanks. In Afghanistan in 2004, it was office equipment.

tobyhanna army depot forward repair facility, bagram:
the embedded training team

> The main foundations of every state, new states as well as ancient or composite ones, are good laws and good arms. You cannot have good laws without good arms, and where there are good arms, good laws inevitably follow . . .
>
> —Niccolo Machiavelli

It was an early, dark night on the fringes of Camp Julien. Major Brian Hynes, formerly of the Royal Canadian Regiment and now of the Princess Patricia's Canadian Light Infantry, coughed up some phlegm as he lit another cigarette and the USMC gunnery sergeant handed me a beer. I first met Major Hynes in 1990, right after his battalion came back from the Oka insurrection in Quebec: I was an observer accompanying his platoon on a live-fire airmobile exercise, and we were nearly shelled by our own guns that time. That was like a century ago as we reminisced in the shadow of the Queen's Palace.

Brian has the most interesting job this side of the mountains splitting Kabul in half: he is the lead for Operation Archer, the Canadian Embedded Training Team, supporting the emergent Afghan National Army. And he is the best man for the task: fit, wise, and experienced, Brian has served everywhere in the past fourteen years, from Oka to Bosnia during the bad old days of UNPROFOR to the NATO Stabilisation Force, then to Operation Apollo with Colonel Pat Stogran's 3 PPCLI in Kandahar, and now Op Archer. He knows this country and knows the people; he is out there advising the new Afghan battalions while they conduct operations against Al Qaeda–trained terrorists and against recalcitrant chieftains. This, of course, makes him and the Op Archer team outcasts in the Canadian camp. Jealous that the ETTs have freedom of movement and are permitted to wear desert CADPAT uniforms, the pettier minds in Camp Julien bleat on about their lot and in some cases bureaucratically obstruct support to Op Archer. *Plus ça change, plus c'est la même chose.* It wouldn't be a Canadian operation if the deployed subunits weren't carping about the others.

Brian brushed it all off; he had more important things to do. Raising, training, and deploying the Afghan National Army was the *Schwerpunkt* of the international effort in Afghanistan, a major cog in the Chessgame. A professional, multiethnic army at the disposal of a legitimate democratic government is absolutely critical for success and, as Brian explained, the exit strategy. The absurdity of people at Camp Julien over how Op Archer personnel are dressed or who controls who or reports to who is irrelevant. The ETT had bigger fish to fry. And they were, indeed, frying them.

"The ETT was based on a construct given by General Leslie when he was deputy commander of ISAF and then it evolved from there," Brian explained. "The ETT has fifteen personnel and is designed to support a battalion on operations, from mentoring and advising the battalion commander down to all company commanders. We can also coordinate health services support and all the battalion sustainment activities when the battalion is deployed."

"Is it ISAF or OEF?"

"We fall under Task Force PHOENIX, which is OEF." TF PHOENIX is usually under the command of a reserve U.S. Special Forces group that is a mix of the 19th Special Forces Group and the 20th Special Forces Group.

"When I was here in 2003, it was a real mess: French officer training, British NCO training—a real mishmash."

"Yeah, they had only been set up for about six months at that time. It's like a child growing. It shits itself for about a year and half and then after that it knows how to do it properly. Basically the Afghan National Army gets stood up in 2002, and commences operations in fall 2002–spring 2003. We're talking a purely volunteer force, multiethnic, with no command staff, no staff. The crucial part is the lack of staff, no ability to organize and plan ahead. When you saw it, it was in its infancy stage. They eventually started to work with OEF doing conventional-type ops: peace support framework patrolling, cordon and search, vehicle checkpoints. They did those things with the U.S. Marines in RC East. The ANA also did cordon support for OEF special operations, but then were used by OEF Special Forces for specific point mission target attack. They also do special operations FOB protection in the Pakistani border areas. Now they're getting into PSYOPS and HUMINT."

"How many of them have previous experience, Brian? I assume some were with the Northern Alliance."

"You have officers that are Soviet-trained, you have some Northern Alliance. Their experience goes from conventional ops to guerrilla ops. Some fought for the Taliban against the Northern Alliance. We've had to remove guys. The others just won't accept that."

Brian laid out the structure of the Afghan army. The basic unit was called a Kandak, which was essentially a battalion. There were at this point four corps, one for each region—RC North, South, East, and West—and there were seven brigades spread out among them. Each brigade had three infantry Kandaks and two support Kandaks. The units were trained and equipped as light infantry, though the Germans were training an ANA armored Kandak equipped with T-55s. Canada was involved in training the first brigade for the corps whose operating area included Herat, Mazar-e Sharif, Gardez, and Jalalabad. The ETT had a close relationship with the 1st Kandak, 1st Brigade: it was employed during the fall 2003 loya jirga and handled inner security for this critical event. Op Archer then worked with the 4th Kandak, a support unit that transitioned into a pure infantry battalion.

"That unit went to Herat, but we weren't allowed to go," Brian ruefully explained. "Down in Shindand, near Herat, there were two warlords posturing. It was internal, territorial, a lot of personal stuff. They were moving their tanks back and forth, get out of my territory, get out of my face or I'll kill you. This was Ismael Khan and Aminullah Khan. Both were anti-Taliban. Having two AMF commanders going at it, though, destabilizes the whole northwestern part of the country, so it became a huge issue. The ANA surged into Shindand, seized the airhead, and moved on to Herat. This was the largest air movement of Afghan forces in history and demonstrated Karzai's resolve. So about a brigade's worth of troops arrived in Shindand over three days' time. Herc after Herc after Herc. We reloaded nine Hercs in one day."

Brian related what happened when the Kandaks got on the ground. "There had been some sporadic shooting. The airhead became an FOB for the operation. They moved out, showed the flag, did a lot of presence patrols, and let everybody there know that the ANA existed and was operating. This was a big issue. Ismael Khan was the Governor, and he was running along a precipice. If he goes against the national forces, he can lose his 'green' status and not be eligible to join the electoral process. If he goes 'red' he can be taken out, he can be DDR'd. This was all explained to them in spades. The ANA was put in there almost à la Blue Beret. It made them think when all the big airplanes start showing up."

The most galling thing was that Brian and his ETT crew were prevented from accompanying "their" Kandak to Herat. "We prepped them, did all the training. They were really upset when orders came that we couldn't go with them. They felt Canada was abandoning them. They were crying. You have to understand that our relationship with them is based on trust. Without that trust, you cannot function. The message was 'we only support you so far and when the going gets tough, we back up.' It took awhile to reestablish the trust. The message got out that if you're trained by Canadians, you'll go and they'll stay behind. Remember, in training we are with them 24/7."

I knew from talking with the Canadian Ambassador Chris Alexander that he had done his damndest to let the ETTs go on the Herat mission, but was getting blocked by people in Ottawa. Was it Foreign Affairs? Or was it skittish staff in National Defence Headquarters who were anticipating the bureaucrats and politicians? The order instructing Brian not to participate came from the Deputy Chief of the Defence Staff's office. It had all the hallmarks of a risk-adverse bureaucracy out of touch with the implications of their caution on Canada's reputation.[6] These people may have saved their bureaucratic masters' asses from potential (yes, *potential*) media questioning and the slippery-slope possibility (again, *possibility*) of having to take public responsibility if people got killed, but in doing so they embarrassed us in front of the Afghans, our allies, and our enemies. You do the math as to what is more important. You think people in Afghanistan and Pakistan aren't paying attention? Think again.

Brian gave me another example of risk-adverse bureaucratic problems that he was peripherally involved with. On 2 October 2003 Corporal Robbie Beerenfenger and Sergeant Robert Short were killed and three wounded when their vehicle "struck an explosive device" in a rural area near Camp Julien. These were the first Canadian deaths in Kabul. There were attempts to downplay the first attack and claim it was a mine left over from the war, but that didn't wash with the troops who knew the road had been remined after it had been "proven" by the same patrol earlier. Sergeant Short worked for Brian for three years, so this wasn't some remote death of an unknown to him. In another attack on 27 January 2004, an insurgent walked up to a Canadian Iltis jeep that had slowed down for a speed bump and detonated a mortar round on the hood, which set off other explosives he was carrying. That attack killed Corporal Jamie Murphy and wounded three others. The perpetrators of the first attack were dealt with using special operations forces during a previous rotation. The crew that orchestrated the second attack, however, was not the result of ISAF red tape.

"We were doing the outer cordon security for the presidential inauguration last week. We were working with 23rd Kandak. There were a number of checkpoints, there was some presence patrolling—the usual framework stabilization operations. We had a bubble around the city—you saw it driving around. We found out the whereabouts of the guys who killed our people. They were in a place called Tanji Sidan, about five kilometers from Camp Julien. These guys had been out of the country after the killing but had come back. They were locals. We confirmed this with non-PHOENIX resources. I offered our services to ISAF since the area was under their control: we could do it, the Kandak and us. Take them down. They were not enthusiastic. But ISAF does not control the ANA. It can go where it wants."

Brian was circumspect—he didn't want to cause trouble—but I found out elsewhere there was a pretty skittish response. Somebody didn't want Canada involved in capturing terrorists that killed Canadians. For the life of me, I will never understand this craven mentality.

"I asked the Afghan Kandak commander if he would be willing to do a cordon and search to get those guys and without a doubt he said yes, in a split second. He knew it was important to me, he knew it was important to Canada. I told him this wasn't coming from brigade, or corps, or the Afghan Ministry of Defence. He said, point-blank, that he'd do it. You are willing to help us, so I'll help you. He was doing this as a personal favor."

Brian sketched out the operation. "Once we got some more visibility on the target and defined it a bit better, we found out the street number the guys were living at. Twenty-third Kandak did all the rehearsals and procedures. It became a full battalion operation. We expected casualties: it was Afghans against Afghans, and the odds were there was not going to be strict fire control.

"It was a textbook cordon and search. The cordon was put in place, communications were put in place, there was observation in the high ground. No Coyotes, all Afghan sources. The Afghan commander walked in his inner cordon, went up to the house, knocked on the door, and the guys gave up. The compound had sixteen people in it, full of kids. The two guys were removed. When they saw that there were Canadians with the Afghans, when they saw the Canadian flags on their uniforms, they literally shit themselves. They realized it wasn't just a random Afghan search operation. They saw the flag and knew why they were being picked up.

"The Afghans turned them over to OEF, who worked on them and found out that they had connections to HiG, Al Qaeda, and the Taliban. That link was very tight in Kabul. One of the two guys, it turned out, was number four in the entire city, a very big fish. It had a huge impact on the enemy's future operations, including possible assassination attempts against Karzai, attempts against other ministers, planned bombing against infrastructure and buildings. This seizure shut them right down. They couldn't do anything."

If certain skittish bureaucrats had their way, the takedown wouldn't have happened at all and this guy would still be on the streets and some of those attacks would have taken place.

Major Hynes, the ETTs, and their Kandak played a major role in providing security for the fall 2004 presidential election. This vast effort was the very reason the Coyote squadron remained in Kabul after the bulk of the Canadian ISAF contingent returned home in the summer of 2004. Practically everybody in uniform who was armed was part of this mission. The election presented the enemy with an opportunity to interfere with several critical things. First, the elections were going to be closely monitored by the international community. If the perception existed that Karzai was an American puppet in a rigged election, he, and thus the international effort, would lack credibility. Second, the election would be the first true measurement of what the Afghan people as a whole believed and in what direction they wanted to go—if the turnout was high enough. The enemy had the opportunity to influence the number of people voting through violent action: the fewer voters, the less representative the elections would be, and thus Karzai would lack a mandate from the people. He would lack legitimacy. The election had to be fair, it had to be representative. It had to be transparent.

Canadian aspects of election security involved overt and some more discrete operations. TF PHOENIX, which was part of CFC-A, became a critical component in Kabul: it was absolutely critical that the "Afghan face" be present everywhere, that the security was not something imposed by outside forces. Afghan citizens protected by the Afghan National Army. This presence was critical long before the election, especially during the voter registration process. If the enemy could interfere with the registration process, the elections would be undermined even before they were held. Wherever there was a ANA presence, voter registration turnout was 75 to 80 percent. In the hot areas with no ANA presence, the registration turnout was 30 percent. OEF and ISAF assisted the ANA with helicopters and transport aircraft to get them out into the rural areas to increase those numbers.

Brian's Kandak was assigned to Kabul province. The loya jirga site was selected as the counting facility for what amounted to 55 percent of the ballots for the country and therefore had to be protected. "It was a security sieve," Brian explained. "It is a university campus, you can't track who comes in and out, there are squatters. We moved in there and assessed it. They moved the site to Camp Darulaman, which is the ANA facility right next to Camp Julien. We were part of the plan to use the Kandaks to secure the province; people forgot there is a Kabul province outside of Kabul city. That was overlooked, so we fixed it. The Kandak, with augmentation, went from seven hundred to eighteen hundred, plus my band of fifteen ETTs."

ISAF played a supporting role, with the ANA and the police up front. The UN, to ensure impartiality, provided its own security in the counting facilities, while the Kandak provided outer cordon security and the provincial security. "It was a circle within a circle within a circle," as Brian put it. This went on for three weeks as the ANA, OEF, and ISAF deterred the enemy's attempts to counter the election process.

In the election run-up, a local individual approached the authorities at Camp Julien and told them that he was being coerced by the Taliban into assisting them with a terrorist attack to be directed against the counting facility. The Taliban cell was about to move a large propane tank bomb to his compound and use it as a staging area. An operation was put together to establish surveillance on the house in an effort to identify the terrorist cell members. Another plan was set up to raid the compound once the bomb was prepared. The raiding force was based on the Hungarian mechanized infantry company based out of Camp Julien, with a variety of Canadian surveillance capabilities in support. Unfortunately the Hungarians got lost (there were language-barrier issues) and the enemy fled before the search force arrived. The bomb was intercepted and disarmed, but the man who blew the whistle disappeared. He is believed to have been murdered by the terrorists in retaliation.

There was serious concern about antigovernment forces rocketing the Daru- laman counting facility. The Afghan brigadier general who normally operated from Darulaman became a sort of theater commander for Kabul province. He was a former Northern Alliance commander who also fought south of the city. "He knew where all the rocket launch sites were," Brian said as he lit a cigarette and pulled a map out. "He had used them himself against the Taliban. We created a map trace/patrol route based on his information. We checked and confirmed from historical documentation and by our other observation platforms. We patrolled those areas with the Kandak. In the lead-up to the election, there were about two or three rockets fired due east of Kabul—and that was from the area the AMF were given to patrol for political reasons." Brian and the ETTs knew it was not a glamorous task, but understood it was one that contributed to the success of the emergent political process. The establishment of a legitimate government was the first step to countering an insurgency operating against the backdrop of chaos.

PART THREE

the german PRTs: konduz and feyzabad, 2004

An appeal to fear never finds an echo in German hearts.

—OTTO VON BISMARCK

y contacts at the International Security Assistance Force (ISAF) had sorted out the arrangements for the flight to Konduz. The whole thing was complicated by the presidential inauguration security operation, Operation Magnum. Intelligence estimates suggested that the HTB (Hostile Taliban), the HiG, and AQ might take another shot at generating disruption. They failed during the presidential elections, but the inauguration would bring international dignitaries to Kabul and crowds in the streets. One of the security measures was a closure of airspace over Kabul for about forty-eight hours, coupled with a shutdown of Kabul International Airport (KAIA). Captain Eghtedar Manouchehri transported me in his LAV III through the deserted streets of Kabul; on the approach route to the airport, there was one Afghan soldier stationed every twenty-five feet on both sides of the road. Gray Russian-built jeeps of the NDS moved about. The security tower at Massoud circle was packed to the brim with armed police.

I met up with the Luftwaffe air movement people at KAIA and settled in with an espresso at the bar. In time a flustered, balding German captain joined me.

"I am Dr. Baray. You are also flying to Konduz?

"Yes. I am Dr. Maloney."

"Well, I don't understand this. I was supposed to be in Kabul for another three days and suddenly I have orders to fly to Konduz today."

The bewildered doctor was an interesting guy. He was originally from Afghanistan and left for West Germany when the Soviets took over in 1979.

"How many German-Afghans are there?"

"Oh, many. Recall that hundreds of Afghans were sent to East Germany to be trained in engineering and agriculture during the 1970s and 1980s. Some remained in Germany, others came back in 1989 before *die Mauer* fell. The German government has been tracking us all down and asking us to join the effort here."

"So they put you in uniform and give you a rank?"

"Exactly. But no responsibility!" he joked.

I also learned that many East Germans had been in Afghanistan during the bad old days: Stasi interrogators and security experts helped train KHAD, the infamous Afghan secret police that was backed by the KGB. These descendants of the Nazi Gestapo had contributed to the carnage at the Pol-e Charki Prison, the closest thing to Dachau in Communist Afghanistan.

Taken as a whole, Germany had numerous opportunities to access the Afghan population throughout the country. As I discovered on my last trip in 2003, there were more than a few Afghans who spoke German. If the Germans could "plug in" to those who had connections to Deutschland, this could be a valuable element in the stabilization campaign for Afghanistan.

Dr. Baray and I trooped out to the Luftwaffe C-160 Transall transport, essentially a Herc with two engines. An RAF Globemaster III was landing; an SOF Close Protection Party complete with snipers on the roof of the KAIA terminal, plus the presence of a number of young, long-haired blond female Belgian soldiers equipped with FN Minimi light machine guns indicated that someone important was aboard.

Thirty seconds after the Transall took off, the machine without warning banked into g-force-producing turn that compressed my internal organs together. *Bang! Bang-bang-bang!* The plane started to pop flares. The plane lurched to the left, then to the right, and climbed and dropped like an elevator before leveling out and gaining speed. I was unable to determine whether there was a direct threat to the aircraft or if this was some type of SOP on takeoff from KAIA. There uncertainly was cause for some apprehension until it was clear that we were above the Hindu Kush.

The rest of the flight was uneventful, and we lined up for the Konduz runway. On the ground, there was a clutch of AMF troops, some ISAF Germans. Two Mi-17 helicopters with camouflage patterns were under tarps, while a UN Mi-17 or Mi-8 was unloading. Konduz terminal was built in the 1960s using U.S. aid money; the airfield was subsequently appropriated by the Soviets and became the base for the 201st Motor Rifle Division. The irony of a modern German army taking control over an area surrendered by a modern Soviet army was amusing. Most of the military accommodation from that period was rubble. I walked down the road outside the terminal while we awaited transport.

It was a bright day—at first. I noticed an Mi-24 HIND attack helicopter. The aluminum carcass was broken in two: the front half with the cabin was still on a concrete arm; the tail was broken off and lying on the ground. This HIND was a monument of some kind to the Soviet forces that had operated here. The carcass had been stripped for spares by somebody trying to keep helicopters running after their patrons had departed the scene. As I was standing there, a cold, dark fog roiled in. The astonishing thing was how quickly it moved. In seconds the scene changed from a sunny day to a boiling envelope that blocked out the light and whirled around the HIND monument-wreck. My spine felt like it was being probed with a million tiny needles and the hair on the back of my neck stood up. It was an eerie experience: Was it the ghosts of dead Soviet pilots telling me to get away? Was it the specters of the killed mujahideen jealously guarding a trophy of the defeated enemy? I attempted to find the terminal, but I could not see two inches in front of me. Oh, and I forgot to mention: the road was cleared, but there were mines everywhere else. I was reduced to either standing still or feeling my way along the roadbed. Halfway back to the terminal, the fog roiled away, as if it had never been there. I looked back at the HIND; it was almost as if I had gone back in time or to some other place for the past ten minutes. Some hellish facsimile of Konduz. And returned.

My contact was Oberstleutnant Bokelman, the PRT spinmeister. His right arm, Oberstabsfeldwebel Christian Kaiser, brought the vehicle up. Bokelman was the shorter of the two, with a bristling haircut and a chain-smoker's hands. Bokelman welcomed me to Konduz. Kaiser, an experienced senior NCO bear of a man, also shook hands. I could easily picture Kaiser as a member of Kaiser Wilhelm's army, while it wasn't too much of a leap to envisage Bokelman behind the controls of an ME-109 in the Battle of Britain.

We proceeded through the skeletons of the former Soviet base. Tank turrets with their barrels removed by a giant's hand lay along the road. Destroyed BTR-60s and piles of BMP tracks were in evidence in uncleared areas. We drove down a winding road; the whole base was on a broad plateau that was nearly at a higher elevation than the city.

"So what is the situation in Konduz? I understand there have been some incidents."

"Yes. We had a jeep attacked. A command-detonated roadside bomb."

We pulled onto the MSR from the airport to the city; the road was extremely rough and we slowed down.

"Where was the attack?"

"Just up here."

I could see where the road had been filled in. Children played on the remains of a D-30 artillery piece next to an AMF checkpoint.

"A Wolf jeep with crew was driving along here. The detonation was, fortunately, mistimed. The explosion went off under the rear wheel well. The body of the vehicle protected the crew and explosion was vented away. It was extremely close. We brought in a CH-53 to evacuate the wounded to Termez, where we have a hospital. Three wounded."

It was easy to see why the insurgents hit the Germans along here. An attack here was predictable: It was the only route from the city to the airport, and it was arrow-straight. There was plenty of cover at either end (the entrances to the airport and the city proper) but almost none along the elevated road. The frequency of ISAF vehicle movement made it ideal.

Konduz was like a northern, colder Kandahar. The roads were pretty screwed up and forced us to a crawl in places. Vehicular traffic was a combination of NGO, ISAF, AMF, ANA, and security forces, though there was a Chinese road construction crew with shiny new rollers and paving machines.

"The Chinese got hit too last summer. Insurgents killed thirteen members of a road crew." I also heard elsewhere that the Chinese figured out who did it and attacked a training camp just inside the Pakistani border opposite Badakhshan province with a retaliatory raid. That didn't make the media.

This road crew was escorted by local security forces.

The journey was interrupted by numerous "Taliban speed bumps." These consisted of BMP treads unraveled with the teeth up across the road, obviously to slow down movement. They were a two-edged sword: for security forces, it inhibited and controlled movement; for the insurgents, it forced vehicles to slow down so they became better targets. I kept a watchful eye out whenever we slowed down.

The streets were choked with horse-drawn carts. In a jarring way, the horses were all decorated. Red predominated, but the horses had garlands and flourishes, as did the carts. Indeed, they made better time than we did, I would suspect. The odd tuk-tuk three-wheeler bounced by. We passed the AMF compound: it had a (crewed) 23-mm antiaircraft (AA) gun mounted on the roof. The ANA compound was right across the street. I inquired as to the relations between the two organizations.

"We have had some significant developments in that area," he said. "An AMF soldier got out of control with, I think, a pistol. Instead of engaging him, the ANA gate guards actually called the local police after apprehending him. In the old days, there probably would have been a shoot-out between the AMF and ANA."

The fact that the ANA in Konduz was professional enough to know to call the police is an important development. And the fact that the AMF didn't mount an armed raid to get him back is another. I understand that the AMF had to be talked out of it and that some higher leadership was involved, but this is a step in the right direction. It demonstrated to all that the ANA has confidence in the local police, the AMF have learned that there are methods for resolving conflict other than immediately resorting to violence. Encouraging.

konduz PRT

The Konduz PRT was tucked away in a cluster of buildings well off the MSR in a built-up area on the outskirts of the city. The obvious problem here was the possibility of ambushes from the compounds and alleyways in this confined space. The Germans were constructing a battalion-sized base out at the Konduz airport. Bokelman explained that there were advantages and disadvantages. With the PRT in the town, they had direct access to the people of the city; they had an immediate presence. Out at the airport, they were more secure, but they would lose the intimacy they had down here. Again, this was a mirror of the Canadian problem in Kabul. What is the best balance between security and contact?

There was local security at the gate; this was strange. They handled all the vehicle searches and identity confirmations. There was some level of trust here. In no way would Canadians permit local security to handle gate duties like this.

Oberst Reinhardt Barz, the PRT commander, was not back from the field yet, but there was a familiar face: Oberstleutnant Matthias Reibold, the Chief of Staff.

"Well, well, well. It has been some time. You finally made it. Still getting into trouble, eh?" The good Oberstleutnant had seen me talk in Canada when he attended our staff college, the time I was nearly bodily removed for daring to suggest that we weren't learning from the past as well as we might. "You came at an interesting time. Three attacks! It's been busy!"

"I only heard about the RSB on the jeep."

"You missed the rocket attack on our ops center!"

We went outside. Matthias pointed up at a series of aluminum C-160 pallets arranged in a protective posture around the first and second floor of the PRT HQ building.

"Second round hit. The first dropped into a field."

"Casualties?"

"Five. No dead, fortunately. It made a mess of the ops center, though."

"OK, I'll bite. Who did it?"

"This remains unclear and we have our suspicions, but I'll let you have a talk with the intelligence people about it."

So it wasn't as straightforward as an HTB/AQ insurgent attack against the infidel ISAF.

There had been at least two other incidents as well; when Bokelman was driving me around, he pointed to blast damage at the base of an electrical transmission tower that was right in the middle of a residential area.

"Another roadside bomb was detonated. We think its intended target was one of our patrols, with a secondary target being the tower. Two birds with one stone, so to speak. The bomb missed our people but shredded several innocent bystanders. We had another one like that too, but since there are no ISAF dead or wounded, it is accorded less interest by some of our superiors in Kabul."

the konduz PRT: structure and operations

Using the ISAF concept of operations, which established as its primary tasks security, reconstruction, and development, the German PRT at Konduz had two pillars: a military contingent (Security Assistance) led by Oberst Barz, and a civilian component (Reconstruction Development) led by Thomas Shultze from the Federal Foreign Office. The badges worn by PRT Konduz personnel cleverly reflected this: A white letter "K" on its side with the flat back supported by both legs. Four German government agencies supplied the PRT: Ministry of Defence; Ministry of the Interior; MECD, the German developmental aid agency; and the Federal Foreign Office. The bulk of the personnel were from the armed forces (321) with three from MOI and three from FFO.

The PRT, as we will recall, transitioned from an American-led OEF PRT in December 2003. The Americans had a Department of State representative at the PRT who acted as a link to USAID, which still retained projects in Konduz province. A representative from the U.S. Department of Agriculture was also on strength.

In keeping with the multinational character of the ISAF PRT concepts, the staff had two German staff members and two Slovak deputies; they were collectively responsible for human rights training, civil service training, and economic issues. Related to this was the hunt for Kabul-based investment in Konduz-area enterprises at the small and medium level.

Militarily the Konduz PRT was predominantly German, based on an infantry company, plus support for a total of 321. There were thirty-nine personnel from ten other countries, mostly in staff positions: France, Belgium, Denmark,

Italy, the Netherlands, Slovakia, and Romania—all were represented. Notably, and to my surprise, Switzerland contributed intelligence personnel. The Bundesnach-richtendienst, the German intelligence service, also supplied a significant number of agents. Nearly sixty locally employed Afghan security guards rounded out the numbers. Some five CH-53 helicopters supported the German effort in the northeast.

There was a (barely) manned outstation in the town of Taloqan to the east in Takhar province, and a separate but not separate PRT in Feyzabad in neighboring Badakhshan province. Collectively this constituted PRT Group Northeast. The importance of these three provinces in the Afghan-ISAF effort related to three things. First, the main north-south artery from the former Soviet "Stans" to the Salang tunnel and thence Kabul ran through Konduz. The main east-west route from essentially China to Mazar-e Sharif and then Uzbekistan and ultimately Iraq also ran through Konduz. Unlike the mountainous southern and eastern provinces, Konduz province was a fertile plain and thus a potential breadbasket for the country. Cotton, rice, corn, and fruits could be grown here. Feyzabad province connects China with Afghanistan.

The primary security threats to stability varied and were ambiguous. Konduz was a former Taliban stronghold during the 1996–2001 period. Indeed, as I discovered from knowledgeable people, the Taliban was behind the attack on the Chinese road workers back in June 2004. Hekmatyar's HiG also had a local following. Mullah Omar himself had some form of personal link to Konduz. The attitudinal makeup, not surprising after twenty-five years of war, was a reflexive fear of outsiders. The narcotics problem was mostly in Feyzabad province. Corruption, in Western terms, was everywhere and ranged from simple baksheesh to black market activities (I was, of course, shocked, *shocked* that there was corruption here). Ethnically the friction points appeared to revolve around Uzbeks and Tajiks on one side, and Pashtuns on the other, though Uzbek and Tajik informants tended to label *all* Pashtuns as "Taliban," which complicated PRT efforts to understand the situation. The intelligence personnel determined that the situation in the northeast was "Calm but not stable." There were some external influencers from Iran and Russia, but for the most part the combination of a high administrative capacity, a moderate NGO presence, a moderate health care presence, and significant natural resources made Konduz a good base area for expansion of central government power. The main deficiency was a poor road net and the possibility of interfactional fighting.

And then there were the chieftains and the AMF, aka "warlords" to the Western media. The victors here were led by General Daoud Khan. His Northern Alliance fighters, supported by a U.S. Special Forces ODA team, TEXAS 11, who called in B-52s and AC-130s to assist the breakout of the Northern Alliance forces, took the city of Taloqan after some reversals by Al Qaeda conventional forces and moved on to seize Konduz in concert with Rashid Dostum's forces in November 2001.

The AMF were, after the war, grouped into "VI Corps," which, of course, is merely a Western imposition of terminology to give it a collective name. VI Corps, technically under the acting command of General Golestan in late 2004, had three "divisions": the 54th, in Konduz (General Mir Allam); the 55th, in Taloqan (General Mawen Sobhan Qol); and the 29th, in Feyzabad (General Sardar Khan). Another division, the 20th, commanded by General Mustaffa, was located in Baghlan, where the New Zealand PRT operated. There was no baseline numbers, so the sizes of the formations could not be accurately determined. The approximate numbers of cantoned heavy weapons included thirty T-55s, twenty T-62s, thirty-eight artillery pieces, twenty MRLs, and about sixty APCs.

I was told that the overlap between the AMF and the narcotics enterprise was extensive and that all high-level personalities were involved—*all* of them, Dostum, Daoud, and so on. Again, this was a wartime expedient critical for the continuation of anti-Taliban resistance, but it was an expedient that became, in a word, addictive. The majority of the population had some involvement in growth and sale, but was increasingly convinced, according to PRT data, that narcotics was against Islamic law and thus was ready for eradication and the Alternative Livelihoods Program. The farmers were quite prepared to do something other than grow poppies. Local leaders, who had a hand in trafficking and guarding the product, were also wavering. After the fall 2004 elections, they saw that something new was on the horizon and wanted to be part of it. They wanted to be part of the new Afghanistan, but they also wanted to have influence in Kabul—for example, to be a Member of Parliament. They were more and more inclined to being at least *seen* to be cooperative.

The be-turtle-necked Thomas Shultze, the FFO rep, was upbeat about the prospects in Konduz but not in the artificial way many diplomats usually are. I could see that Thomas was wary but at the same time enthusiastic. Using his completely fluent and unaccented English, he immediately recognized my skepticism about a dually commanded PRT with a civilian head who was technically the same rank as the German ambassador in Kabul.

"Yes, it appears convoluted. And it could be convoluted, but personalities drive everything. Oberst Barz and I have an understanding, and I have fantastic relations with my counterpart in Kabul. That is the key: as long as we are all on the same wavelength. I report to Berlin, but I coordinate with the embassy. Because of the Basic Law, the FFO must have the lead. With something like the German-ISAF effort up here, it cannot be effectively controlled from Kabul because of the distances and terrain."

Thomas referred to the German constitutional measures designed to ensure the Bundeswehr remained under civilian control.

I was interested in his views on local attitudes. "That will be the key to any ISAF effort here, yes?"

"Yes. My read on it is that the local people are tired of war. Local leaders here have spent over half of their lives fighting. They all have families; this is a very family-oriented part of the country. They are very, very proud of their part in the anti-Soviet war. We have been told by Afghans that we Germans should be thankful because without the Afghan war, the Soviets would not have left East Germany and there would have been no reunification! I have been told, 'We helped you during the Cold War; help us now!'"

The people were sick and tired of all the infrastructure damage. The German PRT was starting to see splits between the population and the leadership, particularly those exhorting them to continue fighting or use violence. In an increasing number of cases, local people were asking ISAF or UNAMA (United Nations Assistance Mission in Afghanistan) or even American forces passing through to mediate rather than getting into situations that might escalate into clan violence. The election turnout in Konduz was 86 percent: *far* greater than anticipated. That was one of the best indicators. Even the Kutchi, nomadic bands, and their regional leaders wanted to be part of the new political structure; this lead to a shura with Shultze and the Governor assisting the Kutchi leaders. The shura is democracy at its lowest level here, something the Communist regime and the Taliban were never completely able to stamp out.

By PRT measurements, the NSP (National Solidarity Programme) was really working here, and Konduz would be a good candidate for success because it was a crossroads. Active participation by local business leaders was high: 140 proposals were submitted to the Governor's councils for financial and infrastructure support. There remained many transparency and coordination issues, however.

I am usually bemused when somebody gives an optimistic assessment of anything in Afghanistan. Thomas must have had some training in detecting nonverbal cues when it came to skepticism.

"How fragile is the situation up here, Thomas?" I inquired. "There have, after all, been some dramatic attacks against ISAF. There must be a reason for this."

Thomas sighed. "Yes, the situation is fragile. A military presence is a practical necessity and is essential."

In Konduz there was an influx of people who had been refugees in Pakistan. The predominant view was that Mullah Omar's minions had gained some influence with some sectors of them and that this kept the situation somewhat agitated. In Badakhshan, there were rival Maoist groups fighting it out, but this was far away from Feyzabad. ISAF didn't figure in their calculations—yet. Clearly the proximity to China was a factor here. For the most part, it was contained.

As for Takhar, the main issue was rival AMF commanders, local leaders with old grievances from the 1980s and/or 1990s, and people accustomed to using fighting to solve problems. This appeared to affect local security, not the overall security of the three provinces. Some wanted to pull an "Ismael Khan" and "do a Herat" here (target unspecified to me) either officially or unofficially, but there were those in some quarters who were convinced this might lead to trouble.

The DDR/HWC process was a positive move in the region. Thomas explained that Daoud was easy to deal with; he wanted a future and to be a player, like Dostum. But what about the lower-level "generals" who didn't want to play a role? Or who just refused to?

In Thomas' view, provincial and district elections were the last chance for the enemy (HTB, HiG, Al Qaeda) to interfere with the positive evolution in the three provinces, but particularly in Konduz. The momentum was just too great. After that, the secondary challenges of the AMF and crime will attain increased importance, and if progress was not made in these areas, it may afford the enemy more opportunities to interfere at all levels.

intelligence

I was curious. I wanted more detail into the threats to stability in the PRT's areas of operations. Lieutenant Jan and his French and Swiss intelligence personnel were overworked; the manning cap didn't give them enough people to process and sort the huge amount of data they were confronted with. During my initial operations briefing, I was shown an interesting chart: it was shaped as a web, a network. In each juncture of the chart there was a PRT representative or staff: CIMIC (Civil-Military Cooperation), HUMINT, SSR coordination, Military Training Team, and so on. Each was linked to an Afghan organization: HUMINT and NDS, CIMIC, and the NGOs/IOs; MTT and ANA, Barz, Shultze, and Daoud. Essentially this was a web of information gathering and relationships. All of it was fed into the fusion cell in an attempt to build a picture of relationships: who was who, who wanted what, who dealt with whom on the back channel. The staff's computer systems were not structured for basic link analysis, so this was done manually.

The int staff had to keep track of this web *plus* enemy activity in its various forms. As discussed earlier, Badakhshan's problems were narcotics oriented, but

Konduz was referred to as "Taliban North." Jan explained that Pashtun returns were not necessarily HTB, but locals referred to any Pashtun refugees as "Taliban." As we had all seen in the Balkans, local enmities could be portrayed to the security forces as terrorist threats and ISAF, like SFOR, could be "used" to settle some local score or dispute going back, say, to the 1980s.

The int cell tried to keep track of developments in several areas: force protection; crime; ANA operations; political, social, and economic trends. Counternarcotics was problematic because of the wishy-washy ISAF policy on CN operations. UK counternarcotics operations conducted by the SAS, the SBS, or the Increment or whatever UK SOF was evolving into, had used certain PRT facilities as base areas for counternarco ops. This confused local leaders, though I had conflicting views. Some told me they understood the difference between German ISAF and counternarco operators; others claimed they did not.

Jan and his staff were no fools. They learned early on that they needed to understand the *historical* connections and relationships between the protagonists in their area of operations. This was a daunting task: "Everybody knows everybody!" an exasperated Jan told me. This was defeating link analysis. They had to focus on key players living in the region. Kabul had to remain a separate issue for them.

What about the attacks against ISAF forces in and around Konduz? What was that all about? Jan explained that it was not totally clear what these attacks were supposed to achieve. The IED against the jeep came two days after a major British counternarcotics operation. Was this a coincidence or not? All of the attacks in and around Konduz occurred during the full moon part of the month. Coincidence? The rocket attack against the PRT headquarters coincided with German parliamentary debates over German Afghan involvement. Coincidence? Earlier attacks involved innocent bystanders; the two latest attacks did not. Was this evidence of improved targeting? Did it signal a doctrinal shift in enemy thinking?

Jan's people knew there were cells of former HTB and Al Qaeda, or former HTB trained by Al Qaeda in town. His money, however, was on HiG and HiG's appeal to basic human greed. Their information was that HiG established bounties in Konduz: 50,000 for a car attack, 10,000 for killing an ISAF soldier, 5,000 for wounding an ISAF soldier.

The Konduz PRT was always on the alert for increased enemy activity during elections. Konduz voted 70 percent for Karzai and therefore was considered at a higher level of risk for disruption by enemy forces. Intelligence staff discovered an Internet note that depicted a planned HTB attack in Konduz. A four-man suicide bomber team was caught infiltrating from Pakistan north of Jalalabad; its target was something in Konduz.

With regards to the IED attack on the jeep, a search of the area turned up a letter signed by a "Mohammed Al-Bashir" of the "Revolutionary Islamic Mujahideen Army of Afghanistan," a group not know to anybody in the ISAF system. Unexploded ordnance (UXO) had been used, with a sophisticated firing point and detonation mechanism. It was a deliberate attack and not some accident. The footprints of three insurgents were found around the firing point. Jan believed it was an "I'm still here!" attack, a demonstration of capability. The rocket attack was professional: tripod launcher, second-round hot, with the firing point located five hundred meters from the AMF compound, either to try and pin the attack on corrupt AMF and cast suspicion on them or, as an analyst in Kabul believed, as payback for successful DDR/HWC efforts. Jan's people favored the former. As is the case in Afghanistan, the "message" being conveyed by the attacks remained unclear beyond "get out."

So much for the insurgent "front." The narcotics nexus was another "front" to Jan and his staff. Their analysis of this problem was best explained by a Venn diagram that had three overlapping circles: police, drug barons, and AMF. There was overlap, but not all key players were corrupt. Jan emphasized that the HiG/HTB front did not appear to overlap with this particular nexus, they had no evidence of it. An emergent trend in Konduz and Badakhshan, however, was a police unit of ten to twelve members that had initiated, on their own, a fight against the drug nexus. They took President Karzai's antinarcotics declarations to southern leaders when he visited Kandahar the previous fall as their starting point. This police action was, the staff explained, being conducted out of shame and because of religious reasons: narcotics was against Islam. The PRT's analysis was positive: Karzai was having an impact in the provinces.

That Monday evening, with cold, damp frost on the duckboards and a quarter moon, the PRT alert state increased. Intelligence warned that ISAF was going to be targeted at locations outside of Kabul. The PRT Quick-Reaction Force (QRF) collected at the gate with a six-wheeled APC and jeeps. Vehicles were manned; light discipline was enforced. Alcohol consumption was suspended by Oberstleutnant Reibold, who was in command when Barz was away. The Afghan guards were quietly replaced in the sentry positions on the walls of the camp. The Wiesel mini-tanks, with their 20-mm guns, were readied. Outside movement was minimized: two-vehicle patrols only, protective equipment worn at all times. The intelligence staff "plugged in" to their web: nothing was coming back yet from the sources.

I had dinner with Reibold.

"We're going on a night patrol. Are you coming?"

night patrol, konduz

I had been told by Canadians in Camp Julien that "Germans don't patrol at night" and that "Rommel was turning over in his grave." Well, this wasn't the Wehrmacht; it was the Bundeswehr, and it did patrol at night. Reibold outlined the problem:

"Attacks on the Konduz-airport MSR will probably increase: we have to use it, our movements will remain predictable in that area. There have been three attacks on it thus far. We will, therefore, conduct night surveillance, overwatching the entire MSR."

Another problem was that the Konduz runway had deteriorated: C-130 and C-160 landings weakened the portion of the runway where the aircraft touched down. An Afghan work party would be refurbishing the runway that night and for about four days. "Work party" was not ten or fifteen guys: it was about a hundred workers and a myriad of irreplaceable construction vehicles. Without the airport in operation, resupply or casualty evacuation suddenly became a significant issue. The airport and the MSR, therefore, constituted the vital ground of the German effort not only in Konduz but in Taloqan and Feyzabad. It was a case of a tactical problem having operational and potentially strategic implications: the "flattening" of the levels of command and operations was a feature of stabilization operations, as we have seen in Kosovo, Bosnia, and Afghanistan.

The night operations around Konduz were not as simple as sneaking across no-man's-land to raid the opposing trench in Flanders or Korea, or grabbing a VC shadow government leader in Vietnam. These night operations in and around Konduz succeeded whether or not they encountered enemy forces; or, put another way, the operations succeeded if enemy forces were deterred from conducting an attack against the MSR or the airport. There were other contradictions to those who were caught up in war-fighting mode: the patrols and observation positions had to be covert, but at the same time potential adversaries had to know that there were forces in place. This was the delicate part of missions like this: some patrol locations could be revealed through movement from one position to another, while others remained in place concealed. Night-vision equipment was de rigueur.

For the soldier, and the leader, keeping focused was difficult and, in a larger sense, explaining to troops that sitting in location with no action was important had its problems. The near-deaths of their comrades and the possible future threat to themselves became motivating factors, in addition to sheer professionalism.

I went with Reibold in a G-Wagon jeep. The driver used night vision and blackout drive once we got through the built-up areas of town. Again, the need to slow down on the rutted roads generated more engine noise, which made stealth more difficult. In time, we bounced through a series of tracks and reentrants, past a destroyed tank, and rendezvoused with a small dismounted patrol. They were the "rear door," covering a Wiesel that was hull down, its 20-mm gun turret moving slowly back and forth in an arc. From this position on the edge of the plateau, the Wiesel, with its improved night-vision optics, could cover the portion of the MSR that left Konduz, to a point about halfway to the airport. I was told that the ROE that night was to shoot at, with the 20 mm, anybody seen to be placing an explosive device on the MSR.

Our movement in the jeep ensured that "they" knew that ISAF had a patrol or patrols in the area. Unless "they" had night vision and were actively patrolling or had a local informant net, the positions of *all* of the overwatch positions would be difficult to determine.

We moved to another position and walked in; this Wiesel overwatched another segment of the MSR. Reibold and the patrol commanders were careful to ensure that clear fields of fire existed so there would be no blue on blue with 20 mm. Any vehicles that stopped on the MSR were closely observed, the information recorded, and, I presume, stopped in the town. Any green blobs that resembled people were checked out using other systems and means.

I noted this operation did not involve the ANA or the AMF at all.

The construction party at the airport had to work with white light to get the job done effectively. There was an edginess among the Germans at the airport; they knew how easy it would be to lob a couple or three mortar rounds into the construction teams. Snipers were stationed in the tower and in other locations, and night-vision-equipped teams silently moved about the perimeter; the latter was problematic in some areas because of the mine and UXO threat. A QRF was based in the airport terminal.

I had been on similar patrols with the German *Gebirgsjäger* in Kabul, and I knew what it was like to watch something and have nothing happen. I empathized with the German troops in Konduz: not everything that is important is exciting. It is not always possible to measure effectiveness. Was HiG or HTB deterred? No IEDs exploded for months on the MSR; the runway was repaired and mortars did not rain down. Operations continued as per normal. It was the closest thing to success that could be measured.

concepts of operations

The Konduz and Feyzabad PRT concepts of operations were closely derivative of the ISAF concepts of operations discussed earlier: I mention this to distinguish the situation up north from the convoluted nature of the KMNB concept of operations and its relationship to subordinate units in Kabul. Conceptually the

Germans up north viewed their spectrum of tasks as five interlocking pieces of a puzzle. These included DDR/HWC; ANA; alternative livelihoods; and election. The centerpiece holding the other four together was development and reconstruction. The military tasks and civilian tasks, of course, overlapped in all five areas. The military component provided for a safe environment, worked with the ANA, and was involved in civil reconstruction. I would suggest that the bulk of the activity was weighted toward force protection, in all of its forms. The civilian tasks, again derivative of concepts from Kabul, included the strengthening of the central government's influence in the region; the buildup and then development of political-administrative institutions; the consolidation of democratic institutions; and most important, the planning of short, medium, and long-term developmental projects.

In practical terms, what did all this mean?

The ISAF Security Sector Reform tasks, as stated, involved police development, ANA, DDR/HWC, the judiciary, and counternarcotics ops. At Konduz, however, the German PRT was not involved in all of these. German police did train Afghan police in Kabul, and these policemen were deployed to the north. There was literacy training for the police up north: only 50 percent were literate. Local police, slowly over time, quietly took up their roles of traffic management and local neighborhood patrols. Highway police also slowly and quietly appeared. Of note, the Kabul government's first special police unit, a counterterrorism unit belonging to the fledgling federal police, had on occasion quietly deployed to the north. Border police were starting to appear north of Konduz, but not in Feyzabad. German-specific programs in the north included the construction of several police headquarters (Konduz, Pol-e-Khomri, and Ali Abad), management courses for police leaders, equipment support to all police units, plus bikes and cars for patrolling. The highway patrol base at Pol-e-Khomri was critical because of its proximity to the Salang tunnel.

As far as I could tell, the Italian-run judiciary reform was in complete chaos. I could find little out about its progress. The obvious problem here was that if the police arrested an individual, and there was no functional judiciary or detainment facility, what to do? And what law? Sharia? Pre-1970 constitutional law? And what of the relationship to local tribal dispute-resolution mechanisms in remote locations where they have been doing that for hundreds of years? A lot of unanswered questions.

As for counternarcotics operations, I assumed based on the mysterious visitors and the raids in Badakhshan that that task was being handled by other agencies ex cathedra to the German operations in the region.

As for the ANA, the local Kandak was trained in Kabul. It did not appear as though the Germans deployed a purely German Embedded Training Team with this Kandak. The eleven-man ETT was from Enduring Freedom; two members were Germans who were involved in signals training so that the local ANA Kandak could communicate more effectively with the German PRT. The Konduz Kandak had four companies for the region.

DDR/HWC: this was a point of main effort. There were two VI Corps cantonment sites: Konduz, out near the airport, and Feyzabad, at 29 Division HQ. The Konduz site handled HWC from Konduz, Takhar, and Baghlan provinces. Oberstleutnant Bokelman and Oberstabsfeldwebel Kaiser and I dropped by the Konduz HWC site. The weapons were grouped by type. There was at least a regiment of tanks: all appeared to be T-54/55s and T-62s. All were in good shape, no rust. There were piles, and I mean *piles,* of multiple rocket launchers of all types. The MRL was clearly the favored weapon, though there were rows and rows of [Sov guns]. I would have estimated that about a Soviet regiment's worth of artillery was stored there. What intrigued me the most were the BMP variants, of which there was about a battalion minus worth. I was, of course, familiar with the BMP-1 and BMP-2. Both types were present, but there were locally modified BMPs too: one was turretless and mounted a 76-mm (World War II vintage) gun with a crude box structure around it; there were numerous turretless BMPs with twin 23-mm AA guns on them (these were not for AA use, necessarily). In mountainous terrain, the high elevation of these weapons made them ideal for dealing with enemies at higher levels ambushing you. Some BMP-2s boasted night-fighting equipment. All were painted in a standard camouflage, dark green and black pattern, with unit insignias present. Again, the stereotype of a ragtag, disorganized force could be called into question. There were maintainers all over the HWC site, so this material was not just rusting away. Essentially there was a mechanized regiment (minus) and an artillery regiment equivalent stored in the HWC.

There were no ISAF guards on the HWC site; it was all local security. ISAF handled logistics for the site and provided consultation for the safe storage of ammunition. DDR observers, who appeared to be Japanese civilians, drove around in a white Land Rover. I assumed that they were the international community's "eyes and ears" who kept the statistics on what was where and as close an eye as possible on activities. That said, movement of any armored vehicles out of the site would be noticed given its proximity to ISAF facilities at the airport.

What was not clear to me was the disposition of mortars, heavy machine guns, MANPADS, and guided antitank missiles, that is, the weapons of choice for a place like Afghanistan. I understood that the buildings in HWC housed this kit, but our limited time there prevented me from examining further. My concern was that it was easy to count tanks, APCs, and artillery—easy for a Western mind used to counting these things from satellite images taken of kit on the other side of the Iron Curtain—and easy to claim success because X number had been cantoned. And it would be easy to mistake this for progress. On the other hand, starting with the big kit, which ISAF was not equipped to deal with if confronted with it, was a smart move. One layer at a time: tanks and APC, then MRLs, the mortars . . . and eventually down to, it was hoped, AK-47s. It was an incremental process. I was looking at the first increments in that HWC site.

But what of those AK-47s? And how did ISAF and the Afghan government prevent an individual with an AK from joining a Badakhshan narcotics production concern? The Alternative Livelihoods Program was supposed to cater to this and the counternarcotics program with some synergy. The leadership of the PRT recognized in their briefings that there were, simply put, no quick fixes. The main effort was to provide some alternative to poppy. There were several elements to Alternative Livelihoods. The starting point was a combination of legal and moral pressure in the communities down as far as possible in the local governance structure. It is bad to grow and sell poppy, and it is illegal to grow and sell poppy, and we will enforce this. Second, understanding that this was a long-term effort was absolutely critical and all involved had to realize that that was the way it was. Third, when deploying reconstruction resources, it was critical not to use aid as a reward to those communities that were not involved in narcotics production; punishing "the people" was a bad move. At the same time, closer attention and coordination of counternarcotics intervention and the deployment of reconstruction aid in poppy production areas could have an effect. A balance was critical so as not to irritate the fragile balance in the region. Another element was the provision of alternative crops to poppy coupled with improved marketing and access, as the briefers put it, to "legal, non-exploitative credit."

This was, as usual, all very well in theory. And putting in the "long-term effort" caveat was brilliant. Without it, there would be no wiggle room when things started to go wrong. The "moving parts" in the Alternative Livelihoods Program were well thought out. From what I could tell, however, the means of implementing all of the programs to get the synergy required was the challenge. And the challenge to *that* was what the theorists euphemistically call "governance."

You are what the Western media have labeled a "warlord." Your troops have fought for years against a vicious radical Islamist army, after having spent your formative years watching your family fight and die against the atheistic Communist Soviet and Afghan forces. The bulk of your adult life has been spent in hiding, practicing deceit and treachery, and fending off manipulation in a bid for outright physical survival. You have, with the assistance of American air support and special operations forces, triumphed against the foreigner-backed Taliban. You command the adulation of your tribe, and others in your region who were abused over the past twenty-five years.

Then some Western guy (or maybe some Asian guy) wearing a safari suit shows up and tells you that the methods you used for the survival of yourself and your war-hardened people are no longer permitted. You can no longer torture those who have infiltrated your movement in a bid to assassinate you. You can no longer deny humanitarian aid to clans who supported your enemies. Your heavy weapons, needed for prestige as much as for fighting, have been locked up. Your security forces are being replaced by outsiders from the south and west led by men from the east. Oh, and some stupid Canadian lawyer wants to put you on trial for something called "war crimes."

Pop quiz, hotshot. What do you do? What *do* you do?

Governance. You adapt to survive again.

the J-9: explaining development and governance

Oberstleutnant Michael Meyer was an extremely busy man; he coordinated the Civil-Military Cooperation cell for the Konduz PRT deep in the bowels of the HQ building. Meyer was an expert; he served in Bosnia, Croatia, and Afghanistan.

"To understand what we do here, one must understand the difference between 'Quick Impact Projects' and the long-term nation building. CIMIC handles the Quick Impact jobs, while the civilian side of the PRT is more involved with development."

"Where does one stop and the other take off?"

"That, my friend, is a good question."

"And how do you do all of this without pissing off the Governor and imposing Western values and culture on the Afghans?"

"That is an even better question."

As usual, one of the main problems was the UN and the NGOs. In theory, Meyer told me, UNAMA should handle NGO coordination. The Governor and the government in Kabul, however, were suspicious of UNAMA and many NGOs. They believed that there were hidden agendas within UNAMA; this reflected long-term distrust of the UN that was engendered back in the early 1990s. Essentially, in some places the UN was viewed as supporting the Taliban, even though the OIC (Organization of the Islamic Conference) and its supporters—i.e., Saudi Arabia and Pakistan—were believed to have sabotaged UN efforts in Afghanistan in 1994 for their ends. Indeed, Al Qaeda has infiltrated many Islamic NGOs and even created its own NGOs. I saw this in Kosovo and Bosnia. In the main, the German PRT preferred to deal with German NGOs for obvious reasons: it was easier for the FFO and MECD to communicate with their various headquarters in Germany, they spoke the same language, and they were more responsive.

What most people involved in humanitarian aid and development (and even in NATO armies) don't understand is that CIMIC activities conducted by NATO military forces have as their primary function force protection. It is designed as a tool to assist in the success of the military mission. CIMIC helps with the initial stabilization of an area the military force is operating in. First, this facilitates movement in the area. Second, it facilitates information flow from the local population vis-à-vis enemy forces operating in the area. Feeding people and stabilizing infrastructure like clean-water sources and sewage disposal addresses Maslowian needs. If those are met, the population is more likely to cooperate with the military force and, at one end of the spectrum, not shoot at them and, at the other, actively provide information. Period.

On operations like the ISAF PRTs, however, the distinction between force protection, immediate aid, humanitarian relief, reconstruction, and development becomes increasingly blurred. NGOs refuse to understand that they are part of a NATO-led effort that stabilizes and then flows into reconstruction and development. They believe, incorrectly, that they are somehow neutral. If the NATO forces are supporting the government, then, and are suppressing insurgents trying to disrupt the government, what are the implications for NGO neutrality in Afghanistan? Logically NGOs would have to support both the government/NATO on one "side" *and* the insurgent effort on the other, just to retain balance. The illogic is, of course, absurd.

Another argument NGOs use is that if they are too closely associated with the "military forces," they will be targeted by the insurgents. Well, yes. But they are part of the effort to stymie the insurgents, after all. Despite this, numerous NGOs continue to behave in a rogue fashion and are in fact quite disruptive to the stabilization effort when they refuse to coordinate with the dominant, and legitimate, powers that be.

Oberstleutnant Meyer explained that CIMIC activity and the "civil" part of the PRT was delineated by projects costing less than 2,500 euros and assistance provided by private donors. For example, rebuilding wells, purchasing furniture for schools, and providing stopgap medical support for local hospitals were handled by the CIMIC cell. Quick Impact Projects were not, he emphasized, economic development. Larger projects were handed off to NGOs through a more complex mechanism or, as it emerged, a series of mechanisms.

The J-9 (Joint Concept Development and Experimentation Directorate) was to evaluate and assess the civil situation. Meyer's predecessors discovered that the primary problem in the coordination of aid and development was that there was a lot of information, but most of it was out of date. The military side, with its resources, could develop a better picture on what was going on in the provinces. It could act as an information broker between the military and civilian sides. This is where any distinction between "information" and "intelligence" was virtually eliminated. A "piece" of information collected by an ISAF patrol walking through a market could have many end users, for example: there was social, economic, and security information to be derived from such a journey.

How, then, to coordinate the activities of the NGOs, the PRT, and the provincial and local governments while at the same time not taking over and running the show? That, according to Meyer, was another challenge. The earlier iterations of the PRT attempted to use UNAMA to coordinate the NGOs. The problem was that numerous NGOs would not cooperate with UNAMA. Indeed, it was unclear exactly how many NGOs were operating in the region. The Governors were annoyed by this; they were the government, and therefore they wanted to be involved with the processes. Conceptually the Provincial Development Committee was supposed to handle all of this, but the PDC had yet to be implemented in Konduz. It was, Meyer explained, a critical decision point. A January 2005 conference was supposed to bring everybody to the table. The ISAF military component could ask people to come to the meeting, but could not lead it. It was like herding cats. Oberst Barz had some success in cajoling local leaders, while the PRT was run off its feet trying to identify all of the NGOs "playing" in the Konduz area. Barz, Reibold, Bokelman, and the other staff members were even invited to watch the traditional Buzkashi game, where a headless calf with two legs still attached was moved around a field, pololike, by teams of Afghan horse masters. I reminded Meyer and Bokelman that Dostum invited Soviet advisers once to a similar event and *they* wound up beheaded instead of the calf. Bokelman wryly pointed to the Close Protection Party "discretely" blending into the crowd: "Did they have these guys with them?" he asked.

The Governors themselves were still learning "governance." The transition from anti-Taliban military leaders in "wartime" to civilian leaders in "peacetime" was not easy for some. The German PRT leadership and staff had trouble determining exactly what motivated the Afghan Governors and chieftains. The Afghans played games with ISAF and the international community. Western concepts of trust did not compute. Most of the Germans believed that the only objective that the Governors had was to maintain power, pure and simple, and that they were adapting to the new circumstances. The Governors grasped the concept of legitimacy and had a working understanding of democracy, but they saw chieftains in other parts of Afghanistan who were unwilling to give up power. The primary culprits in the German areas were the AMF division commanders. Unlike the Governors, these leaders did not quite grasp that they were military "middle management" and not politicians, that not everybody could be the Governor.

There were other complications. The regional power structure, as understood by the Germans, consisted of the Governors (the "big" warlords); the division commanders and leaders ("small" warlords); and local militias that were related to these two groups by ethnicity and clans. Not all of the division commanders were problematic, but those below them were, particularly in Mazar-e Sharif and to the south of Konduz. Some were "running silent," not sure who they would side with.

Unlike Western governments, there is no concept of separation of military and civilian leadership, and no concept of separation of church and state. The mullahs played a role in this system. Most but not all wanted to participate in the new order. The power of the mullahs was starkly demonstrated to the German PRT leadership in Badakhshan province. A mullah alleged that an NGO member raped Afghan women. In no time at all thousands of people sacked that NGO's offices. A single mullah was able to stir this up.

As Meyer explained, "Western rationality is not effective here. This is the Middle Ages with cell phones and AK-47s. The winners here will be the ones keen to learn and develop, but the concept of progress is not operative in Afghanistan. We must focus on the next generation. They want to be involved. The old men are the problem, the 'Generalissimos.' We have to put up with a lot of bullshit from them, and it's frustrating."

The last piece of the "puzzle" was election support. Elections, of course, are absolutely critical in maintaining the legitimacy of the Afghan government. The insurgent targeting of electoral processes and facilities was of serious concern to ISAF commanders, and a lot of resources went into security measures. In addition, the PRT provided liaison officers to the Joint Electoral Management Body (JEMB), an organization that was critical to ensuring that the elections were free, fair, and transparent. A significant effort was mounted by ISAF with respect to protection, transport, and relationship building when it came to the JEMB and the governors. This included logistic support to international election monitors, armed escort for the ballots, and the protection of the ballot-counting facility from both the insurgents and the AMF.

the family as *schwerpunkt*: PSYOPS in koduz

I always drop by PSYOPS units on trips like these. PSYOPS tends to be technologically based, and I am always curious how PSYOPS operates in societies that have adopted some, but not all, Western communications technologies, particularly an Internet-less society. How does a stabilization force communicate with the masses in such an environment? Hauptmann Helmar Koch was going to explain this to me.

"Essentially our objective is to see that the population accepts ISAF as a legitimate information source and that this is a permanent effect. This will, hopefully, facilitate the acceptance of ISAF's presence by the community and thereby contribute to force protection."

The German PSYOPS section had access to a portable radio studio, a printing press, and loudspeakers on vehicles. These last were deployed during emergencies as part of the QRF to reassure the population and provide them with immediate information on the ongoing operation. A Target Audience Analysis (TAA) section worked on demographics and other ethnographic information to assist the effort.

PSYOPS main task in the fall of 2004 was to help the Governor and the people in the region prepare for the national elections. The other tasks involved the QRF role and feeding the PRT analytical sections with PSYOPS' unique data. Though the German PRT was not permitted to engage in counternarcotics operations, the PSYOPS section was not prohibited from supporting antinarcotics information campaigns.

The TAA identified that the leaders of ethnic groups, the regional security forces, the local power brokers, and the opium farmers were the primary groups of people that should be influenced. It took the permission of the commander of the Bundeswehr to permit this type of targeting; own and allied troops and adjacent countries were off limits. Clearly there remained sensitivities to the Goebbels era . . .

The ISAF radio station was called Sada-e-Azadi, literally "the Voice of Freedom." There were seven hours of local programming and seventeen hours of Kabul-based programming. The Taliban had, at this point, no radio stations (though one opened up again in 2005). Two birds were killed with one stone: the enemy had no capability in this area, and the local population now had a connection with events in Kabul, events that demonstrated to them that Konduz was not alone and was part of a larger polity called Afghanistan. Local and national programming was supplemented with international programming; the outside world suddenly became accessible to those who had lost touch over years of war. Where there were no radios, ISAF patrols and CIMIC teams brought newspapers with them for distribution. These were also distributed through the education system: essentially they were in Dari and English.

One problem identified by the PSYOPS unit was that it knew that a lot of locals had radios, but, because of the terrain, it was unclear how many were able to hear the programming. Polling indicated, however, that 80 percent of the population accepted the ISAF radio programming as genuine. In one instance, a series of controlled explosions of UXO at the airport could have been mistaken for terrorist attacks; the ISAF radio station was able to soothe the locals and explain that this was a controlled event. In other feedback, the audience indicated it did not like international programming from Kabul and wanted more modern music, particularly Indian music as opposed to Afghan music. More important, there were demands for local weather broadcasts, not Kabul weather broadcasts.

The PSYOPS unit analysis revealed interesting and nonintuitive things. One might assume that the primary information provider in the family would be the father: he was out working, his wife was at home, he would come home and tell the family what was going on. The analysts found that, in fact, it was the kids (who were more technologically savvy) who were feeding the family, followed by the mother, who listened to the radio at home while she was working. Consequently the best routes for influencing the fathers—and this included chieftains, drug warlords, working stiffs, and military commanders—was through the family. How to measure the effects, however, was a difficult and a long-term proposition. There were no easy solutions, no quick fixes.

in the "mountains above the falcon": feyzabad

Oberst Barz was heading up to the Feyzabad PRT, and Bokelman ensured that we were able to join him for the day. The trip would be made in two German CH-53 helicopters, weather permitting. It was one thing to look at Feyzabad on the map; it was quite another to fly there. Only then does one realize the strategic importance of controlling it.

The fog finally burned off. Our bird, which had a Pegasus and Maltese Cross squadron insignia painted on the side, cranked up and the machine gunners got behind their MG-3 weapons on either side of the fuselage. The SAM spotter-observer sat down on the rear ramp and roped himself in. Bokelman hummed a certain classical piece by Wagner that gained notoriety in a certain movie about Vietnam. The crew started humming Johnny Cash's "Ring of Fire." In minutes we were ascending. Sitting on the end seat, I had an amazing view. On takeoff, I could see the scars of Soviet doctrinally based defensive positions on the edges of the airport: tank run-ups, trenches, bunkers. Right out of the manual, except it was real. I could see the plateau, with Konduz in the distance. We flew low, headed east. It was all fields and plains: completely flat, like Saskatchewan. Then I saw a tank wreck: a T-55. And another. And another, all along an unimproved road. It wasn't exactly El Alamein or Kursk, but there had been an armored battle here. Looking at the map, this road theoretically terminated somewhere near Feyzabad.

The CH-53's partner aircraft flew off back and forth behind us, then it pulled onto a parallel course, We entered a reentrant and suddenly we were flying at low level through hoodoos and canyons. It was cold, but the streams were not frozen. There was no sign of habitation. It was desolate, isolated, and lonely. Not even a shepherd. The elevation increased, but we stayed close to the ground, maneuvering in the gorges. And up again. It was as if we were stepping up a huge staircase. And then I saw white caps. We were flying through mountains. Gray, white, misty. It reminded me of the Lord of the Rings movie *Return of the King* when the warning bonfires are progressively lit from Minas Tirith to Rohan. It felt medieval, even Teutonic. I expected Odin or Thor to drop by for a chat with the rotored intruders. Or Richard Burton and Clint Eastwood to parachute out of a Junkers Ju-52 over Austria in *Where Eagles Dare*. Come to think of it, this aircraft was carrying similar markings. At the very least, it looked like a dangerous set from 1950s *Heimatfilme*.

Banking and turning, we made our way up another "step"; once over these white caps, though, we saw green. Not evergreens like I expected, but more like grass or lichen. It reminded me of a clear-cut Rocky Mountains in British Columbia. Cold, hard rock. I learned later that centuries of grazing had reduced the forests around the city; erosion in Feyzabad was a problem, along with the floods it facilitated.

The CH-53 pilots brought the machines in; we orbited the Feyzabad airstrip. How best to describe it? On aerial photos, one can distinguish the runway only because it is the only completely straight object in the picture. It was camouflaged, deliberately so by the Soviet construction engineers who built it. Once we were on the ground, I looked at the Soviet pierced-steel planking; it was painted in a mottled green pattern to lower its signature. PSP is an amazing thing: this strip was built in the early 1980s to handle An-12 and Su-25 aircraft and Mi-8 and Mi-24 helicopters, and it could still take C-130 and C-160 transports.

Like Konduz airport, the remains of Soviet-era hard shelters were everywhere. I saw in the distance the picked-over carcass of one of those huge scraper trucks. It was not much of a leap to see that this machine had either been flown in or parachuted in in parts and assembled to clear the ground for the strip. And then abandoned by its owners to the ravages of time eternal. A machine that size would probably rust for the next hundred years before disintegrating.

As we waited for our transport into town, an unmarked dual-propeller aircraft landed and disgorged several fit men wearing commercial body armor. The aircraft had some type of lateral sensor slung underneath—either that, or a really weird conformal cargo bay. These people did not intermix with the Germans. In fact, the Germans didn't know who they were and didn't ask.

The Feyzabad ex-Soviet forward operating base and Feyzabad city were located along a river that ran snakelike through a huge mountain valley. It was truly a mountain citadel. I was told that there was an MSR that ran south through a massive gorge; this area was littered with destroyed armored vehicles and nearly impassible. The Taliban tried to force its way in that way and failed. To the west toward Taloqan and Konduz, the Taliban was also incapable of gaining access to Feyzabad.

The drive from the airfield to the city was fairly typical: a slow speed because of the washed out and rutted roads. We forded one stream to bypass a wrecked bridge. A German front-end loader rescued a "jingle truck" from a flooded wadi. A large, old, but not ancient fort dominated the medium ground on a small plateau; it housed a Soviet garrison from the 866th MRR (Motor Rifle Regiment) in times past. Now it was housing for the locals. The kids here were reticent; either that, or they were just used to ISAF vehicles passing by. Feyzabad was strung out along the Kowkcheh river, mostly on the south side. The stalls along the market road were well stocked, with dry goods as well as food. There was substantial vehicle traffic, mostly Japanese four-wheel drives, despite the poor road net.

Oberstleutnant Rainer Stadelmann, the S-5 (CIMIC staff officer), briefed me on Feyzabad. There were about a hundred German and allied personnel at the Feyzabad PRT. About a platoon of local Afghans were employed as security. Though on paper it was a separate PRT from Konduz, it was really an outstation of Konduz. The German government, Rainer explained, wanted to say that it had two PRTs but didn't want to deploy more people than necessary. Unlike Konduz, Feyzabad had no foreign affairs or MOI representatives; the armed forces and the police predominated. German governmental caveats and restrictions demanded that the proper medical facilities be present, which increased the size of the PRT, somewhat disproportionately.

The primary means by which Stadelmann acquired situational awareness in the region was theoretically through Liaison Monitoring Teams (LMTs), each consisting of a vehicle and two observers. There was, however, only one LMT for the entire Badakhshan province. The main constraint was freedom of movement. The lack of roads limited where patrols could go and there were only so many helicopters. Feyzabad, because of the manning caps, did not have enough personnel for force protection, which also limited the PRT's ability to exert a presence. German governmental caveats demanded that German personnel be within twenty minutes of medical care; this meant that the LMT was limited to the immediate area of the city and the forward operating base.

Oberstleutnant Stadelmann and his people were, however, able to identify reconstruction projects. The lack of mobility and the constraints forced Stadelmann to work with other entities in Feyzabad more closely than, say, the entities worked in Konduz in some respects. In this the isolation helped. NGOs and the UN reps and the local Governor were able to disperse 700,000 euros for school construction, and a department of education rep from Kabul was also working in Feyzabad. The initiatives, however, had to be seen to be coming from the local leadership; fortunately they were, by whatever means.

Feyzabad was, however, unlike Konduz, Kandahar, and other areas. Rainer insisted that there was no real HTB, AQ, or HiG threat to PRT efforts there and that the town was even safer than Konduz. His argument was compelling: Feyzabad was a Northern Alliance bastion during the wars. Ethnically there were few Pashtuns. The Uzbeks and particularly the Tajiks were dominant, and thus Taliban influence was practically nil. Feyzabad had held out against the Islamist regime in Kabul, though the local leaders were in fact quite conservative, as many mountain people are.

The main problem was, however, criminal activity. Badakhshan province, because of its geography and isolation, was perfect for narcotics production and had in fact been used by the Northern Alliance to fund the anti-Taliban effort. The usual problems of local leadership, legitimacy, and the narcotics trade were in play in Feyzabad. There were private, family feuds in the region that exhibited some violence. Criminal gangs were assumed to be operating in remote villages. Since the German PRT was not mandated to work in the counternarcotics area, others had to take up the slack.

I came away from the discussion seeing Rainer's unstated dilemma. If somebody wanted hostages, the German PRT and the international community effort was perfect. It was dependent on local security, which was of unclear reliability. I saw no evidence of ANA expansion in the area, nor did I see federally trained and equipped police in the city. It was isolated. Goodwill was the only real weapon here—that, and reconstruction aid. It would take time, and the situation there, as in the rest of Afghanistan, was fragile. Rainer explained that the locals were proud to have an ISAF PRT in Feyzabad. Why, I asked? The assistance? The money?

"No. We were shocked at first, given our . . . historical problems."

"What? Are there the descendants of escaped Nazis hiding up here with Adolf Hitler's body or something?"

Rainer chuckled.

"It is because we are Aryan, they say. We are of the same origins and are therefore friends, and they will protect us with Nanawatty."

"Come on!"

"No, no! I'm serious! *They* bring it up!"

I was curious about the counternarcotics effort. This was a sensitive area to get into. Recently British special operations forces had raided and destroyed some six narcotics production facilities and associated arms caches in Badakhshan province. Four high-value targets in the organized crime world were also "lifted." Apparently the British raids were conducted without coordination with the German PRTs. There was a security concern. The probability was high that the locals would not distinguish one element of the international community from another. The German PRT would have to mend fences with aggrieved locals and take the heat for the counternarcotics action. From a British standpoint, there was no way they could allow adjacent provinces to be used after they had cleaned out their own around Mazar-e Sharif. This was yet another dilemma: How could ISAF work with locals who were involved in the narcotics industry and at the same time operate against them?

Afghan government "info ops" was alive and well in Feyzabad. We drove by a large square billboard that featured half of a skull surrounded in red, with a half a poppy surrounded in green. The caption translated to something approximating "drugs are death." Other signs exhorted the population and informed them that it was un-Islamic to use drugs.

Feyzabadians, the PRT people told me, wanted the drugs gone. The Alternative Livelihoods Program was not here yet, though there was a lot of talk about it and even some anticipation. The narcotics mafias were not liked by those in Feyzabad, but the farmers needed money. They were willing to grow other things, but the programs were not yet in place. They needed something as basic as seed. And that led to the infrastructure problem: Badakhshan's districts were so remote that helicopters would be needed to visit outlying areas. Large, powerful helicopters, because of the altitude. Either that, or ISAF should invest in donkey and mule acquisition. Or road building. It was truly a circular problem.

The historian in me is always curious about what happened in Feyzabad during the 1980s. One of the interpreters explained.

"The villages near the airfield suffered the most. The Soviets were afraid that they would be used as infiltration routes and bases for attacks against them. The people there were mistreated badly: beaten, arrested, and imprisoned. There were significant battles around Feyzabad, particularly near Bahrak in the canyons. Tanks, helicopters, it went on for days."

The high ground was all mined; think of the ex-Soviet FOB as Dien Bien Phu with steeper mountains surrounding it. The tops of the hills and mountains had Soviet observation positions. Despite this, the airfield attracted raid after raid; it was easy to rocket and mortar.

Did the experiences with the Soviets predispose the local people against ISAF "foreigners"?

"To the people near the airfield, for a little while. For the rest of us, no. We can tell the difference. We hated the Taliban and we held them off. We can hold anybody off. This was one of Massoud's sanctuaries," he said with some pride.

The flight back to Konduz was uneventful until we reached Taloqan. I was sitting with my back to the flare dispenser when it fired off. The CH-53 lurched to starboard, dropped, and leveled out. As with the C-160 flight, there was no explanation as to why they fired.

We overflew the remains of another old tank battle once we got out of the mountains and hit the plains. There were fields and fields waiting for the right season for cotton. Then the old Soviet trenches, and then we landed.

waypoint: mazar-e sharif PRT

I finished my business with the Germans and made my *auf Wiedersehens*. There was an IED alert, so I traveled by armored vehicle back to the Konduz airfield, where a gray CH-53 was "churning and burning" on the ramp. The handful of desert Flektar'd troops and I boarded, and we were off, flying west at low level through the snow-covered hills, on the way to Mazar-e Sharif. More *Where Eagles Dare* time. The airfield at "Maz" was similar to Konduz, except there were a few Afghan MiG-21 fighter aircraft in various stages of deterioration sitting on the ramp. There were operational jet trainers, however, in better shape. Some young AMF troops lounged about. A couple of bearded AMF honchos smoked silently in a corner.

It wasn't clear how I was getting back to Kabul from here, but an RAF NCO arrived with a jeep and asked me if I had had lunch. I hadn't, so we went to the British PRT camp, which was located down the runway. The reception was interesting; the guy in charge of new arrivals greeted us.

"Welcome to the PRT. We are all friends here and there is no violence, so we wander about in soft hats. Please take off your helmet and body armor and we'll tuck them away until you depart. This way for lunch."

This was part of the British plan here: by announcing that the situation was secure, and making open demonstrations that it was secure, the psychological point was made both on the population and the PRT staff. Most of the camp lacked barbed wire. If things were so safe here, then why was the PRT not located in downtown Maz? Hmmmm . . .

Unfortunately there wasn't time to get a briefing. There was a C-130 coming in that was headed for Kabul, so I had to eat and run. At the terminal I met a clutch of rather pretty Romanian military nurses wearing Kevlar who were headed south for Kandahar via Kabul; they had been working with the military hospital here. We exchanged culture. They were funny and witty and wanted to know all about Canada and asked about English-language idioms. I joked about Ceaușescu's demise and the Securitate. We had a good laugh.

We heard the drone of a Herc coming in. It was silver and marked with a roundel that had three crowns in it.

"Oh no!" one of the nurses exclaimed. "It's the Swedes!" There was a titter in the group. I asked what the problem was.

"The Swedes: they are *crazy* when they fly!" one said, and the others made vomiting noises on cue.

It actually wasn't as bad as all that. I slept for the trip down. At least until we did the "Khe Sahn" into KAIA. The Canadian ISAF guys picking me up saw me get off the Herc surrounded with Romanian nurses.

"Research, my ass! What were you *really* doing up north?" a miffed Major Jim Fitzgerald inquired as we headed for an espresso and a cigar.

the war in afghanistan, 2005

the war in 2005

I traveled back to Afghanistan in the winter of 2005, and the situation had evolved considerably in the intervening year. Operation Enduring Freedom's CJTF-76 remained based on the 25th Infantry Division headquarters until it handed off to the Southern European Task Force (Airborne) (SETAF) headquarters between March and May of 2005. SETAF was the first nondivision headquarters to take over CJTF-76; it is difficult not to conclude that this was a symptom of just how stretched the U.S. Army was in 2005, given the Iraq commitment. Originally SETAF was a Cold War–era nuclear missile unit established in Italy in the 1950s, but by the 1990s this changed when two airborne infantry battalions were assigned to it and the 173rd Airborne Brigade was stood up to command them. SETAF became the U.S. Army's European-based rapid-reaction unit. Its units deployed to Iraq in 1991 for Operation Provide Comfort; there were numerous deployments to Africa, including Uganda and Rwanda; and, of course, there were deployments to the Balkans.[1] Unlike the 25th Infantry Division, SETAF had extensive coalition experience and was used to operating in a variety of conditions with a variety of peoples. For OEF, SETAF was heavily augmented from a variety of V (U.S.) Corps support units.

The concept of two brigade areas in the east and the south with an economy of force battalion group in the west was retained. CTF BRONCO in RC South handed over to CTF BAYONET in June, while in RC East CTF THUNDER was replaced with CTF DEVIL. Over in RC West, and waiting for the Stage II transition to NATO ISAF, CTF LONGHORN assumed control from CTF SABER. CJTF-76 possessed an equally diverse force structure at the battalion level as the 25th Infantry Division: there were Marines and naval forces in addition to Army infantry and cav units, artillery units reroled as infantry, and contributions from coalition allies like the Romanians, who were the only OEF partner to remain continuously committed to OEF with an infantry battalion from 2003 to today.

The SETAF-based CJTF-76 grouped most of its aviation resources into Task Force GRIFFON and its engineering resources into Combined Task Force SWORD. SWORD had engineering units from South Korea, Poland, and Slovakia in addition to American units. Units from GRIFFON and SWORD operated throughout the CJTF-76 operating area.

One unique organization that reported to SETAF was the 74th Long Range Surveillance Detachment (74th LRSD). This unit was a holdover from the Cold War and was originally designed to penetrate deep into Warsaw Pact territory, locate (fixed) high-value targets, and call in nuclear strikes or lay atomic demolition munitions. After the Cold War, SETAF retained 74th LRSD as a long-range recce unit. Though it was not technically a special forces unit, many of its members were qualified Rangers.[2]

CJTF-76 also retained command of a civil affairs brigade, which replaced Task Force VICTORY. In early 2005 OEF operated fourteen PRTs, which were commanded and supported by the various regional commands. Though it didn't belong to CJTF-76, Task Force PHOENIX continued to operate in Kabul training the Afghan National Army. Most of the 19th and 20th Special Forces Group trainers were gone by 2005. PHOENIX continued to assume a more conventional complexion under the 76th Infantry Brigade, a unit from the Indiana National Guard.

For the first quarter of 2005, the 25th Infantry units in RC East and RC South had comparatively little enemy contact and conducted no large-scale operations on par with Operation Lightning Freedom. The Marines, however, kept up the pressure in the Korangal Valley in Kunar province with a series of ground infiltration operations followed by airmobile operations; they learned early on that vehicle-mounted ops had too much of a "signature."[3] The aggressive Marines also mounted Operation Spurs, Operation Maverick, and Operation Celtics. Spurs went after the HiG in the Korangal Valley, while Maverick cleaned out weapons caches and Taliban cells in Laghman province. In Op Maverick, the Marines worked with U.S. Navy SEALS from NAVSOF (Navy Special Operations Forces) and were supported by USN P-3 Orion surveillance aircraft. Celtics was a surprise move into the Tora Bora region of the Towr Ghar Mountains, but there was no significant contact.[4] TF BOBCAT plunged into "Indian territory" in Oruzgan with the ANA on Operation Endgame in April, but that was about it for OEF V.[5]

After SETAF took over, however, the operational tempo increased significantly in preparation for the 2005 provincial elections, which were to be held in September. The enemy stepped up their efforts to influence the southern provinces, as they had in 2004. In effect, the CJTF-76 main efforts in 2005 were to ensure security for the elections; preempt enemy interference during the run-up to them; continue to train and mentor the security forces; and continue with the construction effort through the PRTs.

The pattern of enemy activity in 2005 was slightly different from 2004. The primary "hot" provinces with high levels of violence were Oruzgan, Zabol, Kandahar, and Paktika. They were joined by Helmand, which experienced a dramatic increase in violence in 2005. Traditional hot areas like Kowst and Kunar had reduced levels during this time, as did Paktia and Paktika; clearly there were positive effects of Pakistani operations on the other side of the border. There was a spate of activity up in ISAF's RC North, but it was limited to a couple of incidents in Balkh. Herat had some sporadic violence, but for the most part RC South was the main area of concern, particularly in the run-up for the fall provincial elections.

regional command east

CTF DEVIL consisted of two parachute infantry battalions, the 2-504th and the 1-508th, plus a U.S. Marine battalion (the 2nd Battalion, 3rd Marine Regiment), which was subsequently relieved by the 3rd Battalion, 3rd Marine Regiment in the summer of 2005. Because of a shortage of personnel, Battery A, 3-4 Air Defense Artillery Regiment (Airborne) acted as an infantry company with the 2-504th in TF WHITE DEVIL; the air defense gunners tended to operate in Ghazni. The Marines operated in Kunar province, using Jalalabad in Nangarhar as a base. The White Devils were situated in FOB SALERNO near Khost. The 1-508th, TF RED DEVIL, worked the Orgun-e Valley in Paktika province.

special operations forces in 2005

TF 121, with its mixture of JSOC and CIA SAD personnel, remained in Afghanistan in a reduced capacity in early 2005; its strength may have been only thirty personnel at one point (exclusive of elements of the 3-75th Rangers who acted as the "green box"), and there was a shortage of experienced intelligence personnel for it. The reasons for this are obscure, but it is possible that the hunt for the al-Zarqawi organization in Iraq was a priority effort for TF-121's "Men in Black." Consequently the160th SOAR Night Stalkers operated on reduced strength for most of 2005, though Company B, 3-160th SOAR was in Afghanistan for part of the year. Task Force STORM was designated a "brown" helicopter unit by CJTF-76, and this otherwise conventional CH-47 and AH-64 unit supported the Tier II SOF in RC South. TF STORM lacked the night-flying capabilities of 160th SOAR, which in turn placed limitations on SOF operations in southern Afghanistan during this time.

Elements from three U.S. Special Forces battalions and several coalition SOF units were deployed throughout the CJTF-76 operating area as the Combined Joint Special Operations Task Force–Afghanistan (CJSOTF-A). This organization included personnel from the 1/7th Special Forces Group (Airborne) and 2/3 SFGA, who handled Joint Special Operations Areas in RC East, while 1/3 SFGA and the French 1st RPIMa operated primarily in RC South. Elements of the three U.S. units operated interchangeably as required across boundaries. One operation, for example, was conducted in Herat province.

CJSOTF-A was not limited to Afghanistan. In 2005, one B detachment (ODB) and its three A detachments (ODA or A Teams) were deployed in Tajikistan, Kyrgyzstan, and Pakistan for "regional activities."[6]

CJSOTF-A and TF-121 also drew on a polyglot of U.S. Navy SEALs in 2005. NAVSOF teams were drawn from Naval Special Warfare Groups 2, 3, and 4 and included SEAL Team 10, and both SEAL Delivery Vehicle Teams 1 and 2. It is possible that some SEALs in these units were former DEVGRU (Development Group) personnel who could provide an ad hoc Tier I capability. U.S. Marines, probably from Force Recon, acted as the green box for NAVSOF operations.[7] One of these missions, Operation Red Wings, went tragically wrong in June 2005. A four-man SEAL team tracking an HVT was "rumbled" and engaged in a dramatic firefight. A Night Stalker Chinook from Company B, 3-160th SOAR transporting reinforcements to the battle was shot down by RPG fire, killing all sixteen personnel, mostly SEALs. Three of four SEALs on the ground were killed and one survived.[8] It is unclear exactly who the HVT was, but the commitment of what looks like TF-121 resources indicates that it was someone important.

The CJSOTF-A organization in RC South was called Task Force 31 and based on 1/3 SFGA. It deployed three B detachments supporting nine A detachments. TF-31's main areas of interest were Oruzgan, Zabol, and Helmand. Helmand had an ODA; there were three in Oruzgan and three in Zabol, as well. The Helmand and Oruzgan ODAs worked with the ANA brigades associated with each province. Oruzgan was designated JSOA CAROLINA, northern Helmand was JSOA GEORGIA, while the south eastern half of Zabol was JSOA FLORIDA. The concept of operations involved deploying the ODAs and the ANA to a network of small bases. Each ODA had a special intelligence organization that produced a (somewhat spotty) web over the JSOA that could cue various responses as necessary: the ODAs could sally forth with their ANA associates; coalition SOF was available in small numbers; airpower could be called in; or the ODA could call in conventional forces from TF ROCK or TF GUN DEVIL. If a really significant HVT appeared, then TF-121 was available.

As the situation in Afghanistan evolved in 2005, the United States quietly asked some coalition partners for SOF to "combat the re-grouping of Taliban and al-Qaeda networks."[9] One of the first to reply positively was Australia, and in July the Prime Minister announced that a two-hundred-man Special Operations Task Group (also called the Special Forces Task Group) would be deployed. By the end of August, the SOTG was moved by RAAF (Royal Australian Air Force) C-130s and USAF C-17s to a forward operating base in Oruzgan province to work with 1/3 SFGA. Based around a Special Air Service regiment squadron, the SOTG had a green box subunit from the 4th Battalion, Royal Australian Regiment (a commando battalion), and troops from the Incident Response Regiment. The SOTG also brought CH-47 Chinooks with them.[10]

The Australian task force role was to "actively [target] . . . ACM key leaders in carefully-planned and coordinated direct action operations involving both the SAS and the Commandos."[11] In other missions, the task group conducted shaping operations before the deployment of conventional forces in operations Determined Resolve and Diablo Reach (see below). In another case, Australia planned and led a five-hundred-man multinational operation with forces from six other countries into the Chora Valley near Tarin Kot to clear the Taliban out.

France had already deployed SOF to the CJSOTF back in 2004. In 2005 the French commitment consisted of a 150-man composite unit, mostly based on the 1st RPIMa. Occupying JSOA ARES, which was centered on Spin Boldak on the border, 1st RPIMa conducted border interdiction operations from the city all the way to JSOA FLORIDA in Zabol.

The Dutch committed a 250-man SF *taakgroep*, which included elements of the Korps Commando Troops unit, some SFMARNS (a Dutch marine unit acting as the green box),and four CH-47 Chinooks. This organization became responsible for JSOA WINDMILL in southern Kandahar province bordering with Pakistan. Its job was to interdict enemy elements trying to bypass the French SOF-controlled JSOA ARES.[12]

Germany also recommitted its KSK special operations unit[13] to OEF after it had been unceremoniously asked to leave Bagram by the 25th Infantry Division commander in 2004.[14] The KSK detachment operated as part of the CJSOTF-A in southeastern Afghanistan from June to October, mostly in Helmand and Oruzgan. It was augmented with American SOF forward air controllers.[15]

And last but not least, New Zealand sent back a fifty-man Special Air Service group for what would be its third rotation to Afghanistan. NZ SAS also worked as part of CJSOTF-A[16] and conducted operations in Oruzgan alongside 1/3 SFGA.[17]

regional command south

CTF BAYONET, the 173rd Airborne Brigade headquarters, commanded RC South. A Romanian mechanized infantry battalion, the 300th Mechanized Infantry (Saint Andrew) Battalion, handled Kandahar Airfield (KAF) security for the first half of 2005 and was relieved by the 151st Infantry Battalion (Black Wolves) for the second half of the year. CTF BAYONET had two other task forces: TF ROCK, operating in Zabol and based on 2-503rd Airborne Infantry; and TF GUN DEVIL, the 3rd Battalion, 319th Airborne Field Artillery Regiment, reroled as infantry. The Gun Devils were responsible for operations in Kandahar province. American PRTs operated in all four RC South provinces. The 74th LRSD operated from Gereshk in Helmand, but elements were brought back to KAF to work with the Afghan Militia Forces and BAYONET's artillery to suppress enemy rocket attacks.

BAYONET's task was "to conduct offensive operations in Zabol, Kandahar, and Helmand provinces in order to deny the Taliban and its allies sanctuary and thus set the conditions for election security."[18] Note that the priority in 2005 was election security, not reconstruction. The legitimacy of the elections and preventing enemy interference with them trumped all other activities, as it had with the national elections in 2004. When it came to PRTs, CTF BAYONET inherited organizations that were not fully manned and, in the cases of Oruzgan and Zabol, unable to operate effectively because of the security situation. Helmand's PRT was undermanned, and the Kandahar PRT was essentially used as a civil affairs company.[19]

Operation Determined Resolve, conducted in the Arghandab Valley in May by TF ROCK, was a typical battalion-level sanctuary-denial operation. Afghan police and the TF ROCK recce soldiers working with them had a contact that escalated into a significant firefight, which in turn cued a larger response to clear out the valley.[20]

CTF BAYONET developed an operational concept to prepare Zabol and Kandahar for the provincial elections. From August to September TF ROCK and TF GUN DEVIL with Civil Affairs, PSYOPS, and medical personnel simultaneously deployed in small dispersed groups to practically every district in the two provinces on sequential, named operations. For example, TF ROCK conducted Operations

Rimini, Anzio, Enchanted, Como, and Verona, while TF GUN DEVIL did Legion, Flood, Falcon, Gambit, Demon, and Force.

"Good works" were done in all locations under the protective eyes of the security forces, who maintained constant patrolling. Additional units were surged in. These operations prompted a significant spike in enemy action in some of those districts as the Taliban sought to confront the coalition effort, which was specifically designed to gain the allegiance of the embattled populations in the election run-up. The lack of adequate forces precluded similar operations in Helmand, while Oruzgan "belonged" to the CJSOTF-A.[21]

In Zabol, TF ROCK, the TF-31 ODAs, and the Afghan National Army battalions worked hard to turn around a situation that had deteriorated since the 2004 elections. The Qalat PRT was reinforced and the road-building efforts into the Shinkay area initiated by CTF BRONCO were redoubled. Zabol was turned into a model, a case study in how the coalition effort could work.[22]

TF GUN DEVIL was faced with a different situation. Kandahar province was larger and more diverse than Zabol. Qalat was nowhere near the same size as Kandahar City. In May the Gun Devils conducted Operation Diablo Reach, which was analogous to Determined Resolve. Diablo Reach focused on northern Kandahar province, specifically the Shah Wali Kot district. Shah Wali Kot's importance revolved around the main road from Kandahar City to Oruzgan province, which ran through the district.

Enemy activity dramatically increased in the tri-provincial border area throughout 2005, which produced several actions. The enemy occupied this area for several reasons. First, it was on the command "seam" between three different provincial commands, which complicated a coalition response, particularly between CJSOTF-A and CTF BAYONET. Second, it is a rugged, mountainous area. Third, it was Pashtun and ideologically hard-core Taliban; Mullah Omar was originally from Deh Rahwod. Enemy forces could sortie from the area and interfere with the elections in all three provinces.

In addition to Shah Wali Kot, the Mianishin district in Kandahar was problematic for OEF. In June Taliban forces were preparing to seize the district center, but pressure applied from President Karzai after a series of police killings convinced BAYONET to take a closer look. When the appropriate special resources were focused on the area, BAYONET learned that regional enemy leadership was going to meet in Zabol to plan future operations against Mianishin. TF ROCK and coalition forces mounted Operation Catania, which killed more than fifty enemy fighters and captured more than twenty. The enemy leadership dispersed during this action. In follow-on operations, coalition forces interdicted the backup meeting site and the targets fled to Pakistan, which suppressed enemy activity for the elections.[23]

TF GUN DEVIL, with the ANA's 2nd Kandak, 1st Brigade, mounted Operation Diablo Reach Back into Shah Wali Kot at the same time to keep the enemy off balance. The Gun Devils encountered a dispersed enemy that fought back in Gumbad, Chenartu, and two other valleys, but then melted away. In time a Gun Devils FOB was established at Gumbad to assert a Coalition presence and act as a mounting base to conduct operations in the mountainous area called the "Belly Button" situated to the west.[24] The combination of the operations drove the enemy into the arms of TF-31 and their Afghans in JSOA CAROLINA. CTF BAYONET used its artillery to support TF-31's forces on occasion.[25]

regional command west

RC West tends to be overlooked: it was relatively quiet after the removal of Ismael Khan in 2004, and the lack of a majority Pashtun population deterred Taliban religious/political mobilization. Task Force LONGHORN was a battalion-sized cavalry unit, the 3-4 Cavalry, which had both ground and helicopter units. LONGHORN acted as the rapid-reaction organization for the OEF PRTs in Herat and Farah provinces. In February 2005 a record snowfall caused havoc in Ghor. Coalition C-130s conducted food airdrops in support of the Ghor Governor's forces in feeding stricken areas.[26] The Taliban did, however, attempt to penetrate Farah province. Mullah Sultan, a Taliban leader, was organizing this effort. U.S. Marine SOF detachments were brought in to assist RC West in tracking down this cell and eventually captured Sultan. NAVSOF forces working with TF-121 were also active in Farah at this time tracking an HVT, but missed him by hours.[27] TF LONGHORN would handle the transition from OEF to NATO ISAF in May 2005.

canada commits to RC south

The Canadian decision to recommit forces to OEF in 2005 was the result of a nearly two-year process.[28] Between February and May 2003, CENTCOM canvassed its coalition partners, asking for PRT lead nations. At this time Canada was busy mounting Operation Athena in Kabul, but it looked at the possibility that a PRT commitment could be taken up at the end of the ISAF commitment. Some thought was given to looking at the Parwan PRT because of its proximity to the other Canadian operations in Kabul, but this option wasn't explored in detail. The main issues were technical and related to chain of command vis-à-vis OEF. Toward the end of 2003, CENTCOM was informally sounded out about a possible Canadian PRT contribution, and a PRT investigation team was established.

In 2004 Canadian planners were looking at the future of the Canadian contribution to Afghanistan because the ISAF commitment could not be sustained after August 2004. The options on the table were to continue with ISAF operations in Kabul or reduce them; close down Kabul and take over a PRT; do both at the same time; or pull out altogether. Closer investigation into which PRT Canada might take over centered on two options: an ISAF PRT in Herat or an OEF PRT in Kandahar.

The problem was that other NATO nations were bidding for Herat and were more advanced in building their cases to assume command of RC West, which was part of the deal since OEF was transitioning to ISAF in what was called "Stage 2 expansion." Canadian Ambassador Chris Alexander leaned toward Kandahar. His reasoning was that the PRT was the "delivery system" at the provincial level for the national reconstruction programs he was working on with another Canadian mission, the Strategic Advisory Team–Afghanistan (SAT-A).

Kandahar was the critical province in RC South, and at some point RC South was going to transition to ISAF anyway. The British were expressing interest in commanding RC South during the planned transition in 2006. That was where the action was going to be. It was a place that demanded high-quality forces. RC North and RC West were comparatively benign environments and, in the words of some planners, "coat-holding exercises," while OEF did all the dirty work.

Canadian politics played a role in this decision. The Chrétien government had antagonized the Americans by doing a volte-face and not committing troops to the Iraq operation after giving indications that it would. The new Martin government was interested in repairing Canadian-American relations, having a more robust Canadian global presence, and distancing itself from the naive "peacekeeping" mythology that permeated the Chrétien government's policy outlook. It was possible that if Canada contributed to the OEF PRT in Kandahar, several objectives could be met all at once. The primary objective remained, however: Afghanistan could not be permitted to be used as a base for international terrorism, and the best way to accomplish this was to continue military operations to shield the reconstruction effort and extend the reach of the Afghan government. The risks were understood. The insurgency was stronger in RC South than anywhere else. There would be attacks. The enemy would try to disrupt reconstruction and capacity-building operations. The Martin government agreed to go to Kandahar, and by the spring of 2005 the PRT recce was under way. In June the PRT was declared operationally ready and its personnel started to deploy.

Canadian special operations forces were also recommitted in a parallel process. By the summer of 2005, JTF-2 was back in Afghanistan working alongside the CJSOTF-A units in RC South.

the 2005 elections

The most important strategic event in 2005 was the lower house (Wolesi Jirga) and provincial council elections. As with the national elections, these elections were a critical part in measuring the legitimacy of the government and conversely served as a tool to measure the extent of Taliban influence in the country.

The Joint Electoral Management Body in Kabul, building on the success of the 2004 elections, brought in the UN to assist in the arrangements. It was a more complex task than in 2004 because of the changes to Afghan political institutions and the need to educate the voters in the complexity of how the provincial elections related to what went on in Kabul. In effect, the stages of the election included the candidate nomination process (conducted in May), followed by the voter-registration process. There were already 11 million registered voters from 2004, but this list had to be updated and expanded as much as possible. Registration took place in June and July; 1.7 million people were added.[29]

Concerns about election security prompted requests to OEF and ISAF to boost their troop levels again. The Election Support Force brought in several thousand troops and specialized capabilities. For example, numerous electronic warfare aircraft like EC-130s and EA-6B Prowlers were deployed to counter Taliban propaganda broadcasts and jam other enemy electronic systems.[30] The Dutch and the Belgians sent F-16s equipped with the LANTIRN (Low-Altitude Navigation and Targeting Infrared for Night) surveillance system.[31] A French KC-135 tanker and a brace of Mirage F-1s operated from Kyrgyzstan.[32] ISAF also received the 26th Infantry Battalion (Red Scorpions) from Romania.[33] An entire U.S. airborne infantry battalion, the 1st Battalion, 325th Airborne Infantry Regiment, surged in during July. TF RED FALCON, as it was called, split into four company groups; two each were assigned to RC East and RC South so that there were more rural patrols available.[34]

At first glance, the voter turnout for the 2005 elections was about 51 percent, which was significantly lower than the 2004 elections. Reasons for this varied. One analysis suggested that the election rules that prohibited political party affiliation on the ballots confused people who wanted to vote for parties instead of individuals. There were only names. It is possible that many people were confused and just didn't vote.[35]

Overall, nine provinces had a turnout below 40 percent; 13 had 60 percent, and two exceeded 70 percent. How was this reflected in the "frontline" provinces of RC East and RC South?[36]

RC East
Khost: 56.1 percent
Kunar: 46.0 percent

Laghman: 37.9 percent
Logar: 38.6 percent
Nangarhar: 47.6 percent
Paktia: 63.7 percent
Paktika: 52.9 percent

RC South
Helmand: 36.8 percent
Kandahar: 25.3 percent
Oruzgan: 23.4 percent
Zabol: 20.0 percent

In other words, RC South had the worst voter turnout in the country. There is a correlation between the level of violence after June 2005, including the increase in suicide attacks, and the low voter turnout in RC South. What proportion of nonvoters was owing to a confused voting process, and what proportion was violence related? RC North and RC West provinces, which suffered from the same process, reported in the 60 percent range, while half of the RC East areas were two and three times higher than in RC South. All of these areas experienced fewer incidences of terrorist violence than RC South. Additionally, voter turnout was down in all Pashtun areas across the country, but most particularly in RC South. It is difficult to conclude that Taliban violence did not have an impact on the 2005 elections in RC South. Out of twenty-four Afghan provinces, fifteen had a significant voter turnout.

Taken together, the data confirmed that there was a serious problem in RC South and that it had grown since 2004. The Canadian-led Provincial Reconstruction Team and CTF BAYONET were about to find out how bad it was in Kandahar province.

the strategic advisory team–afghanistan:
kabul, 2005

[The Iron Amir] Abdur Rahman's immediate concern was lack of money. There was none in the treasury; indeed . . . there was no treasury. A large British subvention helped him on his way. Indeed, the British reaction to any problem tended to be to buy his acquiescence by throwing money at him. His other main concern was to establish his authority across a country that was yet again split into a constellation of independent fiefdoms. Kandahar was the first object of his attentions.

—MARTIN EWANS, *AFGHANISTAN: A SHORT HISTORY OF ITS PEOPLE AND POLITICS*

operation argus: the strategic advisory team–afghanistan

It was late 2005, and I was in Kabul. I had known the caustic and combative gunner Colonel Mike Capstick for many years. Mike conducted, and had the balls to publish, army-wide studies that indicated, approximately, half the Canadian Army was xenophobic, while the other half were racists. Another half was homophobic, and the fourth half was sexist. But everybody got along anyway.* This was the kind of study that made the Politically Correct Gestapo crazy, because if the forces were so racist and xenophobic, they couldn't really be effective in conducting operations while representing Canada's diversity, could they? It was the sort of provocative work I respected. When I heard he was in Kabul with a

---

* *Canada's Soldiers: Military Ethos and Canadian Values in the 21st Century.* (Ottawa: Director General, Land Force Development, 2005.)

bunch of people that he essentially recruited from the "outdoor cigarette smoking club" of National Defence Headquarters,[1] I was intrigued.

While the Canadian ISAF contingent moved around Kabul in LAV III and Bison convoys, Mike picked me up at Kabul International Airport in a SUV driven by another *alt Kamerad*, Major James McKay, whom I knew from the doctrine and training system headquarters. "Security through obscurity," Mike said as he lit a cigarette and headed into the Kabulian street maw. Mike and James were in civvies but were wearing "body armor lite" (a protective plate that barely covered the vital organs) and carried their weapons.

We drove through Kabul's version of the Green Zone, past DynCorp mercs and locally employed embassy guards toting various types of AKs.

"What exactly are you guys called?" I asked as James weaved his way through the barricades.

"The group is called Strategic Advisory Team–Afghanistan, or SAT-A."

"So are you part of the embassy?"

"Nope. SAT-A is independent of the embassy, though the SAT House backs onto the property and our offices are nearby. SAT-A is even independent of ISAF and OEF. We're the best-kept secret in Afghanistan, even more obscure than CANSOF." That I didn't know.

The SAT House was guarded by local security, who opened the gate. The vehicle proceeded inside. As I emerged from the back of the SUV, I was assaulted by a large, friendly black dog.

"Down, Wu-Tan!" Mike ordered, and Wu-Tan slunk back to his kennel. I noticed the dog had the nub of a tail.

"Wu-Tan? Like the clan?"

"Yeah: he was a mine-clearance dog. We found him starving and took him in. His ribs were showing. His tail was cropped to stop him from accidentally detonating mines."

The SAT House was actually two compounds. On the back veranda and in the common room, several members were picking away at laptops. I recognized almost everybody: Major Duart Townshend, a daring helicopter pilot; Lieutenant Colonel Christian Drouin, another daring helicopter pilot; Dr. Elizabeth Speed, an analyst from NDHQ (whose specialty *is not* quantitative analysis);[2] Lieutenant Commander Albert Wong, late of the public affairs world; Commander Mark Chupick. And there were others. Mike had gone for the best and brightest, and he had them in Kabul. But what for? What was SAT-A? Why did it exist?

The primary problem in stabilizing Afghanistan, apart from the Taliban, the HiG, and Al Qaeda and all the violence they brought with them, was money. This should be no surprise to the accomplished cynics among us. But where was it going to come from? The only real sources for the amounts required to get Afghanistan back up and running were the International Monetary Fund and the World Bank. The IMF and the World Bank, however, would not commit monies to Afghanistan if there were no means of distribution and accounting for it. That's what governments usually do, but at this point in history the Afghan government was not in a position to. There was only the semblance of a bureaucracy after the Taliban—and what was there were the remnants of the Communist-era bureaucracy. Which was worse? The Taliban had so disenabled the country that little worked. I was told that the only thing that kept Afghanistan functioning as a state from 1996 to 2001 was that some of the Communist-era bureaucrats showed up for work even though they weren't being paid by the Taliban. Now *that's* a civil service!

SAT-A, as Mike explained in a briefing, was set up to assist the emergent Afghan government "in the development of the human capacity and processes needed to design the strategic plans necessary to attain the objectives of Afghanistan's National Development Strategy." Translation: SAT-A was to assist the government in improving its bureaucracy and planning, and at the same time mentor the Afghan government in the creation of a national strategy. The purpose was not only to help Afghanistan build the institutions it needed to function as a country, but to get the money necessary to do it at the same time. ISAF could stabilize all it liked, OEF could capture/kill all the terrorists it wanted to, but without the money and a plan, there was no future for Afghanistan. And SAT-A was going to play a major part in getting the money. Not the U.S. State Department, not the vaunted UN, not the Canadian International Development Agency (CIDA). Not the NGOs. SAT-A was going to do it.

But wait a minute. Here I was talking to Mike in 2005. What the hell had been going on in the four years since 2001? Hadn't somebody figured this out yet? Well, yes and no. In 2001 the rapid collapse of the Taliban regime months ahead of when U.S. CENTCOM anticipated it precipitated a crisis. CENTCOM, in its quest to destroy the Taliban regime and root out Al Qaeda, had done little or no planning for postconflict reconstruction. Indeed, a number of coalition representatives at CENTCOM—the Canadians, British, and Australians—pointed this out. Out of this emerged a vague idea that the UN would move in behind OEF and "take care of things," but the Northern Alliance didn't want the UN. The UN, on the other hand, would play only if it had a non-U.S.-commanded security force. This became ISAF, which was established under the Bonn Agreement.

But the Northern Alliance didn't want a strong ISAF and discouraged extensive Western planning. Karzai was in charge of the interim and transitional administrations, but he had no real power yet. The British took the ISAF lead and adopted the "pillar" approach that NATO used in the Balkans to fulfill the pledges made at Bonn in December 2001: there would be a lead nation or international agency responsible for assisting Afghanistan build its various government departments. Consequently, as we have seen, Germany took the police pillar, Italy handled justice, Britain counternarcotics, and so on. Unlike the international effort in Bosnia and Kosovo, however, there was no lead headquarters, nor was there a real overarching plan other than the Bonn Agreement. In Bosnia there was an institution called the Office of the High Representative (OHR). The OHR was imposed on the fragmented Bosnian province, and NATO SFOR was used as the OHR "muscle" when the "children" got out of hand.

Afghanistan was not and is not Bosnia. The Bosnians fought for a couple of years; the Afghans for decades. We were siding with the anti-Taliban forces and could not impose anything on them with an organization as small as ISAF, even if we wanted to. There was no OHR equivalent, so the "pillars" continued in a fairly uncoordinated fashion. Now, in Bosnia the OHR was responsible for implementing what amounted to a national strategy. Created by staff in NATO SFOR (because no other international agency had the competence to do so) the Multi-Year Road Map, or MYRM (pronounced "merm"), was established to synchronize all international community activity in Bosnia. MYRM set priorities and established benchmarks and measurements of effectiveness. All the pillars worked off of (or tried to) this strategic plan, which had as its goal peace and prosperity in Bosnia. Since there was no OHR-like structure for Afghanistan, there was no MYRM-like strategic plan for Afghanistan. ISAF was not SFOR.

When Canada took over Kabul Multinational Brigade lead in 2003, and then NATO-ized the ISAF mission headquarters, almost all of the Canadian officers serving in it had experience from multiple tours in the Balkans with either SFOR, KFOR, or both. Once NATO ISAF was more established as an institution in late 2003, the first question the Canadians asked was, "Where is MYRM to coordinate all this activity?" The answer, of course, was there wasn't one. ISAF had been languishing.

In conversations between Lieutenant General Rick Hillier, the commander of ISAF, and President Karzai in early 2004, Hillier suggested that ISAF help Karzai with national-level planning. A small group, including Major Ian Hope, who would later lead Task Force ORION in Kandahar in 2006, Major Howard Coombs, and Lieutenant Colonel Kevin Moore, did an estimate and started working with Dr. Ashraf Ghani, the Finance Minister. Part of this work included creation of what was called the Investment Management Framework, which was essentially a predecessor document to the Afghanistan National Development Strategy (ANDS). The Canadian Ambassador, Chris Alexander, also played a role in facilitating connectivity between Hillier's group and Karzai's people.

When the French-led Eurocorps took over ISAF in the summer of 2004, however, all this work ground to a halt because the new leadership thought that ISAF should remain confined to security activity (narrowly defined), stay out of strategic and financial planning, and not get involved in capacity building. Hillier's former superior in the NATO HQ at Brunssum, a German general, took the opportunity to jettison the progress that was made once the Canadians were no longer in command. The Investment Management Framework was binned. OEF was too busy fighting the war to be seriously interested in things like the IMF and by this time had gutted the CJCMOTF (Coalition Joint Civil-Military Operations Task Force) organization, which could have provided a home for the job.[3] General Hillier then became Chief of the Defence Staff back in Canada after his time in Kabul. He then directed Mike Capstick to put together SAT-A in the summer of 2005 to pick up the pieces that had been left by his ISAF successors.

Mike and the SAT-A crew attacked the problem from several angles. SAT-A had two planning teams: one addressed the strategic development plan issue (Chupik, Townshend, and Haynes), while the other worked on civil-service reform (Drouin, McKay, Lannen, and Delano). The teams were backed up by Dr. Elizabeth Speed, who handled policy analysis; Albert Wong, who was the "strategic communications" guru; and Andy Tamas, a Canadian International Development Agency "cooperant" who specialized in institutional capacity development. SAT-A also had a support cell led by Sergeant Macpherson, a bevy of interpreters led by Ahmad, and the redoubtable Mario the Chef. And, of course, Wu-Tan.

SAT-A had several secret weapons in support of these activities. The first was the fire pit out back. The second was beer. The third was Mario's food. The fourth was Wu-Tan. The combination attracted the powerful, the influential, the near powerful, and the wannabe influential to the SAT House, where the smiling, smooth, polished Albert Wong would go to work on them to counterbalance Mike Capstick's gruff down-home commander persona. Mike didn't have to fake it either; he just played himself. These secret weapons provided an informal atmosphere to meet and parley some, Western fashion, outside of the formal pressures of the bureaucratic workplace.

The most important secret weapon, though, was that SAT-A had no ulterior motive, no hidden national agenda, and substantial credibility with Karzai and the Afghans. Canada gave Afghanistan SAT-A. This was not just bullshit; indeed, it was hilarious to see the Americans, the British, the Iranians, and others try to figure out "what SAT-A was *really* doing." State, being populated with overly competitive people from Ivy League universities, went absolutely crazy over SAT-A's activities because it was more effective than it was in this field. The Iranians kept trying to spy on it, probably thinking it was some secret intelligence organization. But when all was said and done, the sole purpose of SAT-A's operations was to stabilize the government and get the cash to run it. Period.

the afghanistan national development strategy

The most critical SAT-A success, in my opinion, was in the development and acceptance of the Afghanistan National Development Strategy. In effect, the ANDS was Afghanistan's equivalent to MYRM. (Yes, yes, I know: acronyms are confusing, but that's what the things are called.) To understand the ANDS story, you need to understand that there was an interim ANDS (IANDS) and then the ANDS itself; these were the actual plans, "living documents," designed to prioritize how reconstruction and aid money would be used by the Afghan government. The Afghanistan Compact was an agreement signed in London in 2006 between Afghanistan and the international community that essentially turned the money taps on; the money would, theoretically, flow into the ANDS. From there, projects would be funded at the provincial level. This is where the Provincial Reconstruction Teams came into play: they would work with the provincial governors and governments to implement the projects. Before the ANDS, the PRTs were handling provincial coordination between the national development agencies like USAID, nongovernmental organizations, and military forces operating in the area, with little or no reference to the national government in Kabul and its programs. Now it would all be linked: the PRTs were needed to coordinate local aid, and also to help the provincial governments in mentoring tasks so that the money coming in from national sources could be employed effectively at the provincial level. In theory, at least.

The Afghanistan Compact process was led by Chris Alexander, who was by late 2005 the former Canadian Ambassador to Afghanistan. Chris's character had been assassinated, and he had been purged from Foreign Affairs because he was too young and too effective. There were too many jealous people, so they cooked up some bullshit to remove him. He would never agree with my characterization of his circumstances (he's too . . . diplomatic), but I believe it to be accurate based on information I developed. Chris landed on his feet with the United Nations organization in Kabul (he was on leave without pay from Foreign Affairs), where he put his formidable talents to work. SAT-A worked with Chris to "scribe" the original ANDS drafts so that the Afghanistan Compact and the ANDS were compatible.

As Mike explained, "Chris Alexander made a major contribution in terms of the wording of the compact, but the document was flopping all over the place.

Elizabeth Speed worked on a 'straw man' [draft] document. When the final document was accepted, it included 90 percent of Elizabeth's straw man. It was an important breakthrough."

Another Kabul character, the energetic Nipa Bannerjee, who was the Head of Aid at the Canadian embassy in Kabul, also played a role. She led the External Advisory Group, which was the "connective tissue" between the IMF, the Asian Development Bank, and the Afghan government. The IMF had been asking about a national reconstruction plan and was discussing it in the advisory group when Nepa connected with Mike Capstick, who offered planning horsepower. This web of personal relationships, and the staff work and mentoring by the SAT-A planning teams, chauffeured the IANDS into the ANDS, which then became part of the Afghanistan Compact.

James McKay and Christian Drouin explained where they fit into the schema. "Initially we were here to support Nipa Bannerjee, who was in the External Advisory Group. We worked with Chris Alexander, and another CIDA rep, Christina Green," James told me. Dr. Nadiri asked Nipa to oversee and coordinate the ANDS because he had nobody who was capable of doing it. This was not really a CIDA task; it involved coordinating eleven institutions or countries as diverse as the UN, IMF, the European Community, and so on, but he trusted Nipa, so she wound up with the job. Team Alpha essentially coordinated and rationalized all of the discussion notes and got everybody to agree on what was said, so that a streamlined and clear understanding existed. CIDA had no staff or planning process that could adapt to the ANDS process, so James and Christian were part of that "translation."

Our conversation was interrupted by two large explosions somewhere in the city. We waited for a phone call or a security alert, but none came, so we resumed.

Christian explained to me that the advisory group's objective was to ensure "buy-in" to the ANDS process from donors (those institutions providing the money) and nondonors, who wanted a say in how the money was used. Sometimes these people forgot that the Afghans were involved in the process. One of the biggest problems was with the UN Assistance Mission in Afghanistan (UNAMA), an organization whose leadership adopted a "first among equals" attitude in the process, which annoyed the Afghans. And, incidentally, the Canadians. Christian cautioned me, however: "The Afghans are playing both sides, and they are trying to get the most out of everything. But they are getting played too." This Tower of Babel had to be minimized, egos had to be massaged, and overweening outside influence had to be muted.

Even Norway wanted in. "I don't think the power of Asne Seierstad's *The Bookseller of Kabul* can be underestimated," James noted.

"That book has had an impact on Norwegian aid policy in Afghanistan?" I exclaimed.

"That's a hypothesis, not a proven thing, but we can't wish it away."

Christian learned very quickly that the bulk of the job involved "unraveling the spaghetti": "It's a tangled network of people, of connections. It takes time to get to know who's who in the zoo. To make the connections, to know what door to kick open." James told me, "My image of the development community was that it is far more unified and monolithic than it actually is. You run the gamut from very earnest, very well-meaning people who are fundamentally devoted to helping the people of Afghanistan. You have others who like helping, but are territorial and resent additional international assistance coming into what they think is their patch. You can never be quite sure until you've spent some time with them about what type of individual you are dealing with."

Team A had help, Christian said. "We work with Andy Tamas from CIDA. He's been in development for fifteen years. We call him a one-man recce platoon. He knows who to meet, who to contact . . . inviting people for dinner does the trick. We have people over for dinner five times a week. That's how we build relationships. A lot of the relationships are, however, built on what you can give me and what I can give you back, though."

So what did the ANDS look like? I asked my old friend Duart Townshend to explain it to me. Now, Duart is a real Renaissance man: he can fly a Griffon within an inch of its life, fix a fuel leak in a diesel generator in the dark on a freezing night in Kabul, and mentor the Afghans on how to write the ANDS. We hopped in an SUV and drove to an Afghan government compound that housed several organizations. He took me over to the working-group office, a high-ceilinged, wood-paneled room full of foldout tables and computers. Duart was part of Team Bravo, the group that handled the mentoring process that physically produced the ANDS.

Duart attempted to introduce me to one of the bearded fellows picking away at a computer. "This is Ahmad," he said. Ahmad waved in the air with one hand while typing with the other. A man in a suit seemingly burst out of a conference room, looked around, and dove back in from whence he came. The heaters and fans kept the room at a comfortable temperature but produced some background noise. Other people looked around suspiciously.

"What gives?"

"There's a natural level of suspicion in here. They know how important the ANDS is, and they know there are a lot of people who want to influence it or meddle in the process. Or spy on it. They don't know you yet." Duart laughed mock-evilly and assumed his characteristic "Sam the Eagle" look.[4]

Duart's desk was unassuming. It was his intention to be in the background and not run the show. Periodically staff would approach and ask various questions. There was a draft ANDS on the computer screen. He explained to me how it was supposed to work.

"We have to get the language right. We can't just dive into macroeconomic theory, so we lead in with where we were, where we are, and set up where we want to go." He pointed to a paper draft. The ANDS was firmly rooted in Islamic history and started off with a quote from Ibn Qutaybah, who hailed from the ninth century.

> There can be no governance without an army
> No army without money
> No money without prosperity
> And no prosperity without justice and good administration

Yes, that was from the *ninth century*. Implication: whatever goes against this plan is un-Islamic. Then the ANDS moves on to Afghanistan and quotes a tenth-century Sultan from Ghazni (no coincidence he was Pashtun).

> The first thing you should do is keep the private and public treasuries in a prosperous condition; for a kingdom can only be retained by wealth. Wealth cannot be acquired except by good government and wise statesmanship, and good government cannot be achieved except through justice and righteousness.

Implication: there is an Afghan tradition of good governance. It was called, historically, "the Circle of Justice." This concept was specifically equated with, as the ANDS puts it, "building roads and keeping them safe for travelers and trade, building irrigation works to make farmers more productive, assuring honest weights and measures, resolving disputes justly, and protecting the poor and weak." Indeed, the Afghan Constitution is fully consistent with the Circle of Justice. The subtextual message: those opposing the ANDS are blaspheming against Allah and Islam. The ANDS also uses language like "our country" and "we." It is not antiseptically disconnected from the people with a lot of legal jargon. It is a document for the people. Dates are in the Islamic calendar: 1384 is 2005 to us. Importantly the ANDS notes that "unlike the Bonn Agreement, which was a pact among Afghans to be monitored and assisted by the United Nations, the Afghanistan Compact is a political commitment of *both* Afghanistan and the international community." Partners, not subordinate children.

After extolling the success since 2001 (the 2004 elections, the DDR/HWC and DIAG [Disbandment of Illegal Armed Groups] programs, a new currency, school enrollments), the ANDS lays out in stark terms the challenges faced by Afghanistan. First, security: "porous borders" and the "ability of illegally armed groups and terrorists to exercise force," shortages in the army and police. Second, "our civil service has been decimated [and] the legal and regulatory framework necessary for Government to function effectively, ensure the rule of law, and protect our citizens is still nascent or absent. . . . Our ability to enforce those laws is compromised." One of the biggest problems involved aid: "the way in which aid is channeled (less than 25 percent goes through government channels) also constrains Government's ability to gain the capacity to lead its development effort. The unpredictability of donor funding and insufficient progress in developing managerial skills of Government staff has slowed many larger projects." Translation: NGO and IO (International Organization) aid at the provincial level was having a detrimental effect on the ability of the federal government in Kabul to exert influence and transition from a failed state. I would parenthetically note that some of those organizations might have a vested interest in keeping Afghanistan a failed state for their own purposes, as might some provincial-level leaders.

The heart of the ANDS looked identical to the MYRM from Bosnia. This synchronization matrix depicted three "pillars": Security; Governance, Rule of Law, and Human Rights; and Economic and Social Development. Each pillar had a "sector" or "sectors": in the case of the ANDS, security was a sector and a pillar, but pillar 3 had sectors 3 to 8, or infrastructure to social protection. Each sector had programs. The planners had also developed five "crosscutting themes": gender equity; counternarcotics; regional cooperation; anticorruption; and environment. These themes were to be part of any plan developed by the sectors/pillars. The themes, as depicted, supported the pillars in the diagram.

Everything the government did had to fit within this framework, so the ANDS also acted as a prioritization tool. For the most part, the ANDS was geared toward five-year goals. Since it is a living document, there are expansion joints for ten- and fifteen-year benchmarks. Examining the whole ANDS is problematic here, so I'll just look at the security pillar as an example. There were National Defence, Internal Security and Law Enforcement, Disbandment of Illegal Armed Groups, and De-mining programs. All had a five-year or earlier benchmark: by Jaddi 1389 (the end of 2010), the Afghan National Army was to have 70,000 personnel, trained, equipped, and capable of meeting the security needs of the country. It was to be ethnically balanced. All illegally armed groups were to be disbanded by Jaddi 1386 (2007). As for demining, 70 percent of all stockpiled mines were to be destroyed by the same period. Each program had to have a plan to meet the goal, thought this was problematic given the state of the civil service. Duart passed me on to Andy Tamas.

civil-service reform

SAT-A anticipated that one of the biggest obstacles to implementing the ANDS after the Afghanistan Compact was signed would be the Afghan civil service. It was completely dysfunctional after years of abuse, neglect, attrition, and ideological swings. Andy Tamas was moving over to the Civil Service Commission to assess what was going on and relationship-build.

The best word to describe Andy was "sage": he looked like a sage (though he needed a Gandalfian staff to pull it off completely), and he had been involved in development since the 1970s. Initially he was to bring a development and cross-cultural capacity building focus to assist SAT-A. He was, in technical terms, a cooperant, which was CIDA-speak for contractor. "My role has evolved in the past three months," he told me. "I'm invited into government organizations, primarily the training unit for the independent Administrative Reform, and the Civil Service Commission. I've been working with the director. They were training the civil service in the basics of the interim ANDS, and they wanted feedback on how to teach the strategy in their institution. I read the document and it looked like a fine strategy for a place like Saskatchewan, but it wasn't suited to the recovery of a fragile postconflict state. So I made a bunch of comments on it and it caught the attention of the director, so now I've become what one person calls a chief of staff."

"Of the civil-service training unit?"

"Yes. I just finished helping put together the budget and assisted in selection of senior posts. The guy I'm dealing with, he's a lonely leader of a very large and complex unit. He's a physics prof, Afghan, who has returned. He's good at analysis but not in turning it into an action plan." Clearly, if there was no civil service, the ANDS could not function. Anything that could be done to build up the civil service went a long way in Kabul.

Andy and I discussed some of the problems that the emergent Afghan government was encountering. There was, for example, friction between expatriate Afghans who left either in 1979, 1993, or 1996 and returned after 2001 and the men who stayed and fought against the Soviets, the Najibullah regime, and the Taliban. They were, in many ways, two separate cultures. Andy had experience in this sort of cross-cultural interpretation; he even had to apply his expertise at the SAT-A, which was a fusion of a military and civilian culture. "One of these [differences] is the notion of command and hierarchy. The military is happy with this notion, but the concept of command doesn't really apply within CIDA's hierarchy. If you get a senior person who is an obedience-command sort of person, you'll find unhappy staff who will cycle out of subordinate positions. It is more collegial. Development is not hierarchically programmed like the military is."

"What other differences are there that affect things here in Kabul?"

"Both systems are trying to intervene in a system or introduce something into a system, a society, or country, a village or whatever to alter trajectories through time, to improve conditions. So development and the military have things in common. The military's planning process appears to me to be far crisper and cleaner in terms of the role, and clarity of objectives, the definition of who does what. The military's Effects-Based Planning is very similar to results-based planning in development. It's far more nimble. If something isn't working, they can alter course. In CIDA the role clarity is fuzzier. You have to 'invite' the target to the table and help design the intervention. You don't know how the other guy's system works, so you have to let that system express itself first. Once you do that you lose clarity and a measure of control over the situation. Also, the CIDA process is laborious and takes a lot longer to get up to speed, maybe a year or eighteen months."

The Afghan development situation was easily one of the most complex interventions in the past decade. There was so much damage, so much dislocation. As Andy explained, "The institutions of the state are sometimes out of touch with their own people. Yet who are we to tell these folks that they don't know how to govern their country? There's a delicate thing there, and I don't know how to deal with that. Ashraf Ghani said, 'The best road to security is a well-functioning state.' So we have to work with the instruments of the state, but I don't think that means you blindly and unquestioningly support the agenda of whatever politician or senior bureaucrat comes your way."

Christian and James at this point were tasked with supporting civil-service reform now that their coordinating function with Nipa and the External Working Group was finished. It took the two almost three weeks of working with the head of the Civil Service Commission to realize they had a problem. "We started mapping public administration reform," Christian explained. "We mapped it the Western way, the way we were taught in staff college. We presented it to him, but it wasn't Afghanized enough. It took half an hour for us to understand what he was getting at. Afghans see the world in images a lot more than we do, and they link these images to their culture, to their history. For them the word 'efficiency' doesn't mean anything, so we have to try to image 'efficiency.' We looked at Afghan poetry to try and get a sense of how Afghan writers see the world. Strategic planning for them would mean something like the sun gets up in the east, travels across the sky all day, and goes down in the west. Its very abstract."

"But it has to be tangible," James interjected. "Most Afghans don't think in time very far. This is a learned thing from the experience of war: survive now, worry about the longer-term stuff later, because that day will come. You could sit there and discuss a work plan with milestones, but they haven't been exposed to that, and they haven't been in an environment to have the liberty to think that way. The expatriate Afghans have, but then there can be clashes between the two groups."

"Right now, we are trying to explain the concept of a line of operations." Christian sketched out on paper. "We are using carpet weaving as an analogy, comparing the use of a single thread as a line of operations that is part of a whole. James went out and checked to see and make sure that carpet weaving was not unmasculine in the culture; the recipient of the presentation is an ex-mujahideen commander from the north! We didn't want to insult him by comparing what he is doing to something a woman does in this culture. It turns out that carpet work is done by children of both sexes, so it is acceptable to use it."

James pulled out a PowerPoint slide. "We liken the spreading of public administration reform to the light of the sun spreading across the Afghan culture and society. We have a slide with a sun in the middle (the Civil Service Commission) and the rays going to the ministries, and the outer light going out to the provinces. It took us a couple of weeks to figure this out."

Christian reached for his laptop. "Then one of the guys came up with the five-pillar chart, like the one we used in Bosnia, and realized that there were five pillars in Islam, so he drew something that looked like the Parthenon, put the ANDS as the base, and redrew it so it looked like a mosque. We took the draft to our people and asked them what should be used to label the pillars." James pointed to the chart. "We even found Islamic principles in the Koran that support development. And then we collected Afghan proverbs, in both Dari and Pashto. Then we found a document produced by an aid worker who took Western expressions of effectiveness, went into the Koran and poetry, translated them into both languages, and then *wrote a poem* explaining the usefulness of service to the community. If I had to recommend books for successive rotations, I'd have people read Rumi; he was a Sufist from Balkh and is beloved by Afghans. I bought a copy six years ago out of sheer dumb luck," James added.

implementation

I went with Mike and Elizabeth on a run to Blue, a facility located near the British base at Camp Souter. Blue was a low-profile grocery store/liquor store/smoke shop/kit shop for the private military corporation guys, UN, NATO, whoever had hard currency. I needed cigars, Elizabeth needed cigarettes, and the SAT House was running low on beer.

"So why aren't the Americans doing what SAT-A is doing? I mean, they have all the money, all the influence here," I asked.

"The Americans have a lot of consultants here making a lot of money from USAID, but most of them seem to be working in the Ministry of the Interior, Defence, and security-oriented areas. OEF is fighting the war. But Professor Nadiri, Karzai's senior economic adviser, needs support, so we've been working with him to establish priorities. Nobody else offered. We don't do it for them; we help them articulate the strategic objectives in language these international organizations understand."

Mike explained that there were visionaries, like Karzai, but, as he put it, the big gap is turning those visions into something comprehensible, something that could be articulated and so they could be communicated. "We're giving them a vocabulary and tools."

So what gives Canada the credibility here with the Afghans? The fact that we have no apparent agenda? I pondered. That was part of it. The fact that we had an effective, visible, and constant military presence in Afghanistan: SOF, the PRT, the OEF and ISAF commitments, the ETTs. We had been there pretty much since the beginning, in one way or another. All of it—that's what allowed SAT-A to function. We were committed across the spectrum, and the SAT-A was the·cherry on the sundae.

Before I left, I accompanied Ahmad, Mike's best interpreter, on a shopping trip. We took an armored SUV but had no weapons. We kept our body armor in the back. With my beard, I could blend in to a certain extent if I kept my mouth shut. Security through obscurity.

Kabul was a very different city than it was when I visited in 2003. It was bustling, and there was a lot of commerce. Ahmad needed to find lanterns for the SAT-A, in case the generator failed again, so we went to a street that was full of electronic items and appliances. Crowds of people moved in and out of the stores, carrying huge parcels, debating over prices. There were a few burkas, but not as many as there would have been back in 2003. Tea shops were crowded. "That's the movie theater," Ahmad pointed out. "It was closed by the Taliban. Now it shows Indian movies, some Hollywood. There is a theater in Kabul that shows nothing but the Rambo movies. *Rambo III* is the favorite." Bollywood exploded from the poster box.

Ahmad put a CD into the truck's player as we moved through the streets. The melancholic music, sung by an Afghan with a powerful voice and accompanied by instruments that I couldn't name, penetrated my soul and acted as a sound track for the experience.

"Who is that?"

"That is Ahmad Zahir."

"Man, he's good. Where is he now?"

"He's dead. He was killed by the Communists. Then his music was banned by the Taliban, his records were destroyed." Ahmad showed me his stash of CDs. "But we have people who have transferred his music. It is not lost. Ahmad Zahir will live on."

Would somebody, someday, write songs about us in Afghanistan? Would somebody in the future transfer those songs from CDs to whatever technology would exist? Would our efforts here be remembered? It all seemed so far away from the action down south in Kandahar province. Without international money and the means of turning that money into development projects, the soldiers of Operation Enduring Freedom would have to hold the line. And that included the men and women from the Provincial Reconstruction Team in Kandahar, whom I would visit next.

the canadian PRT: kandahar, 2005

kandahar airfield, december 2005: task force afghanistan

I passed through the gate where the SAW machine gun–equipped dune buggy sat under overhead cover in order to keep off the desert heat. On arrival at Camp Mirage, I smoked a cigar (Cohiba this time!), collected my body armor, and repacked my kit, the usual ritual for entry into Afghanistan with the Canadian Forces (CF). At breakfast there were hushed conversations: Canadians in Kandahar from the Provincial Reconstruction Team had been hit with an IED. There were no details forthcoming, however, so I trudged out to the C-130 Hercules, past the Royal New Zealand Air Force Airbus and the Australian P-3 Orion maritime patrol aircraft that were sitting on the apron.

Three hours later, the loadie shook me awake from my slumber on the canvas bench right before the usual gut-wrenching defensive maneuvers were undertaken by the Herc on approach to Kandahar Airfield. I was surprised to find, upon debarkation, that we were on a remote concrete pad and not at the KAF terminal that I was familiar with from my previous trips. The only other passenger on the nearly empty aircraft, a noncommunicative MP Major, just lit out and started walking away, while I waited with the crew for ground transport. An RAF C-17 landed and taxied by us. I noticed, parenthetically, that there were around nine tinted-windowed SUVs parked in a row next to the pad, with a number of bearded guys equipped with exotic weapons kicking the dirt in a bored fashion and regarding the scene through Goyle sunglasses.

Then the weirdest ex-Soviet aircraft I've ever seen landed and taxied up to the adjacent pad. The SUVs moved off slowly, and a number of the obviously SOF people then deployed in an all-round defense around the unmarked Antonov An-32. A small number of corpulent men in shiny-new American desert camouflage uniforms emerged from the ramp and were whisked away, along with a quantity of boxed equipment. The Goyle'd guys mounted up and the SUV convoy departed. Just one of the weird spooky things that happens in Afghanistan . . .

Two white SUVs arrived, and we loaded our kit. KAF had dramatically changed since I was last there in 2003. The tent lines where I had lived and the nearby holding facility were all gone and replaced with permanent barracks buildings. The KAF terminal had been given back to Afghan government control and was isolated from the rest of the base by HESCO Bastion walls and guard towers. An Ariana jet sat forlornly on the apron near where the inuksuk memorial to our dead used to stand. RAF Harriers screamed off, USAF C-17s flared and landed, and Dutch CH-47s whirled off to parts unknown. Two USAF Air Police Hummers faced the terminal and guarded the taxiway. Radar antennas rotated away and the smell of jet fuel wafted the scene in pulses.

As we drove through the base, I noticed that the SOF still occupied the same facility as the last time. It was located on ground of tactical importance near the AAFES (American Armed Forces Exchange Service) complex, which boasted the only place you could get cappuccino and espresso: the Green Beans franchise. KAF had expanded nearly fivefold from 2003.

I walked through one of the old vaulted concrete Afghan air force buildings, which acted as the terminal for military personnel. Somebody had spray-painted "Osama bin Laden was here!" to the blacked roof. I passed out into the heat amid several chalks of Canadian soldiers who were getting a briefing: this was an HLTA (Home Leave Travel Assistance) group that would take my place on the Herc back down to Mirage and then on leave. Dragoons and Royals in arid CADPAT clustered in small groups smoking and joking, while a group of special operators, which included a woman with long braided hair, had their Merrell hiking boots propped up on the backs of chairs as they chilled and watched impassively through Ray-Bans and Goyles. The excitement of leave in exotic places permeated the air.

The Canadian compound, or Task Force Afghanistan (TFA), was in transition from a collection of tents and wooden plywood buildings inherited from the 82nd Airborne or its descendants to a more permanent structure that was under construction. The ASIC (All-Source Intelligence Centre) was isolated behind mounds of concertina wire. A row of shiny MP G-Wagon patrol vehicles, without a speck of dust on them, sat outside the fence. American Hummers rolled by. Across the road was a plywood building with a sign bearing a white wing transporting a bayonet: the 173rd Airborne Brigade HQ, or Combined Task Force BAYONET, was housed there.

I dumped my kit on the gravel, stripped off my body armor, and strode toward the temporary building where I was to meet Lieutenant Colonel Dave Anderson, the Chief of Staff for TFA.

"Welcome back to Kandahar!" Dave exclaimed as he emerged from the building.

Dave had been handling the administrative arrangements for this trip, a feat for which I was grateful once we sorted out some misunderstandings with the help of Colonel Mike Capstick and Brigadier General Mike Ward. After getting some coffee, we launched right into a briefing. I had a lot of catching up to do. Dave is an intense guy, and it was clear that he was relishing the practical application of what he learned at the staff college in Toronto to real life in Afghanistan. I like infectious enthusiasm, particularly when I'm jet-lagged.

Since I had been in Kabul in 2004, the situation regarding Canada's commitment to the war in Afghanistan had changed significantly. The decision had been made to close out Canadian ISAF operations in Kabul (Op Athena) and relocate to Kandahar with Operation Enduring Freedom. In time Canada would take over command of RC South under OEF and then affect the transition from OEF to ISAF in RC South. Before that, however, Canada committed to take over the Kandahar Provincial Reconstruction Team; this occurred back in July–August 2005 while the Canadian ISAF contingent in Kabul (Task Force Kabul, or TFK) was still operating out of Stalag . . . errr, Camp (yeah, that's it) Julien. By the time I arrived in December, Canada had just pulled out of the ISAF mission in Kabul and, in a road move, convoyed a surveillance squadron of the Royal Canadian Dragoons, an infantry company from the Royal Canadian Regiment, and the bulk of a logistics battalion from Kabul to Kandahar Airfield. There were still Canadian instructors at the Kabul Military Training Centre, and a strange organization called Strategic Advisory Team–Afghanistan (SAT-A) in Kabul led by the aforementioned Colonel Mike Capstick. Down south, there was the PRT and a contingent of Canadian special operations forces, both of which were part of Enduring Freedom. TFA operations, including the PRT, were called Operation Archer, which was a bit confusing since that was what the Canadian Embedded Training Team was called back in Kabul.

Dave Anderson was acting commander of TFA (his boss, Colonel Steve Noonan, was on leave) and proud of the challenges TFA had met in the past three months. The former Canadian ISAF contingent, based around the Royal Canadian Dragoons Surveillance Squadron Group and a Royal Canadian Regiment infantry company, had conducted a series of road moves all the way from Kabul to KAF, something not really seen since the Soviet period. A "bubble of steel," as Dave put it, was placed around the softer transport trucks. The staff studied Les Grau's historical work on the Soviets' war in Afghanistan to determine which areas posed problems when the Soviets moved *their* hundred-vehicle resupply convoys along the ring road in the southeast. From there, likely ambush areas were determined and contingency plans made to deal with them. Convoys moved from OEF- or ANA-controlled forward operating base to forward operating base, or FOB to FOB, would laager at night in a defensive "crouch" and then move on. Attacks were anticipated in Zabol, but surprisingly there was no enemy action taken against the convoys at all. The biggest apparent threats consisted old minefields off-road and road traffic accidents. The operation was marred only by the rollover of a LAV III Kodiak vehicle, which killed Private Scott Woodfield.

At the same time, TFA was involved in some "drama" over in Iraq. A number of Canadian citizens from a peace group had been taken hostage by either a criminal gang or Islamist extremists; it wasn't clear which, exactly. TFA, because it controlled the theater-level airlift (a number of C-130s), most of the Canadian assets in the region, and the secure undisclosed location, Camp Mirage, had a role in supporting efforts to recover these people—multiagency, multidisciplinary efforts. It was a busy time for TFA. The units from Camp Julien, now based at KAF, had to store their equipment down south for the planned two-thousand-man Canadian force that would take over Kandahar operations in February 2006. They were essentially Hors de Combat, which left the PRT and the SOF as the primary Canadian forces engaging the enemy in Afghanistan at this time in late 2005.

The secretive nature of SOF operations, unfortunately, precluded detailed discussion at this time, but it was clear to me based on my previous trips to Afghanistan that Canadian SOF worked with other OEF coalition SOF units in designated areas doing violent things. *Very* successful violent things, despite the fact that they took a number of casualties on a mission that went down the day I arrived. SOF, however, had its own chain of command and did not report to TFA, so those missions remained outside of TFA's control.

To further complicate matters, TFA had a role in assisting Canada's Disaster Assistance Response Team (DART), which was sent in during the aftermath of the ruinous earthquakes that struck Pakistan in the fall of 2005. DART essentially has medical, engineering, and protective resources. Some bright light in Ottawa came up with a plan to send a Canadian relief convoy from the ISAF force in Kabul, *through the Khyber Pass,* all the way to Kashmir! This plan was pure "optics," a word we use to describe instant-satisfaction, politically driven operations whereby the CF will acquiesce with the minimal commitment knowing full well that the project was ill conceived in the first place and therefore dangerous. Colonel Noonan, Dave, and his staff people were *quite* happy that the mission was called off.

Task Force Afghanistan had other functions. First, the planned transition from OEF to ISAF in the south would be handled by Canada, which would play a major role when the Canadian-led multinational brigade group eventually deployed in February 2006 and took over from the Americans. This move was a radical reorientation of how Canada did business in Afghanistan. Since General Rick Hillier took over as Chief of the Defence Staff, after serving as COM ISAF in 2004, things had been changing. To some, NATO command was becoming more and more like UN command, with too many restrictions and "caveats" placed on the declared national forces. This was having a deleterious effect on what Canadian troops could and could not do.

The constraints on Canadian and NATO operations described in the first section of this book—e.g., "directed" operations, overcontrol and overreaction from National Defence HQ, meddling in operational detail by politicians—would be mitigated as much as possible. The "operations authority matrix," a complicated chart that told commanders in the field when they had to get authority from Ottawa to do particular types of operations, was completely rewritten to reduce interference and, as Dave put it, "clearly delineate TFA battlespace from DCDS battlespace." Translation: Ottawa had for years been overcontrolling units directly from National Defence Headquarters, using the National Command Element as a way station. This was going to change.

The NCE was generally not equipped as an operational command HQ. Task Force Afghanistan was, however, under no such constraint when the brigade group deployed, the commander would have operational control of all Canadian forces in Afghanistan, not staff in Ottawa who hadn't seen the Hindu Kush. This, according to Dave, would "reempower" field commanders. Indeed, as it was explained to me, those who sought overcontrol were cleverly and deliberately distracted by TFA and their sympathizers in the DCDS shop with all the staff work necessary (necessary!) to process a request for Nyala armored patrol vehicles.

The Canadian Provincial Reconstruction Team was part of the American-led Combined Task Force BAYONET. Under the command of Colonel Kevin Owens CTF-173 consisted of the 173rd Airborne Brigade HQ leading a multinational formation that was unique to Afghanistan. Using KAF as its base (which was protected by a Romanian mechanized infantry battalion), CTF-173 controlled a number of elements: three PRTs (Qalat, Lashkar Gah, and Kandahar) and had a relationship with the ISAF PRT at Farah; a mixed aviation battalion (TF STORM), which had AH-64 Apaches, UH-60 Black Hawks, and CH-47 Chinooks; the 1/3 Special Forces battalion, which had ODAs and ODBs deployed in Kandahar and Zabol; a recce company with a special forces ODA at Gereshk; and two composite American infantry battalions. One of these battalions was the reroled 3-319 Field Artillery, called "the Gun Devils," based near Kandahar, while the second was the 2-503rd from the 82nd Airborne (TF ROCK), located in Zabol. An Afghan National Army battalion with an American airborne infantry company (called a Prepare to Deploy Order, or PTDO, company) working in close proximity to it was based in Kandahar, while an ANA brigade with another U.S. airborne infantry company was situated in Zabol. Another ANA brigade was in Helmand province. CTF-173 had the usual collection of PSYOPS, EOD (explosive ordnance disposal), signals, intelligence, logistics, and military police units. An American MP company was deployed in three platoons and was mentoring Afghan National Police in the various American areas of operations.

Unlike the 2003 operations in which TF DEVIL (the 504th Parachute Infantry Regiment) sortied out from KAF cued by intelligence and a network of special forces FOBs, CTF BAYONET's maneuver units were deployed in the hinterland in small groups, either in FOBs or platoon houses. There was a great emphasis on mentoring the ANA units and subunits alongside the CTF BAYONET forces—that is, not having OEF forces do everything. Coalition special operations forces had their own areas of operations separate from CTF BAYONET's: the Dutch KCT, for example, was in the south on the border in a Joint Special Operations Area called WINDMILL, while the French SOF were to the east of Kandahar, also on the border, in a JSOA called ARES. Other coalition SOF worked in the interior: there was JSOA CAROLINA and FLORIDA. For the most part, the main effort in RC South was in Kandahar, Zabol, Oruzgan, and northern Helmand.

When I arrived, the main debate was whether the Dutch would take over the PRT in Oruzgan province. This debate had gone up to the Dutch parliament for discussion, and the enemy was employing information operations in order to convince the Dutch people that the Outgun deployment would be a "second Srebrenica," a reference to the situation in Bosnia when a Dutch UN battalion surrendered to Serbian forces before seven thousand people were murdered in 1995. Up until this point, the Dutch had CH-47 helicopters and special operations forces operating in RC South, but were considering a PRT and associated support forces.

This was a crucial debate. The British were considering taking over the PRT in Helmand and sending a battalion-sized task force and its associated conventional and nonconventional support, and there were fears that if the Dutch didn't commit, the British wouldn't either. Furthermore, since Canada committed to take over from CTF BAYONET with a brigade HQ and an infantry battalion, Canada needed the Dutch and the British to round out the forces necessary to take over from the Americans. If the allies didn't pony up, then Canada would be left holding the bag in RC South with only Canadian and Afghan forces. Since the Liberal governments had gutted the Canadian Army, this would have posed serious problems because there would be enough troops for only one or two rotations before the force was burned out. Everybody was watching this debate very carefully when I arrived.

I needed more coffee and to stretch my legs. Romanian BTR-70s cruised past after picking up takeout at the Burger King semitrailer in the AAFES yard.

"So the Romanians are still in charge of camp security?" I asked an American SOF guy who was also lounging with a cappuccino at Green Beans. He was wearing the new CADPAT-like Army Combat Uniform, or ACU (which was replacing the Battle Dress Uniform, or BDU), which has a big square of Velcro on the shoulder for the easy and rapid removal of unit patches. He had none on at this point.

"Yeah. We call them the 'Romulans.' They're alien and pretty trigger-happy. We got rocketed yesterday. At the same time they thought they had a contact on the wire and let loose with 12.7. It was fairly indiscriminate," he grimaced.

"How active has it been around KAF these days?"

"Sporadic rockets in four attacks, but one of them took out a Harrier jump jet on the pad and severely damaged another one. No friendly casualties, though. The Apaches caught the rocketeers and nailed them with 30 mm before they could get away. Last week seven local fuel trucks waiting to enter KAF exploded, again with no casualties. It's worse in and around the city: lots of IEDs. But it's not as bad as Iraq," he added optimistically.

IEDs, rockets, sabotage. Things were heating up and it was only December, not even the so-called traditional campaign season.

from KAF to camp nathan smith

I met up with the PRT LO to the task force, a friendly captain named Derek Gilchrist, who arranged trans-port. One could not just drive around Kandahar City in a Hilux truck full of para-militaries buying rugs anymore like the "old days" of 2003. The enemy had significantly increased his use of IEDs and, after the German bus incident in Kabul, the mass movement of Canadian personnel was conducted under armor. On the road near the old hanger, an eight-wheeled Bison APC and four LUVW (Light Utility Vehicle, Wheeled) G-Wagons were lined up. The convoy commander started his brief, explaining the route we would take, actions on contact, and so on. I paid rapt attention, despite my fatigue. A woman who seemed buried under body armor and helmet sat down across from me in the Bison.

"Hi, I'm Niki Palmer," she said with a British accent.

"Who are you with?" I inquired.

"DFID: the British government aid agency."

The crew commander leaned back, "If I ask for a rocket, pass it to me. The grenades are in this box here." He pointed. There were M-72 one-shot rocket launchers Velcroed to the ceiling. "Stay in the vehicle, even if the ramp goes down, until we give the word."

And we were off.

I saw nothing. As a former soldier and having some armored vehicle crew commanding experience, it was really difficult to sit in the back under armor with no view out. Niki and I chatted. Apparently I fell asleep in the middle of the conversation while getting decreasingly coherent (jet lag again!), to Niki's amusement, but was awakened when we collided with a civilian vehicle, which tore the mirrors off the Bison. Unlike vehicles involved in previous incidents in Kabul, this one kept moving: no stopping for a fender bender!

The ramp went down, and we were ushered out into the main arrival area for Camp Nathan Smith, home of the Canadian-led Provincial Reconstruction Team in Kandahar.

The PRT camp was situated in an old factory complex that, according to the holes in the sides of the metal roof, had been commandeered by the Taliban or Al Qaeda or both as a military facility in the bad old days and then hit with fire from a variety of automatic weapons. A new wall ran around it, and there were guard towers, arc light trailers, concertina wire, and cameras festooning it. A substantial helipad and vehicle park constituted the open-area part, which was complimented by a small arms range. There were three largish buildings and a number of Weatherhaven temporary buildings, including a CF-pattern mess facility. G-Wagons and Hiluxes (including a certain familiar M-19-equipped Hilux!) were all present, plus a couple of Nyalas and Bisons. Everything was a drab color, either beige, tan, or gray. The Afghan national flag flew from the flagpole, which was situated in the courtyard of the main building.

Niki was met by a tall bearded guy who introduced himself as Mathias. A familiar and smiling face appeared. It was Lieutenant Andy Bone, a former student from RMC (Royal Military College) and a man of many special talents, including master at "SOCOM" on the PlayStation Portable; art imitates life. We shook hands.

"So what do you do here?"

"I'm a platoon commander with Patrol Company. But you'll find out all about that later! We have a long-range patrol coming up, so I have to plan it."

"Where to?" I asked.

"A district called Maruf."

Now that was a hell of a coincidence. I had been to the Rode Maruf Valley in 2003 with the 82nd Airborne, so I was immediately determined to get back up there to see if there had been any changes since. Andy promised to make sure I was on the trip.

I was welcomed to the PRT by Lieutenant Colonel Steve Borland, the deputy commander; Colonel Steve Bowes was away on leave for the time being. Steve Borland, with his shaved head and confidently quiet demeanor, exuded experience. He was a veteran of Operation Apollo in 2002, when he was with 3rd Battalion PPCLI, and a mean Texas Hold 'em poker player, so the political and operational environment of Kandahar was old hat to him.

"Colonel Bowes told us that with you there wasn't to be any dogshit. You've been to Afghanistan before and know the drill. Good to have you here."

We went right into a daily morning brief, where I encountered a whole bunch of acquaintances from previous visits to operations in the Balkans and Afghanistan. This was an experienced team, and I knew immediately there wouldn't be any screwing around like there had been in Kabul in 2004.

I learned in rapid-fire succession that the enemy was now referred to as the "ACM"—anticoalition militants or militias, depending on the interpretation. ACM was a catch-all for Taliban, Al Qaeda, HiG, and the Haqqani Tribal Network. "Elvis," a Kashmiri-looking enemy operative, had been spotted in Kandahar on a motorcycle, "ghosting" Canadian vehicle patrols, while the vociferous Mullah Baqi, the main ACM pain in the ass in the Kandahar area, was causing various forms of trouble. There had been an IED attack on a PRT patrol (forensic details to follow). In an otherwise successful operation conducted the night before in which numerous bad guys were eliminated, coalition forces had two CH-47s shot down, and these had to be recovered. It had been a busy twenty-four hours in RC South. The PRT needed new turret rings for their G-Wagons and the Military Police at KAF wouldn't give theirs up, the Public Affairs Officer had Christmas messages to distribute to the troops, there was an event at a girl's school, Niki described progress on some "best practices" projects, and the USAID rep, whom I will call "Phoenix," complained about intimidation at a school. As usual, it was like drinking from a fire hose, and I know this is how my students in History 271 feel when I lecture on the history of warfare. I had to regroup and get reoriented.

But first things first. Sleep.

I had breakfast early. Stepping out for a morning cigar, I encountered yet another face from the past: Warrant Officer Dan Hitchcock, who I had interviewed about his time in the Balkans centuries ago. Warrant Hitchcock was the CQ, or company quartermaster, the man responsible for the support functions of the PRT and, when it came to what the troops think, a man whose opinion I valued.

"Howz it going, sir? I didn't recognize you with that fuzz on your face," he said with the tone of voice reserved for newly arrived junior officers. As he stubbed out his cigarette, Warrant Hitchcock gave me the basic overview.

"The PRT is mostly based on a company from 3 VP [3 PPCLI], but about 60 percent of the ranks have no overseas experience."

"What about the leadership?"

"Almost all of our officers and senior NCOs have time in with Op Apollo in 2002 here, and/or Op Kinetic in Kosovo, plus two or three other Balkans tours, either UNPROFOR, IFOR, or SFOR. We have a heavy sigs det from Kingston. CIMIC is mostly reserve personnel, the engineers are from 1 Combat Engineer Regiment in Edmonton."

"You like it here, Warrant?"

"At least we're away from the bullshit at KAF. The food is better."

As I was to learn, to the detriment of my waistline until I contracted a GI tract bug in the mountains, the crap that passed for food delivered by Kellogg, Brown and Root at KAF bore absolutely no resemblance to the delicacies created by the master chefs at the PRT, the cardsharp also known as Stefan and his crew. Indeed, I also learned that the PRT personnel were called "the hillbillies" by KAF-bound types. SOF were also called "hillbillies" too, apparently. There was a certain amount of friction, which paralleled the Op Archer ETT/Op Athena TFK friction in Kabul. When I had the misfortune to be stranded at KAF overnight once, I stayed in the PRT transient quarters and was treated by the clean-cut "never pass a fault" KAF people as one of the "hillbillies"—with suspicion and given a wide berth as if I smelled or something. It was an honor, in its own way.

The "we-they" attitude between the KAF and PRT personnel was put to good use by the PRT leadership. The "vibe" at the PRT was a good one and contrasted with KAF. KAF was uptight: Kabul-like uptight, Stalag Julien–like uptight. PRT was a unique organization and much more relaxed but in a self-disciplined way. If there was a happy medium between KAF's uptightness and SOF's "tigers off the leash" looseness, the PRT was it. Some of the troops had beards, but those beards were clean. Whoever was able to cultivate this atmosphere of relaxed competence knew what they were doing. I assumed it was Regimental Sergeant Major Ward Brown and Company Sergeant Major Billy Bolen, with the active concurrence of Colonel Bowes and Lieutenant Colonel Borland. The RSM was a quiet, intense man, while the CSM cultivated an actively intense persona. Both were incredibly experienced, as I learned during my stay, and I came to respect both leadership styles. Nobody was shoving an iron bar up anybody's butt, but nobody (at least the Canadians) was running around smoking hash in the rocket bunkers either.

I proceeded to one of the guard towers. Being in a walled camp can be disconcerting if one doesn't know the lay of the land. I called up to the sentries, who told me to go get my body armor and to come on up. Tower 3 was manned by Adam de Bartok from the Queen's Own Rifles, Tim Northcotte from the Grey and Simcoe Forresters, and Ali, who was a PRT paramilitary. Adam and Tim were part of a composite militia platoon that normally protected Camp Mirage; arrangements had been made to rotate sections to the PRT to give them experience and variety. Tim showed me the ground. The PRT was adjacent to the ubiquitous Afghan house compounds and walled crops, with brown mountains all around the horizon. A greasy, brown, smoky band of haze hung over the slumbering city of Kandahar. "Those are the morning wood fires," Tim explained. "It'll disperse later in the day." A CH-47, escorted by an AH-64, passed in the distance.

"Any activity?"

"No." Adam laughed. "We get the usual kids wanting to sell stuff. There's this old guy down in that compound who complains, though. His wife is only allowed into the garden without her burka. He complains that we're looking at her all the time. It's hard *not* to look in that direction because it's a major approach route along the road, but he doesn't get that we're just *not* interested!"

"It's good to see mixed Afghan-Canadian manning at the towers. Does it afford opportunities for cross-cultural contact?" I wondered.

"Well . . . that was done after the Sergeant Major caught two of the Afghan PRT police boning each other one night in one of the towers. Oh, by the way, Ali here wasn't one of them," Adam added hastily.

Ali seemed to understand what we were talking about and laughed in his own way.

When I went for coffee, there was this stocky guy who obviously lifted weights. The hockey game was on the big-screen TV. I said hello as I walked by. He looked at me and muttered, "Roger, confirmed!" and munched on a banana.

the overall threat situation

Before getting into the details of how the PRT is structured and what it does, it is best to explain the level of danger that the men and women from the unit operated under. As I mentioned before, the HTB (Hostile Taliban) of yesteryear had given way to the ACM of 2005. For the most part, the HiG and the Haqqani Tribal Network were limited to operations east of Kabul and were not factors in Kandahar province. Broadly put, the main problem was from the Taliban and its Al Qaeda support network in Pakistan. In 2003 the Taliban forces were small groups of five or ten, remnants of a defeated army bolstered by Al Qaeda individuals who were also remnants of the dispersed terrorist training camps and conventional Al Qaeda units that had been JDAM'd into nonexistence. Back then, they had attempted to conduct pinprick attacks against aid workers to interfere with the initial reconstruction efforts and were moving weapons into Afghanistan from Pakistan in preparation for more extensive operations later. TF DEVIL had, in those days, successfully prevented any form of buildup, and the enemy was reduced to paying the "non-insurgent insurgents" to lay mines almost randomly. The first IED attacks did take place back in 2003, but they were relatively unsophisticated and didn't cause significant damage to coalition forces.

The situation by 2005 was very different, as the members of the Canadian PRT found out after it deployed in July. RC South had essentially five hot areas: northern Helmand in the mountains; the area west and north of Kandahar City; a sideways C-shaped area encompassing the borders of Oruzgan, Zabol, Kandahar, and Helmand provinces; the critical porte d'entrée of Spin Boldak; and the Zabol-Kandahar-Paktika region on the Pakistan border. The enemy had tribal and family support in the C-shaped area, but not to the same extent elsewhere. Intimidation efforts were used to coerce local support in the other areas, particularly around the city of Kandahar. In all cases, the enemy worked in areas where there was weak or no Afghan government control.

The enemy had different types of forces operating throughout the province. The intelligence world broke it down thus. There were rural groups that used standard guerrilla tactics: ambush with RPGs or gunfire, or IED placement or mining, plus the random shooting at coalition aircraft with small arms or MANPADS. Personnel and equipment was infiltrated in along the Kandahar-Zabol border with Pakistan. There was also some form of information operations or propaganda unit operating north of the city, working on the uncommitted population using "night letters" (which I will detail later) and other forms of planned and organized intimidation. A "facilitation network" assisted infiltration on the border.

Then there were "IED cells," which could consist of a single individual or a two-man team, and maybe up to three or five men depending on location and conditions. These IED cells operated from built-up areas: towns and cities. Their sole function was to lay IEDs to target coalition vehicles and convoys. There did not appear to be any coordination with the guerrilla teams, that is, these IEDs were not covered by fire as part of a larger ambush.

Special note should be made about the IED organization operating in Kandahar City: it was probably several cells, or technically a network. Unlike the rural IED cells, the Kandahar network employed suicide IED attacks, or SIEDs. They were also unique in that vehicle-borne IEDs, or VBIEDs, were also being manufactured somewhere in the city for use against coalition targets. Put the two together and you had an SVBIED, or suicide vehicle-borne IED.

There was a distinct pattern of attacks. Like the situation I described in Konduz, coalition movement was predictable between the airfield and the city, which meant that the statistical probability of the enemy finding a coalition combat service support vehicle to attack was high. Between October and December 2005, there were four suicide IED attacks on the KAF-Kandahar road alone, despite a significant police presence. Between July and November, this amounted to 50 percent of the IEDs detonated in the city itself, compared to thirty IED incidents in the rural parts of the CTF BAYONET operating area. So 25 percent of the IEDs were being detonated in the city, and half were suicide attacks. The butcher's bill for all this was twelve killed and twenty-five wounded, civilians and coalition. Notably, the "dog that didn't bark" included thirty IEDs discovered *before* they could be detonated; ten of these were found inside Kandahar City.

To the west of the city, Mullah Baqi led the ACM effort against the coalition forces. Exploiting weaknesses in local governance and security, Baqi's organization regularly attacked Gun Devil vehicle traffic west of the city in the Zharey and Panjwayi districts and intimidated the locals; this included selective assassination, of which seven had taken place in the July–December period. Assassination tended to be directed against election officials. The proximity of the Baqi organization to Kandahar City and the fact that it straddled the main ring route to Helmand and then Herat was not good for the economy.

As CTF BAYONET—the PRT, the ANA, the ANP, and SOF—pushed its presence out farther and farther into the rural areas of the province, the probability of contact increased. Statistically, there were fifty-five incidents from July to December that were categorized as "troops in contact," or TIC. This was a broad term referring to any incident that involved direct fire between coalition forces and the enemy. There were, surprisingly, relatively few indirect-fire attacks: seven during the same period and, I believe, almost all were against KAF.

At this time, enemy forces in the outlying districts varied. In Ghorak, there was a small but active cell. In Khakriz, there was another one, but up in the mountains. It was less active. In Mianishin, in the northernmost part of the province, the Taliban operated openly throughout the district. In Shah Wali Kot, there was a significant Taliban group in the "Belly Button" mountains (known by the locals as Sahemardan Ghar). They patrolled openly there. Down to the south in Arghandab, there was a small cell that made trouble for the Afghan National Police checkpoints. The largest Taliban groups were in Arghistan and Maruf, up near the Pakistan border.

In addition to its varied tasks, the PRT was made responsible by CTF BAYONET for Kandahar City itself, at least from a quick-reaction force perspective. This QRF task meant that the PRT had to have a group ready to roll in minutes to help secure an incident site or otherwise support coalition forces operating or passing through the city. If there was an attack, the PRT's QRF was rolled out.

The first attack against Canadians occurred on 5 October 2005. An enemy VBIED was going to be used against an American Hummer patrol, but at the last minute it veered off and hit a Canadian patrol. The gray and red Mitsubishi Pajero turned into the lead Canadian G-Wagon and detonated ten feet away, producing a fireball. An Afghan family on a tractor was hit; one child was killed and the father was wounded.

Four days later, on 9 October, another VBIED was detonated next to an SUV used by a British Customs House counternarcotics team. These guys were in civilian clothes and wearing beards; it was thought that the enemy took them for British SAS or SBS special operators. A white Toyota Corolla pulled up behind the vehicle, made as if to pass, and detonated two feet away. The men were seriously wounded and the Land Rover completely destroyed.

The situation changed again as the enemy's tempo increased, despite the fact that the "experts" claimed that attacks would drop off in the winter. On 4 December, the day before I arrived, an enemy suicide bomber attacked another Canadian convoy. This time the explosives were in a wheelbarrow. Two civilians were injured and another was killed.

One of the more intriguing aspects of the campaign against us was the debate that was going on inside the enemy's camp on the efficacy of suicide IED attacks. Taliban leaders closely monitored developments in Iraq, whereby the coupling of spectacularly violent bomb attacks with sophisticated, Al Qaeda–supported information operations was having an effect on American public opinion. There was a split between certain Taliban leaders. The generation of civilian casualties by SIED attacks was deemed acceptable by some but was viewed with skepticism by others. More-experienced Taliban commanders knew that the support of the people was critical to success, while the younger Al Qaeda–trained hotheads from the madrassas in Pakistan didn't care. Mullah Omar, for example, did not want civilian casualties (there may have been religious reasons for this as much as military practicalities), but one of his subordinates believed that since SIEDs worked in Iraq, they would work in Afghanistan. Mullah Baqi, the main antagonist west of Kandahar City, did not agree with Mullah Omar.

The usefulness of this split to the coalition would be obvious to Machiavelli and Sun-tzu: the enemy was divided; therefore exploit the division wherever and whenever possible. We will come back to this later on, but this was one area in which the efforts of the PRT could have a significant effect if handled properly.

The threat spectrum, if we can call it that, had essentially three tiers: there was the ACM on the top, followed by the poppy dealers, and at the bottom there were the traditional smugglers and associated Mafia-like organized crime. This last group tended to be along the borders with Pakistan and used family and tribal connections to conduct business. It turned out that there was seamless movement between all three tiers; family and extended family connections made this possible.

the CA PRT: operations and organization

I wandered around Camp Nathan Smith to get my bearings. CNS had been some sort of factory. The large main buildings were internally subdivided by the engineers to provide living quarters. The Afghan liaison and interpreters had their own building. The mechs had a repair bay, where they also taught Afghan police mechanics how to maintain police vehicles. Several Weatherhavens served as offices, but the Tactical Operations Centre was in a more protected area. The mess was a series of several Weatherhavens linked together. A high wall ran around the whole camp, and there were "stalag" guard towers on the corners.

A number of tents were set aside for "welfare." I saw an Afghan kid deke into one of them. Inside was a big-screen TV blaring away to nobody. A number of computers glowed in the dark. Several soldiers, each equipped with a headset, were seated and working the keyboards and mice.

"Sniper on the oil derrick."

"Roger, confirmed," one muttered.

"Little Bird coming in, watch it," said another as a Gatling gun sprayed pixelated death all over the screen.

The machines were linked in a LAN; the game of choice was "Battlefield: Modern Combat," a first-person shooter set in a fictional Middle East country. One group played the Arab terrorists (I could see C4 explode on the screen as a Hummer was taken out) and the other the Americans or NATO forces. It was positively surreal. Here we were in Afghanistan and the troops were playing a fictionalized version of the war for recreation . . . but what a great training aid!

After checking in with Sergeant Sue "Big Mama" Coupal and Corporal Lora-lai Corsiato at the PRT Orderly Room (the anchors of the administrative side of the PRT; all other activity was futile without them), I set out to learn about how this particular PRT was structured and what it did. I attended an O&I (operations and intelligence) briefing to get the basics, followed by a more detailed interview with Colonel Steve Bowes.

The Canadian-led PRT in Kandahar had 235 people working in it and essentially had four components. One consisted of all of the support elements (vehicle techs, cooks, logistics). The second, the "military function enablers," included the explosive ordnance disposal team, the PSYOPS section, the Civil Military Cooperation section, the signals section, and the intelligence det. These two components supported the other pairing: the Other Government Departments (OGDs) and Patrol Company. The OGDs that were assigned included the Canadian International Development Agency (CIDA); its American equivalent, USAID; its British equivalent, DFID; the Royal Canadian Mounted Police (RCMP); and FAC. Each OGD had between one and three people working for it in the PRT; what they did in the field was a "deliverable," which could include aid and reconstruction money, bureaucratic and governance capacity building, police training, and so on. When these people sortied out to do their job either in Kandahar City or the provincial districts, this was referred to as a "nonkinetic attack." ("Kinetic" attacks, on the other hand, meant that shooting was involved.) The "delivery system" for these nonkinetic attacks was Patrol Company. Based on B Company 3 PPCLI, Patrol Company consisted of a mix of infantrymen, combat engineers, signalers, and medics riding in G-Wagon and Nyala armored patrol vehicles.

A "patrol" was not the more familiar "framework" foot patrol that occurred in stabilization operations. It was more like the Long-Range Desert Group in the Western Desert in that a patrol would deploy to a remote district, do its job, and return, as opposed to conducting a presence patrol by remaining in a particular area. It was a noun, as opposed to a verb. PRT patrols went out every day either to conduct a task inside Kandahar City or in the rural districts of the province. They delivered the designated OGD rep to the place he needed to be and protected him en route and on-site.

The PRT also had a number of "pocket" capabilities. It had its own bevy of interpreters in 2005: I dealt with Habib and Niaz Mahommad most often, but there were others too, like Sammi, Aktar, and The Mullah. Having high-quality interpreters is absolutely crucial in this operational environment. There was a Ministry of the Interior liaison officer, Colonel Hussein, who was the epitome of professionalism and one of the most decent men I've ever met in Afghanistan. Then there was the "PRT police," who were really an Afghan paramilitary force inherited from the previous American owners of the Kandahar PRT. Led by the mysterious "Colonel Tor Jan" or just "Colonel TJ" to the troops, the PRT police handled the security "bubble" around the base in conjunction with the tower guards, but they also accompanied patrols in the field. Colonel TJ, it was rumored, had his own intelligence network in the surrounding neighborhoods that acted as an early warning system. He had his own fighters and vehicles, led by his lieutenants Smiley and Wali. Colonel TJ also had a reputation that acted as its own "force multiplier." Where did he come from? What motivated him? These were questions I was to get answers to later on during this trip. I suspected early on—quite correctly it turned out—that Colonel TJ had connections to our old friends, General Gulalai and Rezik Sherzai.[1]

There were a number of "buzzwords" and "mission statements" associated with PRT operations; this reflected the business culture-speak that was permeating military operations in the 1990s and the first decade of this century. The best slogan, which came from CTF BAYONET, was "Put an Afghan face on every solution" and "Put an Afghan between us and every problem." This appears cynical, but the coalition can't do everything for the Afghans, and it is their country, after all.

Like any military operation, the PRT pursued several "lines of operations," all operating concurrently. First, there was provincial election security, followed by Security Sector Reform: police, army, and judicial system development, plus something called DIAG (Disbandment of Illegal Armed Groups, which will require more detailed explanation later). The "reconstruction" line consisted of numerous subthemes: health, education, agriculture, infrastructure, economic development, human capital, cultural, and recreational programs. These all fit into the CFC-A "strategic" lines of operations: governance and justice; security; and economic and strategic reconstruction.

So, the "kinetic" forces like SOF and airmobile infantry carried out their tasks in hunting the enemy while the PRT conducted "nonkinetic attacks" along these lines of operations. The nonkinetic operations were further subdivided into *immediate* nonkinetic and *long-term* nonkinetic operations. Immediate operations tended to be time-sensitive, while long term were not.

What about NGOs, the saviors of the planet? Most NGOs refused to operate in Kandahar for a number of reasons. First, they did not deem the security situation favorable to their operations. Second, they wanted to be "neutral," and working with the PRT, in their eyes, made them a "belligerent." The logic was ridiculous, of course. If you are helping the people, you are supporting the government. If you are helping the insurgents, you are the enemy. There is no neutral ground here.

The PRT staff used the term "relevant" NGOs: there were numerous small groups claiming NGO status but had no oomph to their activities. Indeed, some were tax shelters or nonprofit groups pretending to be involved in reconstruction. Then there were NGOs that were suspected (quite correctly) of being infiltrated by Al Qaeda and affiliates. The only large nongovernmental aid groups that would work in Kandahar with the PRT were the aid organs of the UNAMA in Afghanistan, and a group called Chemonics. Chemonics was an agribusiness NGO that worked closely with USAID; it had been in Afghanistan since before the Soviet invasion in 1979. There was no inclination to attract NGOs to Kandahar by the PRT; the organization was quite comfortable dealing with the national aid organizations, such as USAID, CIDA, and DFID.

I had the misfortune to attend the O&I briefing with a representative of the U.S. State Department. During the course of the briefing, this individual adamantly stated that Afghanistan needed more "helpers," like NGOs, more aid, and more trainers, and that they needed to seed the countryside with these people. I objected, noting that it was a large foreign "footprint" and attempts at radical societal change that got the Soviets into trouble here. He took extreme offense, believing that I was comparing the "American effort," as he put it (neglecting the coalition members, like us), to the Soviet occupation. I merely reiterated that the Afghans didn't need or desire a large footprint, that it was their country, not ours, and that we needed to take that into consideration. He attacked me rather stridently.

In keeping with a Vietnam-era Ugly American stereotype, he actually said, and I still can't believe it when I write this, that Afghans were "like the American Indians of the nineteenth century," that they "had no work ethic," "couldn't organize anything," and "preferred to drink tea and talk." It was disgusting. He was behaving so arrogantly that I almost brought up Iraq, but I backed off. I later found out he had served time in Al Kut, which just reinforced my view that he should have known better! I wondered aloud if we were *giving* a man a fish to the detriment to *teaching* a man to fish. He discounted my argument in the most aggressive terms, asserting that "the fish was rotting." Attempts to ascertain where he was coming from and what information he was relying on came to naught. When I recounted this to the USAID rep, Phoenix, she went absolutely ballistic and ranted about State in the same way I rant about FAC. I think she used the phrase "that fucking asshole" a few times. Phoenix, who spent a *lot* of time in the hills, had a better appreciation of things than Mr. State-from-Iraq. Afghanistan, I hasten to add, is not and will never be "Iraq." Nor will it be "Vietnam," for that matter. Afghanistan has to be understood on its own terms.

The U.S. Navy's VXS-1 squadron sent an NP-3D to work with the U.S. Geological Survey and the Afghan government in their quest for mineral resources. *Courtesy of the U.S. Navy*

Colonel Mike Capstick, commander of the Strategic Advisory Team–Afghanistan, and Ahmad, the unit's chief interpreter, ready an SUV for a sortie to Blue.

SAT-A's two secret weapons: Wu-Tan and the fire pit, host of many fireside chats between government and international power brokers.

The main Canadian base in Kabul was Camp Julien, adjacent to the Daraluman Palace in the western part of the city.

Detachments from several NATO nations used Camp Julien as a base of operations, including the Belgian special operations forces, mounted here in Pandur APCs while patrolling the police districts north of the camp.

The broken and stripped Mi-24 Hind monument at the Konduz airport. It's haunted, I swear.

This BMP, modified to carry a World War II–era 76-mm gun portee fashion, was part of the Northern Alliance DDR site stash at Konduz.

The war between the Northern Alliance and the Taliban wasn't a guerrilla war. Here is the MRL [multiple rocket launcher] park at the Konduz DDR site.

The DDR program still had to reach parts of Konduz province. Here unassimilated Afghan Militia Forces use a D-30 artillery piece at a checkpoint.

Two of Major Brian Hynes' Embedded Training Team NCOs, Master Warrant Officer Payette and Sergeant Power, show me the sights, including the destroyed former Soviet officers mess up in the hills.

The Canadian ETTs, working with Task Force PHOENIX, were responsible for molding recruits into the multiethnic Afghan National Army. Here part of a new kandak drills at the Kabul Military Training Centre.

Kandahar PRT patrols were subjected to suicide IED attacks starting in October 2005. The frequency of these attacks increased dramatically into the winter. *Courtesy of the Canadian Department of National Defence*

The long-range patrol to the Maruf district mounting up at the PRT. Private Sarah Keller, a medic and the driver of call sign 21A2, does a walk-around of the G-Wagon.

Le *tricolore* flies over the Maruf district at the French special operations forces own Fort Beau Geste.

A collection of .50-cal-armed jeeps belonging to the French SOF working in the Maruf and Arghistan districts.

The success of PRT operations was dependent on competent interpreters. This is Niaz Mohammad, working closely with the police training team.

Corporal Joe Dupuy explains to me why his weapon has been heavily modified. Roger, confirmed.

The PRT had at this time two RCMP officers who worked with the Afghan National Police in the province. Corporal Bob Hart is about to mentor the Khakriz chief of police.

Major Sanchez King from CIMIC, Matthijs Toot from DFID, and Lieutenant Andy Bone from patrol company survey a village in the Maruf district. The force patrol company acted as a "delivery system" for personnel involved in district assessments.

"This is not a good place, Dr. Sean. I feel like I am being watched all the time." Sergeant Wali from the PRT Police on guard against the Taliban (or others . . .) in the Kakriz district center.

Sergeant Smiley of the PRT Police and Corporal Wadleigh during a short halt coming back from Maruf. Wadleigh, an avid motorcyclist, was nearly asked to ride a captured motorcycle back to Kandahar from the Ghorak district.

The Panjwayi *shura*. I'm sitting next to Hajji Agha Lalai, who remains a major power broker in the province. He later became the Peace Through Strength amnesty program coordinator.

The Panjwayi *shura*. From left to right: Leo McKern, Christopher Lee, Anthony Quinn, and Peter Ustinov.

PRT patrols went into Kandahar City daily despite the risk of suicide IED attacks. This was a police substation assessment task.

The reputationally fearsome Colonel Tor Jan, the commander of the PRT Police, and I meet during a weapons seizure operation. But whose weapons were they, exactly?

Ambassador Glyn Berry, the PRT representative from FAC was assassinated by a suicide IED attack in January 2006. *Courtesy of the Canadian Department of National Defence*

The crew was lucky to survive an IED attack on its G-Wagon in the Ghorak district. The vehicle was recovered by a CH-47 to prevent its exploitation by the enemy. *Courtesy of the Canadian Department of National Defence*

After a cooling-off period, I had a meeting with the PRT commander, Colonel Steve Bowes, who was now back from leave. Steve Bowes is an extremely fit, balding armored officer from the 12 RBC (Régiment blindé du Canada). He is Steve Borland's alter ego in that Borland is quiet, commanding and calculating, while Bowes is deep-voiced, commanding, and calculating. The two were a team, and it was obvious their strengths and skills complemented each other's. Again, competence and confidence permeated any briefing I attended. Neither suffered fools gladly. They knew what the challenges were in this environment and were prepared to meet them all.

I asked Steve how he conceptualized the PRT. I knew from visiting other PRTs that there had been attempts to standardize them across the country. The planning staffs in Kingston and Ottawa came up with a concept, but when Steve looked at it and spent some time on the ground, he couldn't apply it fully.

"We didn't want to follow the American model slavishly, but what we wanted to do was focus more on security sector reform and developing the capacity of the local government, so earlier planners had looked at Mazar-e Sharif, but I made a lot of changes to that template. Those who try to standardize PRTs are barking up the wrong tree: We even had people that were trying to template Bosnia onto Kandahar!"

"Why is that?"

"Regions in this country are distinct and challenges to capacity development are really distinct, as are the security challenges. Mazar-e Sharif was a benign security environment compared to Kandahar, so we had to change the structure to accommodate that. At the same time we couldn't, or didn't, want a huge Camp Julien–like logistics tail, so everyone here, techs, mechs, and so on, are soldiers first, and I wanted a full infantry company, not just a security platoon, plus PSYOPS, and more combat engineers. I knew there was a higher preponderance of IEDs, so I wanted a robust EOD capability."

Steve and I discussed the nature of historical counterinsurgency and the role of development. He had studied the British experience in Malaya. One of the things that struck him on his recce here was the need, as he put it, was to "establish relationships between the local elders and between the locals elders and the provincial government to facilitate our ability to work on other issues, exchange information, and develop confidence. It's not about 'development' per se, it's about relationships." And to make those relationships, one had to go out to meet the people—all over the province, if necessary, not just in Kandahar City.

"So this facilitates the 'kinetic' attacks conducted by SOF and the conventional forces?"

"This is counterinsurgency; the nonkinetic ops are the dominant line of operation. CFC-A has forces aggressively hunting the Taliban in the mountains, but they are a supporting effort. The main line is [with the PRT] building Afghan National Army and Police capacity, and that in turn requires good governance."

This was the only way to win: the enemy, Steve asserted and I agreed, was "using tactics that would make Pol Pot and the Khmer Rouge proud. But the population isn't buying into it. We've got the moral high ground."

"But the problem is explaining to people back home," I said.

"Sure, there's some frustration in that this is Roto 0,[2] so everybody would like it to move faster and see results quicker. A journalist asked me in August what changes I'd like to see in three months. Three months! It's very difficult when you're capacity building to say in three months, 'This is what we have accomplished.' We have to build relationships with the people, and that takes time. We have to be in this for the long haul."

Now, there had been a PRT here before this one: was the current staff able to build on existing, established relationships? What had the previous American PRT done? I was always concerned about continuity with the six-month tours. One could lose this easily, especially with a culture that didn't hold to the same timelines as North Americans and their frenetic consumer culture.

The key American PRT staff had pulled out before Steve and his staff could get on the ground. The CTF BAYONET commander wanted them kept in place to effect a proper handover, but someone higher in the food chain withdrew the PRT leadership in June: Steve and his people arrived in July. There were some people "who were keeping the lights on," according to Steve. There was, in his words, a "loss of momentum." The looming fall provincial elections and potential for violence scared a lot of the NGOs, who decamped, and everything started to go into suspended animation. It was almost as if the Canadian PRT had to start from scratch.

On investigation, the PRT strategic recce discovered that TF BRONCO's leadership really didn't seem to understand how to use it or how to exploit the PRT's capabilities effectively. It did some civil affairs work in support of the brigade and some limited force protection patrolling around the PRT base itself, but the organization was much smaller and less capable than the Canadian PRT. They did not have a police mentorship role, but TF BRONCO's PRT didn't have the same level of protection for their OGDs, so the American-led PRT operated with a much-reduced capacity to get out and about in the rural areas. Steve pointed out that not all PRTs "leveraged" their capacities, but some did: the American PRT in Qalat consisted of reservists who made local connections based on their civilian jobs back home. Cops talked to cops, civil engineers with civil engineers, and so on. It was ad hoc, but it worked.

"Isn't the term 'Provincial Reconstruction Team' confusing? You're not 'doing' reconstruction as a primary task."

"Yeah, I'd call it a Provincial Development Team if I had my way, but PRT has become a brand name. People who can't speak a word of English know what 'PRT' means, and they can say those three letters. So let's be cautions and not tamper with success."

Steve Bowes, Steve Borland, and Regimental Sergeant Major Ward Brown were not compound-bound bureaucrats. The PRT commander had other duties, one of which included being the senior coalition liaison to the provincial government. The PRT was also responsible for quick-reaction-force tasks in the city itself. Steve and the PRT RSM sortied out regularly using the element called "Niner Tac," which consisted of three G-Wagons and crews. They traveled all over the place for meetings: the Governor's Palace, the legislature building, the Guest House, and so on. Steve firmly believed that a critical part of the job was operating on the Afghans' turf, since it was their country, after all, and it would look bad having Afghan leaders show up at the PRT all the time and appear subservient. Steve went to them.

On one occasion, Niner Tac was involved in an incident in the city.

"I was meeting with a tribal leader and returning to the PRT when we saw black smoke billowing on the road ahead. We came across an American convoy that had just been hit two or three minutes before by a motorcyclist who threw grenades at the vehicles. They had detonated the fuel-storage bins and the vehicle exploded and caught fire. The crew managed to drive out of the kill zone and then came under secondary attack a few minutes later. It could easily have been us. There was a large crowd, and they were surrounding the three American vehicles and their nine crew members, so we stopped. CTF BAYONET made me on-scene incident commander and requested reinforcements; we were in the middle of a market, and the crowd made it easier for the enemy to conduct further attacks. I turned to the RSM and I wondered aloud how often the Russians had been attacked in the same spot because of the canalizing ground. Once we got the Afghan police organized, we put some of our guys up on the walls and got the sensitive equipment out of the American vehicle. We had to wait for a satchel of grenades to cook off in the burning vehicle, so we had to get the people away from it. Because this was a main service route for the coalition forces, we also had to divert incoming convoys away so they wouldn't pile up and create a larger target. Then the QRF arrived, followed by some Special Ops people that just happened to be moving through. Lesson:

everybody who goes outside the walls needs to protect themselves and needs to be able to assist others as a first responder. Everybody that goes in a vehicle needs to be a shooter. I'm an armored officer: I'd like to think that with my training I can put a tank round through a window at two kilometers, but I couldn't hit the broad side of a barn with a rifle. At the end of the day I carry a rifle because I'm supporting the other guys in the vehicle—the RSM and the driver. I'm covering my arc, and I'm prepared to execute my responsibilities."

It wasn't just a platoon leader's war.

colonel TJ

The PRT had its own Afghan security force, generically called the "PRT Police." The reality was that the PRT maintained its own paramilitary group and were invaluable facilitators. They had translators, static guards, a mobile force, and even their own intelligence system. These men and their leaders had been inherited from the American PRT. The DIAG process, ironically, was a problem for the PRT in that this force was not registered with the program yet. The coalition was demanding DIAG . . . as long as the right people were DIAG'd. The PRT were, fortunately, not the right people.

The troops referred to them as "Colonel TJ's boys." Colonel TJ, whose full nom de guerre was Colonel Tor Jan, had a fearsome reputation. Indeed, his reputation in the neighborhood surrounding the PRT was such that there was a ready-built early warning network among these people, who would warn Colonel TJ if an attack was imminent. He was a diminutive man with a gray turban and a black beard, and it was easy to see how he could pass for a Taliban or even an Al Qaeda operative. He had been a subordinate of either the Sherzai brothers, Gullali, or both during the anti-Taliban operations in 2001–2.[3] His principal lieutenants who went "outside the wire" were Smiley and Wali and their pickup-mounted troops, while "Sergeant Carter" (Qadr) handled the static guards at Camp Nathan Smith.

I had arranged through Wali to visit Colonel TJ and talk about the past and its relationship to the present campaign. Company Sergeant Major Billy Bolen, Sue Coupal, and small group of Canadians escorted me the short distance from the PRT to TJ's compound. After the requisite greetings and deployment of tea, we got down to business. Niaz Mohammed interpreted for me.

"Welcome to my compound. Before we deal with the past, is there any possibility that Colonel Bowes could give us some of the blankets that he is distributing at the shuras? My men could use them. It is cold."

"I'll pass the message on. I am just visiting, so I have no influence with the PRT." This was part of the game. Colonel TJ was also a shrewd businessman, always looking for an angle. Those blankets would not be for his men; they would have some other purpose, like trade for information or influence in a rural area. Or for resale in some market. The room was covered, like Rezik Sherzai's was, with group photos of Colonel TJ with senior American commanders and even Donald Rumsfeld.

"I need to understand your part in operations here against the Taliban. Do you feel comfortable talking to me about this? Rezik Sherzai talked to me when I first came to Kandahar in 2003."

"You know Rezik?"

"Yes."

"What did he tell you?"

I explained the outlines of the U.S.-supported campaign in the south in 2001.

"I was managing a hotel in Spin Boldak then. It was a front for various activities. I had problems with the Taliban when they took over," he said as he drew back a sleeve to show substantial scar tissue. "I wanted to be near the border so I could get away if I had to. Karzai sent a representative to me and asked me if I could provide bomb-damage assessment for the Americans. Anything that was against the Taliban was OK by me, so I said yes. I had some men, and we also protected some journalists who wanted to get into Afghanistan. Later on, the Americans provided us with weapons and encouraged us to organize and fight. Sherzai and Karzai were part of this effort. Then American Special Forces arrived. My group assisted them in getting them into Maruf district, and then we helped get them into Kandahar City. They came in two helicopters, about sixty-five of them. We already had a team of twelve Americans with us at this time. They were interested in several objectives in the city itself. Other American planes dropped food, ammo, and weapons. That was the first time I had seen a chemlite!"

"What was the enemy doing?"

"There were many enemy forces in the south. First, there was the Taliban, but then there were people from Al Qaeda's Brigade 055. There were Pakistani special forces. We even saw Iranian special forces. Then there were the Chechens. Most of these people were in small groups, retreating, but could not get home. They came here to try to get into Pakistan. Over in Herat, Iran sent in special forces to support Ismael Khan. The Americans were very concerned about that. It looked like there would be a fight between Pakistani forces and Iranian forces, with both countries using Afghanistan as a battleground."

"So there were Pakistani troops supporting the Taliban?"

"Of course! But the Americans were more concerned about Al Qaeda and what they were doing in Kandahar. There was a chemical or biological facility at Tarnak Farms. There was another one in a mosque here in the city. My men helped surround the mosque while American Special Forces went in. We were there for several days but did not see what they were doing inside. We did raids with the Americans. We captured about forty Al Qaeda. On one raid we found a Stinger. We captured many Arabs on the Kandahar–Spin Boldak road."

The chemical weapons angle was interesting. "Were chemical weapons ever used here?" I asked.

"I heard that the Taliban used 'stinky gas' on one occasion somewhere on the road to Herat. Many, many people were killed, and they had blood coming from their noses and openings. The Soviets took all their chemical weapons with them, so it had to be Pakistan or Al Qaeda that supplied them to the Taliban. It wasn't used that often, just a couple of times at the beginning when the Taliban took over."

Colonel TJ had no love for the Pakistanis. During our conversation he explained how he got some of his sixteen scars. He described to me how he and some of his men were recruited by the OGA (Other Government Agencies) to conduct operations inside Pakistan. These operations were designed to track Osama bin Laden. He was severely wounded when his team was intercepted and attacked. He wouldn't say who attacked him, but I got the impression it was Pakistani military forces, not Taliban or Al Qaeda remnants. He implied that Pakistan was compromising American operations to get the Al Qaeda leadership.

"But the war is changing. These suicide bombers . . . this is new. The Afghan method is to kill and run, not die. My intelligence network tells me that these suicide bombers are not truly Afghan. They call them 'bastards,' but they appear to be uneducated Afghan orphans from the wars who have been indoctrinated specially inside Pakistan to carry out these attacks. We must do everything we can to counter this."

But Colonel TJ had to ensure that the PRT Police conformed to the new DIAG requirements. That was taking a lot of his time. They police needed to have certain training courses before they could be certified, and the deadline was looming. Contracts had to be signed with the PRT. His vast informant network had to be paid. He was a busy man, on many fronts.

politics and ethnicity in kandahar province

Understanding the political and ethnic environment in Kandahar Province is a sine qua non for understanding the PRT's operational environment, especially when it comes to nonkinetic operations. When I visited Kandahar in 2003, the Civil Affairs personnel had identified three Pashtun tribal groupings in the KAF area. I was astonished to learn in 2005 that there were, in fact, between seventeen and twenty-six. The implications are profound, in that some tribes straddle the so-called border with Pakistan, some support the Taliban, and many do not. Entire dissertations could be written about this, but I don't have the space, so I'll give you the highlights. The PRT interpreters—Niaz Mohammad, Aktar, Habib, and Sammi, among others—assisted in my understanding of how this all worked.

In general, Pashtuns make up 35 to 40 percent of the Afghan population. There are two tribal confederations of Pashtuns in Kandahar province: the Durrani and the Ghilzai. Each has about six tribal groups, but one Ghilzai tribe has some six or seven subtribes. For the most part, they are Sunni Muslims and all claim descendance from a single ancestor, one Qais Abdur Rashid. The Durranis tend to dominate in Kandahar City, but the Ghilzais tend to dominate in the province. The tribes below the conferederacy level also have a myriad of associations, conflicts, and loyalties between each other and their counterparts in the other confederation.

What holds these tribes together? Essentially, a tribal code called Pashtunwali is the basis for interaction between the Pashtun tribes and subtribes. This is a legal and ethical framework for behavior between tribes; an honor system called *rang* is the basis for this. Meetings, called *shura* and *jirga*, are used to regulate disputes, at least in an ideal sense. Under Pashtunwali, all Pashtuns are equal. Part of the honor component relates to land ownership, which in turn relates to social status as much as meeting physical needs like food. Without land, a Pashtun is nothing. If the land is barren, it is worthless. And, importantly, without water there is no cultivation. Hold onto that thought for the rest of the book.

When there is weak government control, the Pashtun tribal system will take up the slack. When institutions are incapable of providing for the needs of the people, the people will fall back on long-established conflict resolution mechanisms and governance at the village, district, and even the provincial level. Indeed, in traditional times, the Pashtuns had their own tribal police, the Arbaki, to handle things, but this system was eroded in Kandahar after decades of war. Tribes had their own *shura*s to resolve intratribal disputes, but more recently any meeting to resolve problems at the village and local level tends to be called a *shura*. Thus, a PRT member might believe that the team is solving intratribal problems, when in fact a *shura* has been convened of only intertribal representatives. A *jirga* may be called at the provincial level to resolve larger issues. A *marakha* is a religious *jirga* and may even act as a parallel legal system since, technically, there is no separation of church and state in Islam.

Instead of looking at the problems in Kandahar province as purely Taliban or ACM versus the government, the PRT members learned that this conflict was superimposed on another one: the Durrani and Ghilzai confederations were locked in a competition for power in the province, and the tribes were competing with each other in various districts as well as at the provincial level. Indeed, it was informally understood that there were two de facto governments in Kandahar, one Durrani and the other Ghilzai, but that this played itself out in jockeying for influence within the various government and economic institutions that were being created after the fall of the Taliban. This included the drug trade, contracts with coalition forces, and so on. Many antagonists in this struggle viewed the coalition forces and even the Taliban merely as resources to be used to enhance their relative power versus the other tribes or the other confederation. Ambitious individuals, like politicians in the United States and in Canada, competed to be the heads of their tribes by all means foul and fair.

An example: the incident that occurred before I arrived that resulted in the destruction of the seven fuel trucks outside of KAF at first glance could be attributed to the Taliban. But on closer examination, nobody was killed and, aside from the trucks, nothing else was damaged. Strange. Was KAF's fuel capacity affected dramatically? Apparently not. The working hypothesis was that the contracted fuel trucking company was owned by a guy who hailed from one tribe. Another tribe, who also possessed a fuel truck delivery company, wanted to reduce their rival's capacity to profit from the coalition forces. Consequently, an IED was placed in the fuel tanks of some of these vehicles. Somehow the drivers knew what was going on and none were even singed. Then somebody started a rumor to blame Kellogg, Brown and Root corruption to deflect investigative attention. How much violence in Kandahar is related to tribal rivalries and how much of it is "political"—that is, Taliban—insurgency? This is a critical question. The media, for example, never ask this question. It amounts to "commercial violence."

The Durrani-Ghilzai Pashtun rivalry dates back to the sixteenth century. The Durranis, known as the Abdalis at the time, and the Ghilzais had moved west from what we know as Pakistan, all the way to Kandahar and Herat. The area of Afghanistan south of the mountains was and remains a crossroads of empires, and at the time the Safawids (Muslims from what we know as Iran) and the Moguls (a Muslim dynasty in control of the bulk of what we know as Pakistan and India) were competing back and forth for control over an area that had been controlled by Alexander the Great's Macedonians centuries before. The Abdali's Pashtun confederation, which had pushed all the way up to Farah and Herat, sided with the Safawids, while the Ghilzai Pashtun confederation sided with the Moguls. Then the two confederations allied to fight off everybody, but the Abdalis were pushed out of Herat by the Safawids into Ghilzai territory. Then the Abdalis were co-opted by a Safawid king and took over Ghilzai-controlled Kandahar in the 1700s. Fractures within the Abdalis (specifically between the Popalzay and Barakzay tribes) existed, but a member of the Muhammadzay clan rose to lead and the Abdalis were renamed after him, becoming the Durranis. Ahmad Shah Durrani led his Pashtun forces (Durrani *and* Ghilzai) to conquor Ghazni and Kabul, and went all the way to the Punjab. Eventually a Mogul army defeated Durrani, but there were several border-defining campaigns to delineate Mogul India and the new Pashtun-controlled territory. In time Durrani took control of most of what we call Afghanistan and Pakistan.

How Ahmad Shah Durrani ran the show is instructive. Historian Willem Vogelsang explained that he "was first of all the leader of his own tribal confederacy. . . . He gave most of the important offices to his own tribesman. To further win their support he granted them special favours. He provided his kinsmen with land in the [Ghilzai-dominated] Qandahar region in return for the provision of armed horsemen for his army. The Qandahar area thus became thoroughly 'Durranized', the native people of other ethnic groups being forced to move." Durrani then established a council that had both Durrani and Ghilzai representatives on it. He bought off the various Pashtun tribes with monies acquired in the military campaigns against Mogul India rather than from directly taxing them, and let the tribes control seized regions of Afghanistan. In other words, Ahmad Shah Durrani exhibited only a loose control over several independent Pashtun tribes, and then only in the military sphere. Afghanistan was, as Vogelsang explained, "an amalgamation of tribes and tribal states headed by the Durranis" well into the nineteenth century. There was no strong central government per se except when military forces were needed to fight the Moguls. By the 1800s Durrani tribes tended to dominate Kabul-centered politics, often in alliance with Tajiks and Hazaras. The Ghilzai slowly moved into control over the trade route provinces between Kandahar, Ghazni, Kabul, Jalalabad, Quetta, and Peshawar.

Pashtun tribal rivalries continued to play a role in whatever system of government existed in Afghanistan in the 1900s. More recently, the Afghan Communist leaders in the 1970s included Noor Mohammad Taraki (a Ghilzai) and his successor Hafizullah Amin (a Ghilzai). But Pakistan supported Ghilzai mujahideen and virtually ignored the Durrani mujahideen. The American special forces in 2001 then supported the Sherzai brothers (who are Durrani) in and around Kandahar. Mullah Omar, the spiritual leader of the Taliban, is a Ghilzai—and he invited both Durrani and Ghilzai to join the upper echelons of the Taliban movement. President Hamid Karzai is Durrani. As Sean Connery put it to Wesley Snipes in the movie *Rising Sun*, "Deep, isn't it?"

This tribal complexity doesn't appear to be replicated in quite the same scale or scope throughout the rest of Afghanistan, which is not dominated by Pashtuns.

I kept hearing the mantra that Kandahar is as different from Kabul as Kabul is from Ottawa. Say it often enough and it becomes true.

For the coalition forces, it became increasingly clear by 2005 that Durranis had taken over from Ghilzais in the governance, security sector, and economic life of Kandahar. How were the coalition forces to determine whether someone a Durrani designated as "Taliban" was, in fact, Taliban? Indeed, Ghilzais rivaled Durranis when it came to poppy cultivation. What were the implications of Durrani-dominated police raiding only Ghilzai-controlled fields? More important, what were the implications of a military commander from one confederation or tribe authorizing air strikes against a "Taliban" village from a different confederation or tribe?

the other government departments

Hatred is gained as much by good works as by evil.
—Niccolò Machiavelli

Disclaimer: OGDs are *not* OGA. In *Enduring the Freedom,* I explained how "OGA" was a euphemism for the intelligence community.

Second disclaimer: "OGD" is not a learning-disabled mix-up of "GOD."

The PRT's OGD community consisted of one British, one American, and three Canadian organizations. The total number of OGD personnel was 7 out of 235 on the full PRT establishment. These people wielded the "nonkinetic" weapons and were as varied in their personalities and approaches to the problems in Kandahar province as a scalpel differs from a hydrogen bomb. During the course of my time at the PRT, I accompanied all of the OGD personnel on one patrol or another and watched them at work. In all cases, and in a small organization like the PRT, strong opinions develop: military opinions on the OGDs, and OGD opinions on the military, each OGD versus other OGDs, and so on. When people are under stress, shit happens and not everybody gets along all the time. My objective is not to recapture all of the *Peyton Place* stuff that develops under such conditions. I believe that all of the people I dealt with had strengths and weaknesses; not all people see the hidden strengths that some have, and many people tend to be dismissive for a variety of superficial reasons. What I want to get across to you is the uniqueness of the people and how they handled the situation they were in, not their foibles. In one of these cases, it would be inappropriate of me to speak ill of the dead.

From the PRT leadership, Steve Bowes and Steve Borland had the challenge of directing, and mediating between, the OGDs when necessary. This was not easy;

there is the Canadian Forces military culture, and then the cultures of the RCMP, CIDA, Foreign Affairs Canada, DFID, and USAID. The RCMP, USAID, and DFID are used to, in varying degrees at least, working in conflict zones, where FAC and CIDA are not. There was a lot of adaptation necessary, and the fact that it was achieved was a tribute to good leadership.

Personally, I have had poor relationships with diplomatic personnel, no matter what the country. The glib arrogance, condescension, sneakiness, and elite mentality gets under my skin as if I were injecting barbed wire. For example, I was sitting in the PRT mess one day writing when this short, balding guy storms into the room. He walked over to me and said, in an unpleasant, interrogative tone of voice, "Who are *you?*" implying that I shouldn't be on that chair/in that tent/at the PRT/in Afghanistan/or on the planet.

"I'm Dr. Sean Maloney. Who are *you?*"

"I'm *the Ambassador!*"

David Sproule, Canada's new Ambassador to Afghanistan, stormed out of the room, and he hasn't spoken to me since. He does, however, glower across rooms at me.

However, when I encounter somebody like Chris Alexander, Canada's former Ambassador to Afghanistan, I see that there can be rough in the diamonds.

glyn berry from DFAIT

I think Glyn Berry from FAC was one of those rough in the diamonds too. Glyn had been our ambassador in Pakistan. One of the Patrol Company guys told me that they had a hell of a time getting Glyn to wear body armor. He wanted to wear a suit to his meetings with the provincial leadership, but after an IED attack that narrowly missed his assistant, Erin Doregan, he acquiesced. CADPAT body armor over a three-piece must have been an interesting sight. I always saw Glyn dressed like the rest of us: open-necked short-sleeved shirt, Mountain Equipment Co-op pants.

Next to my brief initial meeting with Niki from DFID, Glyn was the first OGD rep I had a detailed conversation with. I was lucky I caught him; he was going on leave soon. The best word I could use to describe Glyn's demeanor that day was "exasperated." I walked into the FAC Weatherhaven tent to see this short guy with a beard pacing back and forth, speaking adamantly into a cell phone. Glyn saw me, made his good-byes, and snapped the phone shut. He wanted to vent.

"Those people in Ottawa! They just don't get what is going on here!" he said in his fading Irish accent.

"How so?" I inquired.

"We keep trying to explain that Kandahar is as different from Kabul as Kabul is from Ottawa! You're a military historian; you know all about fighting the last war! It's different here! What we did in Kabul has little or no bearing here!"

"Ottawa" in this case meant "Fort Pearson," or the headquarters of Foreign Affairs Canada. Glyn had some choice words about certain overly ambitious people working the Afghan and regional desks. I knew of or had met some of these people and instantly understood the problem.

"Kabul-centric perceptions are not useful in explaining Kandahar. And I can't get them to understand that. In some cases, even the Karzai government doesn't know what's going on here. Only people with intimate contact with all levels of Kandahari society have *any* inclination . . . and that is why the PRT is so important." Glyn was on a roll.

And then there was the meddling. Glyn explained to me that high-level political interference reached bizarre proportions. When the Kabul-based contingent did its road move, a Cabinet minister in Ottawa wanted to divert the convoy through some small town so that he could assuage some constituent's micro-interests or concerns. This pressure had to be staved off in the strongest terms: putting a whole convoy at risk because of the selfish behavior of a cabinet minister? Glyn and Erin had to resist all sorts of missives and interference.

"A person who shall remain unnamed at FAC has asked us to look at a program list formulated by people in Ottawa, people who have never been here or if they have it was in Kabul for a couple of days. Half of the list, *half*, are bullshit projects that could never be implemented down here, like 'enhancing women networking' schemes. They are forcing us to spend a significant portion of our scarce money on this sort of thing when we have far more critical problems here, like basic governance, policing, and infrastructure. Michael and I are tearing our hair out." (Michael was the CIDA representative; we'll meet him later.)

Talking with Glyn was like talking to a convert. He admitted to me that he had been one of those ambitious guys on the cocktail circuit. He knew the Ottawa mentality. And now he saw that it was all bullshit, that this was where the rubber hit the road. He was starting to "go native" in that he recognized that there were two realities and that the people who understood the Kandahar reality were the military personnel, and the other OGD reps at the PRT, not distant people thousands of miles away. Indeed, each of the OGD reps on one level or another expressed this to me when I was there. Although some would be loath to admit it publicly, the personnel at the PRT had more in common with each other than with their parent organizations.

We discussed history. Glyn told me that he was increasingly drawn to history as a guide here, as opposed to the "analytical crap," as he called it, coming out of

Ottawa or academia. "Here, have you read *A Political Officer in Afghanistan*? It was written in the 1800s by a Brit. Once you strip away the colonial condescension, you can see he really had great insight into what goes on here. Kandahar is almost a separate country, and we need to recognize that and deal with it. There has never been strong central government in this country, and we need to understand that too. History is the way to go." That was the second time this trip that the usefulness of history had been brought up to me by personnel in the field: the planners of the road move used Les Grau's work on the Soviet period, and now the Canadian political officer of Irish descent was taking lessons from a long-dead British political officer.

"What, exactly, is Foreign Affairs doing here anyway?" I politely inquired. "Aren't diplomats really engaged in national government to national government interaction?"

"Well, Erin and I are essentially a recce and are establishing contacts within the provincial government. The idea is to build on those contacts in the future in order to mentor the provincial government, and overseeing the Confidence in Government program. The reality is, we see this as a means to an end: we want to encourage the return of NGO and IO aid support to the province, and we need a certain level of stability within the government to be able to do that. I have been working on establishing contacts in the security area, but more importantly the judicial reform area. I see my role as facilitating: I make contacts, develop the relationship, and bring in the specialists for those tasks." Glyn implied that projects like the Women's Legal Education Group and the Women's Shura were unwelcome distractions imposed by feminists in Ottawa. FAC had some funding (around $200,000 and up to $2 million the next year) and acted as a conduit for those funds, in consultation if not coordination with the PRT and with Michael, the CIDA rep, who in turn had his own projects and money streams.

"What is the current security situation from your perspective?"

"Let me give you some numbers. They don't tell the whole story, and we disagree with one particular one, but here it goes. Fifty-four percent of the population view Pakistan as the main security problem for Afghanistan, with only 2 percent viewing the United States as the problem. Sixty-four percent of Afghans see Afghanistan as able to protect itself from internal terrorism. We were surprised with this figure. Even more surprising, we saw that 24 percent trusted the Afghan National Police as an instrument of security, followed by local shuras and elders who were normally tasked by their communities with handling local security. The people also indicated that they *wanted* the ANP professionalized and put in charge of local security. The ANP was not viewed as corrupt, but I told my superiors that this was counterintuitive for us here at the PRT, given what we've seen. Now this is interesting: 26 percent believed that the main threat to local security came from local 'commanders,' but that the Disbandment of Illegal Armed Groups program, or 'DIAG,' was a key element in reducing this by the people. Thirty-six percent called for expanded security forces, including deployment of the Afghan National Army. We thought there would be more support for the ANA, but the people want police, and they want police that are not corrupt.

"Dispute resolution: what do the people want? They want local dispute resolution in the shuras, but 31 percent wanted the local government involved and only 13 percent wanted the central government involved. Seventy-two percent want the shura system to be the focal point for this role. Note that the current development programs coming out of Kabul and elsewhere practically ignore this in favor of a centralized judiciary and all the apparatus that goes along with it. There has to be a way of acknowledging local mechanisms and making it compatible with good governance. If we insist on one, we will not get the other. It may take decades, particularly in the remote districts. Let me quote for you what I told Ottawa: 'It is perhaps time to reevaluate policies largely formulated outside Afghanistan and that to some degree, in some areas of this country, focus on a goal-central government authority extension whose time frame for "success" is well beyond that of the window for stabilization.'

"In other words, we must stabilize first, then extend government authority, in my view. We should enhance local government first, then bring in central government later. There has to be a feeling of local empowerment, or 'buy-in,' or this isn't going to work. Some people in Ottawa aren't interested in hearing that," he added. "It's too 'micro' for them, they can't measure it. I always spice up my message traffic with quotes from history. We ignore it here at our peril."

Music to a historian's ears.

phoenix from USAID

Phoenix was the PRT's USAID representative and as such carried a large checkbook. "My mom worked for USAID in Laos during the 1960s," she told me. "I guess I come by this honestly, but I worked the Beltway in Washington for a few years too." A fiery, passionate, determined, and intelligent woman, Phoenix and I hit it off right away. I loved her bluntness, which I'm sure got her into trouble with her superiors in USAID and their associates in the State Department, but that kind of bullshit just sluiced off her and didn't leave any detritus behind. Her forthright approach appalled the diplomats, but Phoenix wasn't there to be liked: she was there to get a job done. She spent as much time in the hills as possible and loved working with the American SOF world in the northern areas.

I first met Phoenix in the back of a Bison when she picked up a man she called Bubba the Seed Dude from a flight at KAF. (Bubba was from the U.S. Department of Agriculture in, I think, Iowa, wore a crumpled Cat ball cap with his body armor, and chewed a piece of hay. He had a real ability to connect with Afghan farmers.) The perspectives and ideas just tumbled out of her once she realized I wasn't the media and had been to Afghanistan before. "This province is going to go to hell over the next year. It's going to get bloody," she predicted. "The new bad guys don't care how much carnage they generate amongst the population. This is Pashtunistan, not Afghanistan. Only force rules here right now." I asked her if there would some form of migration from Iraq. "No, this place is too nuanced for that. It's only a superficial comparison. The Afghan opposition won't put up with outsiders actually running things directly. There's a debate going on within the ACM over whether they should use mass casualty suicide attacks in the furtherance of their cause."

"What are we doing right? What are we doing wrong?"

"Well, I think OEF has lost control of the hinterland in Kandahar province over the past year. This occurred when the 25th Infantry was in charge. The 173rd has been trying to correct this since they got on the ground. I have to rely on Ghekho [the SOF base in Kandahar] to do anything up north. If they go, I'll go. We need to push up there and get a better presence in those districts."

"Have you worked with the British SOF in Helmand province?"

"Yeah, but they're too violent. They can get away with it in Helmand, but not here. It needs to be subtler here. The Canadian Forces is great to work with, but some of your other agencies are naive about what's going on here. Then there are the Islamist NGOs; we need to keep a better eye on them." As I've told people for years, not all NGOs are created equal. Some act as intelligence-gathering organizations for our enemies, others recruit, others provide safe havens.

Phoenix was having problems in a district called Khakriz. She had succeeded in getting a school built, but while it was under construction some armed people occupied it. I would eventually accompany her on a patrol to deal with this later in the month.

matthijs from DFID

Matthijs Toot was "the Man from DFID," the British version of USAID, but with a slightly smaller checkbook. Strange: Matthijs was, in fact, Dutch but working for a British governmental aid organization. I had heard from some people that Matthijs had a mysterious past, so I decided to be blunt as I shook his hand:

"Hi, I'm Dr. Sean Maloney. I hear you're a spy."

Matthijs though it was funny and started laughing. He had heard it before, of course. "Well, I have credibility problems with UNAMA: *they* think I'm a spy! In fact, the UNAMA head here is ex-KGB. I lived from 1990 to 1994 in Quetta and I speak Pashtun. I work exclusively with governmental organizations, not NGOs or the UN. For some of those UN people, if you work for a government, you are an extension of government policy and not *their* policy, therefore you are a spy!"

Matthijs could be as blunt as Phoenix, but he was a bit more restrained. His outlook on the OEF effort in RC South revolved around his belief that operations were "too kinetic" and that if it continued we might lose the province. He called for more balance and subtlety, and for increased resources for nonkinetic operations, particularly in the border regions. He was concerned about the Canadians: we needed, he said, to break out of the "peacekeeping" mentality and realize that Canada has taken sides in a war and that the PRT was a weapon in that war.

"You mean Colonel Bowes and his people, or the Canadian political people?"

"No, I mean other Canadian agencies. You people focus too much on orphanage visits, which is nice, but what does it accomplish in the long run in stabilizing Kandahar? We need to advertise the fact when we take out a 'spoiler' and not cry crocodile tears. These people respect it when we have to get kinetic, but there has to be more balance."

"We have people back home who like to 'stovepipe' things: its either war fighting or its peacekeeping. Or there is a difference between information and intelligence. Here it seems seamless."

"Well, this is a problem with NGOs and aid agencies. They get concerned that if they coordinate with military forces, that their information will be used for targeting purposes, or other nefarious purposes by American intelligence agencies. But we need information on what the enemy is doing. Money, properly funded projects, and a presence will win us the border regions. That presence can come from ANA, ANP, SOF, whatever."

"How does development work with SOF?" I wondered.

"Well, it depends on which SOF. There's 'Fort Bragg' SOF, which is really aggressive, and then there is the reserve U.S. Special Forces, which has a better understanding on where development fits into the equation. I still think there is too much kinetic going on, Helmand particularly, and it will explode in our faces eventually. We have to get out there into the hinterland, out of Kandahar City, determine what is going on, and address it."

I would eventually accompany Matthijs on a long-range patrol to the Maruf district and see him in action too.

michael callan and CIDA

> A pessimist sees the difficulty in every opportunity; an optimist sees the opportunity in every difficulty.
>
> —Winston S. Churchill

The Canadian International Development Agency, like its American and British counterparts, was established during the Cold War to counter Soviet influence in the decolonizing Third World using economic assistance and social development. Over the years, CIDA forgot its Cold War roots and incrementally shifted away from acting as an instrument of Canadian policy and toward behaving like a government-funded neutral NGO. Indeed, CIDA refused to help the Canadian and American contingents deployed as part of Operation Enduring Freedom back in 2002 and institutionally resisted involvement in Afghanistan. My impression always was that CIDA's leadership had an African fixation and wasn't really interested in helping Afghans. Unlike USAID and DFID, CIDA was less "operationalized" in that hands-on fieldwork was usually left up to the governments that CIDA bureaucrats were assisting.

I found the PRT CIDA rep to be a refreshing change of pace. The quiet-spoken, extremely fit, and bearded Michael Callan had significant experience in development work and threw himself into the Kandahar maw. I would learn, from dealing with Michael and certain other CIDA personnel, that there was a distinct difference from CIDA field personnel and those who moved money around from computer to computer in the Ottawa headquarters or sat in air-conditioned offices in African capital cities. Michael regularly traveled from Camp Nathan Smith to the Governor's "palace," the Guest House, the provincial council center, and KAF to carry out his duties, which put him at significant risk. He was a one-man "nonkinetic" attack.

"We have never done anything like this before," Michael explained to me in his Weatherhaven office. "There is this big gray area between military operations and development, and CIMIC can only cover part of it."

I had already confronted Michael with my prejudices about CIDA as an institution, and it became a running joke between us. Michael explained that CIDA was becoming more and more open-minded, that there were younger people and fewer baby boomers, that there was increasingly more flexibility in CIDA, but it was still a work in progress. The current minister was willing to accept risk, whereas others before him had not. The possibility that the state of affairs might revert back was still there, however.

"So how does the money flow?" I asked. Always follow the money. I learned that from *All the President's Men*.

"The Canadian government assigns an amount of money and puts it in trust. It's supposed to go to the Kabul government, then to the provincial governments, and then the districts via national-level construction and aid projects. The problem is mentoring the Afghan government at all three of these levels. The SAT-A does this in Kabul, we do it in Kandahar, but the PRTs are not optimized for mentoring the provincial governments. That is where CIDA's Confidence in Government initiative comes into play.

"You have to understand the Kabul-level National Solidarity Programme. CIDA money is supposed to flow into the NSP and then to the NSP representative in Kandahar. But there are significant obstacles. The staff is afraid to go out to the districts. The Afghan leadership here has to be engaged in this; we could bypass it, but the international community can't run everything, so we are engaged in capacity and institution building here through the Confidence in Government initiative. The fact that this has to occur synergistically with military operations is completely new for us—all of us. There is a steep, steep learning curve. We have to address the sources of insecurity here at all levels."

"So what do you see as the sources of insecurity here in Kandahar province?"

"As we explain it, there is active and passive antigovernment behavior here. The active resistance to the government, that is the Taliban, is a response to political marginalization, while the passive aspect is the lack of will to resist the Taliban by the population because there are not enough incentives to do so. These are what we are calling the Tier I problems. The Tier II problems relate to disputes over land registration, water rights, and grazing rights. Youth unemployment is becoming a big problem. Then there are the 'opportunists,' criminal gangs, and government corruption. It is difficult to address the Tier I problems because of the lack of government presence in the insecure districts. The Tier II problems relate to deficiencies in security-related institutions at the district-level. We have a program to address that that we call the Security Sector Initiatives Programme, or SSIP. In theory, National Solidarity Programme and other money, once deployed to the provincial level, will be directed at SSIP, which will be targeted at the district level. But we can't deploy the money until we have an accountable provincial government . . . or government departments."

It was gridlock. The money couldn't be deployed from Kabul because there was a lack of provincial governance, the enemy took advantage of the lack of development in those districts, which in turn prevented government from influencing the populations in those districts. But there were even more fundamental problems. Michael was trying to establish what the baseline was for what was going on in the province itself. Astoundingly, neither the previous PRT nor the

European-led "pillars" in Kabul had assessed critical areas. There was no justice "map" of Kandahar. Michael anticipated it would take two or three months just to establish what the justice system in Kandahar province looked like. Similarly, it would take at least two or three months just to figure out who owned what land. None of this had been done since the Taliban collapsed. The biggest problem with the previous PRT, Michael explained, was the lack of measurement of effectiveness and the inability to pass on what they had done. There was a failure of continuity.

OK, OK, OK. I know it's not combat. It's not exciting. It is, however, absolutely crucial to winning a counterinsurgency war and beating the Taliban and Al Qaeda. We can kill as many Taliban as we like, but without what Michael was working on, the whole effort would be wasted.

Michael explained that the money needed for SSIP, which came from the National Solidarity Programme, was blocked at the provincial level. The Canadian embassy was the signing authority to permit the deployment of monies. It insisted on proper procedure and written proposals, but the Kandahar provincial government was incapable of producing these complex documents. Michael had a dilemma: should he do it himself, or should he mentor an Afghan in the provincial government to do it? That would take time. Was there time?

To further complicate matters, Canada wasn't the only country operating in Kandahar: there was money coming in from DFID and USAID too. How was that supposed to be coordinated? There was also the PRT Commander's Contingency Fund. There was a U.S. Army fund called the Commander's Emergency Response Program (CERP). Some of these monies had strings attached and could be used only in certain places or on certain pet projects. Michael had to explain to his mentorees in the provincial government that some countries deployed aid monies directly to the districts, which bypassed the mechanisms he was trying to establish in Kandahar to coordinate aid and construction. The Americans, as usual, were in a hurry, so Phoenix was applying resources in key hot spots, sometimes in coordination with CTF BAYONET's Civil Affairs. It was "on-demand" aid, whereas CIDA's strength was capacity building in recognition of the need to include the Afghan government people in the distribution process, which to CIDA was as important as the actual deployment of the aid resources. Bringing both approaches together was the challenge, and that was accomplished through the personal contact between the players, which in turn explains why the PRT was so important in this effort. It all boiled down, sometimes, to Michael, Matthijs, and Phoenix having a coffee in the mess. More formally, there was the PRT committee chaired by Steve Bowes, which was also critical, but it is often the informal, off-line discussions that grease the wheels.

In all my discussions with the PRT people, I kept coming back to the possibility that there were two fights here. The first was against the Taliban, but the second was a fight for time to stave off government corruption. It was a recurring theme that I couldn't dispense with, that if "the people" didn't see positive action, then they would take matters into their own hands. And there were still a lot of AKs around. What form would that take? Would they side with the Taliban against the government? Or would they form a third entity? If so, could OEF distinguish between the two? These questions nagged me.

I asked Michael what the sources of power in the province were. He explained that there were the line ministries from Kabul with their bureaucratic "stovepipes"; the Governor; the Provincial Shura; and the Provincial Council. A significant problem was that the Kabul government hadn't really sorted out how it related to the provincial government and kept centralizing things in Kabul. The line ministries' representatives in Kandahar were told what to do by Kabul, and how they related to the Governor wasn't clear. Did they coordinate with the Governor? Did they command the Governor? The result was that the Governor retreated more and more into dealing with security issues and not the other areas of governance. This to me seemed to be the root of the problem: federal-provincial relationships. Just like in Canada.

I learned from Glyn Berry that historically a provincial governor in Afghanistan was the military leader of the province. He was responsible for the military and paramilitary forces, and the maintenance of law and order. We were asking that the Governor act like the Governor of a state in the United States, or a provincial Premier in Canada. At the same time, the line ministries lacked the resources and manpower to do their traditional jobs in the provinces; the security threat was too high for them to assess what was going on in the provinces. It was yet another example of gridlock. And again, this was why the PRT was so valuable. It could conduct assessments in high-threat areas.

The problem of lack of government presence in the districts meant that the PRT could facilitate what CIDA called "knowledge development." What was needed in effect, was a big province-wide recce.

Then the question revolved around prioritization of resources, and how that was to be done. Do you build courthouses? Police stations? Roads? At the same time there was substantial pressure, usually from CFC-A, for measurable successes. The higher headquarters wanted to see change, and they wanted it now. The information operations people needed to be able to *show* that there was progress, that problems were being addressed, that things were *being done*. There was pressure for cosmetic projects to feed the information operations beast.

Michael's Confidence in Government initiative didn't fit that construct. He viewed the situation in Kandahar as a protracted problem requiring protracted solutions. The key areas were the districts, many of which felt disenfranchised. The idea behind CIG was to make aid monies and resources available to the districts' communities and to permit the districts to be part of the priority-establishing process. The communities had to fulfill several requirements, however. The people had to ensure that any decision making was inclusive; that sustainability was built into any project; that the community contributed either financially or in kind; and that the community "demonstrates a willingness to cooperate with other national-level programmes," which I took as coded language to mean assist in the fight against the Taliban.

Ultimately the Confidence in Government initiative was designed "to give remote areas tangible cause to support the direction and legitimacy of the Afghan government"; "to develop networks between insecure communities and the provincial government"; and "to promote the legitimacy of the democratic process through the Provincial Council."

Michael now had to convince the provincial leadership that the mechanisms necessary to carry all this out be established, and that they accept and participate in them. It was all just theory if he couldn't do so. The Provincial Development Committee concept in use up in northern Afghanistan was one model that was promising: that permitted "buy-in" from all provincial and federal agencies. To get buy-in from other NGO aid organizations meant that some form of steering committee be established to coordinate efforts between the PDC and the "internationals." Then he came up with the idea of a Contact Group, which would actually go into the field to explain the process to the people at the district level.

It would not be possible to implement CIG throughout the province all at once. Four districts should be selected: they should be remote districts national programs didn't reach into; they should have strategic provincial importance; and they should be districts that were not secure, but were not openly hostile. At this point, only Panjwayi, Zharey, Maiwand, Dand, Arghandab, Shiga, and Daman districts got national monies. That was the plan in December 2005.

It was evident to me that the Confidence in Government initiative could become a key aspect to success in Afghanistan. Michael Callan would spend the next eight months trying to implement it in Kandahar province and was still trying to do so when I returned in the summer of 2006.

CIMIC operations

For the [Vietnamese] rural peasantry, the prescription was "civic action" by the military forces (handing out goodies and constructing public works) to generate appreciation. But nowhere in the Plan was there a program for pure political action—organizing the population into political groups, articulating a cause that would attract their participation and support . . . in other words, a direct counter to the program the Communists were carrying out in the countryside.

—WILLIAM COLBY, *LOST VICTORY* (1989)

My roommate at the PRT was Major Sanchez King. Sanchez was a thoughtful, low-key bespectacled older reserve officer from Halifax and was in charge of the Civil-Military Cooperation (CIMIC) cell at the PRT. Sanchez had been part of the Emergency Measures Organization (or EMO, which is like FEMA in the United States) and specialized in domestic operations at Land Force Atlantic Area.

"So dealing with disasters isn't much different from dealing with Kandahar?" I joked.

"Well, I've seen worse-organized disasters!"

Colonel Bowes saw CIMIC as his "eyes and ears" in certain quarters of the coalition effort, which diverged from existing (and evolving!) doctrine in that CIMIC is the liaison between a deployed military force conducting operations and the local political leadership. Sanchez told me that among the Canadian Forces, how CIMIC is defined and what role it should play depends on who one talks to, a confusing situation that permitted the PRT to be flexible on how it employed Sanchez and his team.

For example, NATO CIMIC doctrine, like that used in ISAF, asserts that a CIMIC unit assists a deployed unit, supports it, and facilitates military operations. But what happens when CIMIC *becomes* the operation, like in the original concepts of the Joint Regional Teams (JRTs) and PRTs, and doesn't just support an ongoing one?

The confusing state of affairs was important to understand. In theory, CTF BAYONET, if it were conducting conventional operations, would have a Civil Affairs (the American term for CIMIC) unit of company or battalion size to move with the CTF BAYONET maneuver units and liaise with the locals. The CA unit would conduct "quick-action" projects designed specifically to temporarily relieve poor local conditions and show the local population that CTF BAYONET was the "good guy." CA was not supposed to be into long-term development issues. In RC South, however, this thing called a PRT existed that was supposed to liaise with local and provincial authorities, quick-action projects, *and* development. CTF BAYONET wasn't quite sure how to use the PRT, Sanchez explained. The force had its own CA unit that conducted operations farther north with the Gun Devils and the 82nd Airborne. This in turn posed coordination problems: CTF BAYONET's CA unit was doing quick-action projects and the PRTs and OGDs were doing development projects *in the same operating area*. Then there were the NGOs, doing their (uncoordinated) thing. This confused the local people to no end.

And then there were coordination problems with SOF. In RC South, SOF units had their own operating areas that were different from PRT and Gun Devil operating areas, but in some cases they overlapped. The PRT coordinated with the French and Dutch SOF working on the borders, but rarely with the American and Canadian SOF working in the interior. I learned that unlike the French and Dutch SOF who were dispersed in a number of forward operating bases (FOBs), the North American SOF units didn't have a dispersed presence on the ground and were usually seen by the locals to be "passing through." This made it difficult to coordinate CIMIC activity, and in many cases it just wasn't done in certain operating areas.

The first step taken by CTF BAYONET was to make Kandahar City *a* but not *the* PRT operating area, separate from the Gun Devils or SOF, though both "passed through." Colonel Bowes and Sanchez then had to figure out where on the spectrum CIMIC sat: the NGOs and CIDA insisted that CIMIC was "not projects," but then CIMIC became involved in projects. The commander of CTF BAYONET had a pot of money for "projects"; some of this went to the American CA unit, while some went to the PRT. CIMIC, not the OGDs, was tasked with making recommendations for its dispersal.

CIMIC then became a venue to deconflict aid, development, military, and civilian projects. Sanchez decried Ottawa's (in this case, National Defence HQ) lack of understanding about how CIMIC in the PRT had to evolve given the complex situation. Tampering with this delicate instrument could cause no end of problems. To make matters worse, there was UNAMA. Sanchez was blunt: "We don't know what they're doing down here."

The UN was not coordinating with the PRT? I was confused.

"How does all of this interact with the Kandahar provincial government and what the central government in Kabul wants?"

"An excellent question. It all revolves around who sets the priorities. The problem is getting the government to *set* priorities. We recommend, we advise, but . . . We *know* that to succeed, to get anything done, we have to engage the hidden leadership: these are the shuras and the district chiefs. The tribal and family connections. We have to recognize that the Taliban is not necessarily the main issue here. There are people who will use a Taliban cousin with a gun to solve a problem. Not all violence here is 'political.'"

"So how does CIMIC work here? What do you do?"

"We conduct nonkinetic attacks. The repertoire includes agriculture development and water in the border regions, and then health and rule of law development in Kandahar City. We have identified the border regions and the city as the PRT's vital ground. We have only so many resources, and we can't be everywhere. How do we balance them? We roughly split it up this way. Agriculture is handled by USAID—they provide money for tractors and so on, while DFID and some local NGOs are focused on the water issue. USAID has some money earmarked specifically for water issues too. Health: Canadian medics do that at the Kandahar University, 'train the trainers' sort of thing. The American military medics also run something called a VMO, or Village Medical Outreach, whereby medical personnel deploy to outlying areas to assist the Afghanistan Health and Development Service. There were problems with the enemy targeting Afghan medics after the VMOs had gone and the AHDS doesn't want VMOs taking place anymore in some critical areas. We had a clinic burned and four doctors assassinated.

"Rule of law: that is an American-handled thing. It had to be after the eight Italian-trained judges decided to stay in Italy rather than return to scenic Kandahar. The RCMP are part of the rule of law component; they work with the Afghan National Police. But there aren't enough of them.

"The PRT Commander also has a pot of money at his disposal, the PRT Commander's Contingency Fund. We use that to support the ANP. It is Department of National Defence money and subject to strict controls. Colonel Bowes will usually employ it in a unique area, something nobody else is doing."

"How is this all coordinated?"

"The Provincial Development Committee, like the ones up north, doesn't exist here yet. We have something called a 'PRT Synchronization Meeting.' UNAMA doesn't like it and they won't play; *they* think they should control it. We don't and neither do the Afghans. CTF BAYONET Civil Affairs plays to a certain extent. The Dutch SOF are pretty good; they have professional CIMIC. The French SOF don't have a lot of CIMIC with them and ask us for help; they're keen. TF-31, the American SOF, generally don't play; they're short staff and focused on 'kinetic ops. They don't work for CTF BAYONET and the command-control issues are immense. They did ask us for some nonkinetic ops, but the command and control broke down. Bagram was involved, so it didn't happen."

I learned also that there were even more fundamental problems on the Afghan side and this reflected tensions between Kandahar and Kabul, Pashtuns and non-Pashtuns, Durrani and Ghilzai. Kabul was pressuring the provincial government to set up the PDC, but it was being resisted. The provincial government was actually split: there was the Governor and his staff, and there was the provincial council. The Governor was an outsider; he had no power base in Kandahar province, even though he had legitimacy from the central government. My old friend Gul Agha Sherzai had an extensive power base and could get things done, but he had been

"Chessgamed" to the volatile province of Jalalabad. Governor Asadullah Khalid struggled at every turn, and the PRT sometimes had to mediate between him and provincial council. The line ministries from Kabul, like Health, Housing, and so on, were totally stovepiped and tried to do their own thing in Kandahar without coordinating with the provincial authorities, which in turn pissed off the local authorities and inflamed intertribal tensions that were centuries old.

Of course, this state of affairs was not much different from any city, province, or state in the United States or Canada—and to expect instantaneous change to "fix" all of this now was unrealistic. Bureaucratic theorists remind us that when a route is blocked, people will work around the block to get things done. The PRT performed this unstated, unwritten, nondoctrinal role in Kandahar province.

info ops with sergeant thombs's patrol: kandahar city

I met Sergeant Chris Thombs (pronounced "tooms") on my first patrol with the PRT. Nicknamed "the Tomb Raider," Sergeant Thombs initially struck me as a hippie sergeant: he had a beard ("I got a surfing injury on leave and had to cover it up," he explained unconvincingly) and burned incense in his quarters. I believe he had a Buddha stashed in there as well, but I never actually saw it. I learned that B Company allowed the troops to modify their equipment as they saw fit and had a relaxed dress policy, almost SOF-like. Many of them had been with 2 Commando in Somalia as privates, and then as master corporals and sergeants in Kandahar in 2002. They weren't into bullshitting around. Thombs himself had been in Somalia, Bosnia, and Nepal.

Sergeant Thombs and his patrol were initially skeptical about my presence for a time; this patrol was tight—they knew the moves and they knew each other. Outsiders and hangers-on were, quite rightly, regarded with suspicion. Thombs' section was the first PRT patrol hit with an IED back in October, and the attention directed at them because of this novel event must have been a complete pain in the ass.

While I was gearing up for the patrol, another sergeant, Chuck Coté, was assisting. A confidence-inspiring individual, Sergeant Coté seemed to be built out of spare bulldozer parts.[4] Some of the guys said there was a "Chuck Coté Action Figure" somewhere.

"Have you got a tourniquet?"

"Nope. I thought tourniquets were bad for you . . . "

"Only if you use them on your neck. They're back now; we're getting the feed from Iraq. Traumatic amputations can be safely staunched with them." Chuck got one for me. "Keep it in your left-hand pants pocket. That's where everybody has them so they can get at them quick. You have field dressings?"

"Two."

"I'll get you more. Be prepared to hand ammo up to the gunner if he needs it. You know how to use the smoke grenades?"

"Yep."

"Remember: stay in the vehicle if you get hit. Don't flop out until the crew commander says. If you have to get out, check for additional devices on the ground before you do."

This wasn't riding around in an SFOR Iltis in Bosnia or a 1967 pattern jeep in the Sinai. This was serious shit.

The mission today was an "I/O patrol," or Information Operations patrol. The obsidian Sergeant Reginald Obas from the PSYOPS section had multiple objectives: deliver posters and newspapers, conduct street-level interviews, and engage in something called "route designation." This last related to confirming the existence of streets, buildings, and such for navigation and clearance purposes. Oh, and we were going to drop by a "problem" police station to see what was up . . .

This was not just some jaunt into the city; it was a potentially dangerous operation and was treated as such by Sergeant Thombs and his troops. In the threat briefing, we were told that five suicide bombers were known to be in the Kandahar area and that a fairing-equipped motorcycle had been observed tailing Canadian patrols in the city. The ubiquitous Elvis, believed to be a Pakistani intelligence agent, possibly Al Qaeda, had also been dogging the PRT patrols. A gray Land Rover also posed some unspecified threat, and we were to keep an eye out for it. Actions on contact with the enemy were detailed, but I won't go into them here because they work, and the enemy doesn't need to know them. The ROE was "as per," which I took to mean "we will go beyond the ROE if we deem it necessary for our protection but we don't want to say that out loud." Being one of the "protected," I had no problem with that . . . After all, I wasn't a journo looking for scandal. Nobody should be unthinkingly prosecuted by the System for protecting themselves or others.

The patrol consisted of a G-Wagon with a .50-cal mount, another with a 5.56 mount, another support G-Wagon, and a Nyala armored patrol vehicle crewed by the engineers. In terms of personnel, it was a mixture of infantry, sigs, and medics, plus the I/O team. Thombs put me in a G-Wagon with Master Corporal Keith Smith and Private Dan Coté.

"Doc, you have a job when you're with us. We heard you used to be in the Forces. You have a pair of eyes and are part of the defensive system of this patrol even though you are unarmed. Watch your arcs and let us know if you see anything."

We mounted up, gunners cocked their weapons, and we rolled out the gate past the PRT Police. This was my first time "outside the wire" since I arrived at the PRT, so it was the first time I had seen the city since 2003.

Kandahar is more like Mogadishu than Kabul. Steve Bowes in his briefings constantly had to remind people that Kandahar is as different from Kabul as Kabul is from Ottawa. The PRT is situated in the northwest part of the city, in what could be considered a place between "suburbia" (no such construct exists there, but basically the residential areas built more recently than "downtown") and the center of the city. Kandahar is built around an east-west MSR that makes the city more or less elongated. As they do with any regularly traveled area, soldiers develop their own terminology, a shorthand, to describe critical areas. All the routes have code names to facilitate rapid reaction if necessary, In this case, they were named for beer—like "Route Michelob," for example. For Kandahar, there was "Electronic Square," which was a market area specializing in electronics; there was the "Crop Circle," a large traffic circle with food growing in it.

This is one of the PRT's battlefields: a built-up, crowded, vehicle-choked, seemingly endless sea of brown buildings, dusty main streets, muddy side streets, and refuse. Side streets that went nowhere. Cul-de-sacs, alleys, produce stalls, jingle trucks—even jingle bikes! Three-wheel tuk-tuk taxis, mules, donkeys, and the filth associated with them. In other words, unlimited opportunities for ambush. Choke points and canalization: sometimes a vehicle *had* to go through a particular area and there was no choice in the matter. Increased frequency meant increased risk. Routes were varied as much as possible.

Maintaining a high level of alert was exhausting. I attempted on this trip to anticipate potential IED locations. This became futile, since *anything* could house an IED. Indeed, there were so many propane cylinders next to the road that I lost count. But the guys did it: they got used to what everything looked like in this environment and knew what just looked wrong, or outside the context of the freneticism of Kandahar City.

There was no shortage of commerce in Kandahar; shops and stalls were open for business, and there were plenty of them. This was not some city under siege like Sarajevo was. It didn't have the tense feel of Jerusalem under sustained suicide attack that I experienced in 2001. This was a city that was carrying on despite the war. We were locked into our armored conveyances passing through, and they pretty much ignored us. When youths threw stones, it was because they were youths, not terrorists with an ideological agenda. When the gunners waved at people, they generally waved back.

The first part of the patrol was to drop in at a police station without warning and ostensibly inquire as to the maintenance status of their vehicles, in case they needed "help." This particular police district was problematic and suspected of being infiltrated by Taliban supporters. I assumed that dropping in was related to some larger operation collecting information on personalities and what was probably some link analysis related to it. The "police station" bore no resemblance to an equivalent facility in a North American city; it was just a small, one-story house surrounded with a mud wall. Several "officers" lounged about and there appeared to be no uniform, though some had some kind of brassard. There were a few Hungarian AK-47 equivalents in evidence, and two vehicles in various stages of disrepair. The men smiled and superficially appeared friendly, but my time in Afghanistan has taught me the folly of taking any of that at face value. Tea was offered, but we declined, citing the (illusory) need to press on. Help was offered for the vehicles, but it was politely declined by the police. The right people got what they needed, and we mounted up. There was an uneasy vibe in that place; the kids in the street looked cowed.

The patrol drove along the main east-west highway, into the southwestern part of the city. A mountain spur thrust its way north-south like a knife into this residential area. We turned onto what amounted to a narrow dirt road that threatened to be overwhelmed by compounds on either side. Where the hell were we going? After about a klick or two, the road opened up into what could be described as an empty open area to the left and the equivalent of a corner store to the right, with cave-holed hills immediately behind it. One G-Wagon covered the south entrance of the open area with a .50, while another handled the north with the 5.56. The Nyala ground to a halt and Sergeant Obas climbed out the hatch on the back. Sergeant Thombs' guys dismounted and took up positions covering all possible entrance points.

The "corner store" had two poles with large rolls of cellophane blowing in the wind. Reg and the interpreter proceeded to the store and asked if they could put up some posters: I think they had health messages or something akin to that. They also started to hand out a newspaper to whoever wanted it. In seconds there were about fifteen or twenty kids or youths there, coming out of the woodwork. Four girls with green and purple head scarves looked at us and smiled and waved—but from a distance.

The PSYOPS guys, working with interpreters, started asking the adults who were in the store their list of carefully prepared questions. From my vantage point, they didn't appear to have problems getting answers. Nobody was reticent.

"Reg, what are you asking them?"

"Well, we have to collect certain statistical data so we can see how we're doing. It's inexact, but at least we have some measure of what the people think. We can do this almost randomly throughout the city and try to build a picture of what the people need, what they want, and what they think they need and want. We have to be careful, though. We don't want the enemy knowing what *we* want to know since that might assist him in his targeting. Or he could try to influence our perception of what is going on here."

He turned back to give some direction. Thombs' guys were getting a bit antsy.

"The main problem we have is time," Reg explained. "The longer we are in one location, the longer the enemy has to plan and do something to us on the way out. We picked this location, almost at random, and we'll remain as unpredictable as possible on our way out. On the other hand, if we don't stay long enough, we don't get the info we need. It's a balance. So we do a bunch of smaller patrols instead of one long one."

It was time to leave. We loaded up and made our way back to the main highway and the journey back to the PRT compound.

The return trip can in some ways be more tense than the outbound trip: the enemy doesn't know where, exactly, we are going or how we are going to get there. It is a truism to state that what goes out must come back, which makes us predictable within certain canalized areas. There are, essentially, four ways back to the main street that the PRT is on, and then there is the entrance, which makes six possible attack areas. The PRT police are trained to keep an eye on the main drag there, which reduces the odds slightly. After the patrol has gone out and done its job, people are tired and want to get home, so vigilance can lapse if the troops aren't careful. It becomes ingrained to increase the attention span on the way back in.

During my time at the PRT, I got to know Chris Thombs, and he spoke with me about the incidents he had been involved in. Chris explained how things had changed in the fall after the unit got on the ground.

"The 'bad guys' didn't really know how to take us, and we figure they spent a lot of time just to figure out how to hit us. They tried pushing different things, seeing how far we would go. We call this 'templating,' or gathering information on how a patrol works, moves, and so on. They would trail our vehicles, try to break into the packets, ignoring nonverbal communication. They would only react when they were engaged or had a shot fired across their bow."

"You guys had to shoot at them?"

"A couple of other patrols did. But my patrol got hit in October. The suspicious stuff happened in September. We were still learning; we had sensory overload. You're trying to see everything and not filtering yet. It was sort of like driving through Montreal, but heavily armed. We smashed a few mirrors, we played chicken with some people, and 'threaded the needle' a few times."

"I heard the I/O people had to put public service announcements on the radio station?"

"Yeah. We told the locals not to follow us, not to try to get into the packet, and we put signs on the back of the vehicles."

Chris leaned back to collect his thoughts.

"We were doing a straight convoy run from KAF to the PRT; we had a Bison with lots of officers. We 'dialed in' the new guys. So we're rolling, everything's fine, we were pushing the center of the road to keep the locals out of the way. We'd been talking about this donkey that was dead on the side of the road, we were joking about a donkey IED, and just before we got hit we hear, 'Donkey!' I was watching my arcs to the right, and I saw it out of the corner of my eye, in slo-mo, the dirt push from the explosion and then the fireball came back, just at regular speed. 'Gunner, down! Are you okay? Go! Go! Go!' I yelled. We pushed about five hundred meters, broke left. The Charlie 2 vehicle was close enough that they couldn't stop safely so we pushed some more: we were traveling at about 105.

"We did a report and got the cordon set up. Then some other Canadians happened on the scene, so I used them for the cordon. Then the QRF showed up. Damage to the convoy was a broken headlight and the squirty thing that the windshield washer fluid comes out of. The funny thing was, we were delayed at KAF by some rear-echelon guy. If we hadn't been delayed . . . "

"Was it an IED or a suicide bomber?"

"It was a suicide bomber in a Mitsubishi Pajero. I just remember seeing the grille, because he was off on the right-hand side of the road. An American convoy had just passed us going to KAF, we were going to the city, and the guy was on the KAF side. So he chickened out and didn't hit the Americans, he hit us. He pushed out onto the road and was 10 feet away from the median when he detonated. He killed a kid 250 feet away, wounded the father of the kid, and the fireball singed my gunner pretty good from where his gloves ended, up to his forearm and back of his neck. The panel marker on the roof caught fire. The turret shield is angled, so that deflected most of it. It burned him without singing his hair! We figure it was a 122-mm round or maybe a 155.

"There were chunks of the jihadi, like his feet and stuff. There was a bunch of him smeared all over the vehicle and forced into the air conditioning system. It smelled like bad body odor in there for about a week. The lower extremities were left, but the upper torso was eradicated completely.

"Then the crowd started to encroach. We were concerned about secondaries: the enemy might have another device to attack first responders and the crowd to generate more casualties. The QRF moved the crown back, and EOD cleared the area."

"So this was the first hit against the PRT?"

"Yeah. Everybody handled it differently and not everybody shows their emotions on the outside. You have to know your guys. A couple of guys were behaving oddly, and I noticed it and kept an eye on it. My gunner wanted to get back up in the turret, but his burns wouldn't let him for a while. He would roll with us and sit in the same truck. He needed to get back up there. Climb back on the horse sort of thing.

"That was on 5 October. We were involved in another one on the ninth, when the Brits got hit. We were the first on the scene. We were in transit and talk about timing! We were delayed the first time and got hit. This time we got delayed and we didn't get hit. They were a *minute* ahead of us! That KAF-Kandahar road is just a target-rich environment. It's difficult to generate unpredictability on that route.

"It looked like a car accident at first, and all of a sudden I see this smoke. We pushed up and deployed. I had a Bison this time full of officers, so I deployed them to cover arcs and we set up a cordon. The first thing on my mind was securing the site. We called for the QRF. This was another suicide attack, same mechanism as the first one, but they pulled this one off differently. They let the armed vehicles pass by them so the turret guns couldn't be brought to bear; they moved in with an SUV from behind. All the middle vehicles have are rearview mirrors, no gun turrets facing back. This jihadi's lower torso was removed. The funny thing was that he looked like a Klingon from *Star Trek*, because half of his brains were gone, but his head was still up like the big forehead of the Klingons. He was in real bad shape. Again, it was an artillery shell. The Brits were all Pri 3[5] so they lived; they were in an armored SUV."

I asked Chris what were some of the more memorable things he'd seen in Kandahar during his time here.

"I remember doing this night patrol downtown. Everything was green through the night vision. On another occasion, we were flying down the road before anybody was awake through Kandahar and I looked back through the rearview mirror and the three-vehicle packet and it reminded me of *The Italian Job*! It was pretty fricking cool. I also noticed when we were checking bumpers and wheel wells for explosives and I saw a sticker from a civilian skydiving company and wondered how it got to Afghanistan. We also were picking some stuff up at an orphanage when these girls from the grade school kissed the back of my hand. I always try to shake hands with the kids. I learned this was a sign of respect. When we were coming back from that one, I saw the damndest thing: I saw street cricket! Just like street hockey back home. Street cricket? Never would have thunk! That was fucking weird. You'd expect that in India, Pakistan, or Australia, but it just blew my mind. It was a return to normalcy."

police patrol in kandahar city

Superintendent Wayne Martin and Corporal Bob Hart were the Royal Canadian Mounted Police contribution to the PRT. The challenges they faced trying to assess and help train and restructure the police in Kandahar province were immense—in my opinion far too many challenges for two men. It was like trying to divert a river.

Kandahar City was divided into police districts, each with a police substation, and the rural districts each had a police chief. It appeared as if all the rural chiefs were selected by the Governor, but where the substation commanders came from wasn't clear. Chief Wahidi, an Afghan living in the Netherlands, had been convinced to come back to Afghanistan and run the police in the province. He found police substations that were collapsing, that were without bathrooms or holding facilities. When new substations were constructed, there was no bureaucracy to handle building maintenance, so they were falling into disrepair right after they were built. He wanted barbwire to secure the buildings, handheld radios, base station radios. Japan provided SUVs, but they needed maintenance and their drivers needed to be trained. Most police commandeered taxis. I can just see four guys with automatic weapons piling into a Toyota Corolla: "Follow that car!" which was approximately what was happening.

Wayne and Bob encountered what they called "fortress policing," whereby the police were barricaded in Fort Apache and the locals had to go to the substation if they needed help. The goal was to move the police away from this toward "community policing" through patrols and presence. This was a problem in that the police weapons were centralized at the main police headquarters downtown and not distributed to the officers. As a consequence, most policemen brought their own AK-47s to work. If they lacked uniforms, they looked like paramilitaries, not policemen, so there was an image problem too. In one incident in 2006, this led to police being accidentally shot by Canadian troops.

Removal of police for corruption was problematic. In one critical police substation along a coalition main service route, the commander was a corrupt pedophile that Wahidi refused to sack. It was not clear why. The main problem areas, however, were the southwestern police substations in the city. These were known to be penetrated by the Taliban, and numerous intelligence-gathering operations were run to determine just who was who in the zoo.

The Kandahar police could have benefited from direct mentoring by the German police trainers in Kabul, but they were forbidden by their government from doing so. They needed a ministerial order to allow them to travel to the provinces.

Bob Hart was going to drop in on a substation in the west end to check out an infrastructure issue, so I went along. The patrol was led by Sergeant Jamie Bradley and consisted of four G-Wagons and their crews. It was cold and dusty that morning as we passed through Tech Square, around Martyr Circle, and on to the Crop Circle. In the patrol briefing, which was extremely detailed and dealt with every conceivable contingency, we learned that there were motorcycles shadowing PRT patrols, and that there were two inbound VBIEDs that used white Toyota Corollas as delivery systems. The crews were cynical: "We get *that* all the time!" There were, of course, hundreds of white Corollas in Kandahar.

The preparations were elaborate; they had to be. We had been told there were a number of suicide bombers in the city and briefed about the methodology that they will probably use, in this case a car bomb or VBIED. This patrol had already been "templated'"; the enemy had already run observation on its movements and activities. Indeed, the enemy was spotted doing so. Sergeant Bradley's crews were not visibly nervous; this patrol was like every other, and the risks were the same every time they rolled out the gate of the PRT. Machine guns were mounted, loaded, and cocked. Radios were checked. A crewman opened his M-203 grenade launcher and inserted a 40-mm grenade, while the exposed turret gunners wrapped themselves in SAS shemagh scarves to ward off the cold. Body armor was mandatory. "Do you have a tourniquet?" asked the mustachioed crew commander, Master Corporal Andrew Forbes. I had the latest field dressings, but not the new tourniquet that can be applied one-handed if a limb has been traumatically amputated. All of Sergeant Bradley's crews were under the age of twenty-five. And they knew their shit. I was with Master Corporal Forbes, Corporal Terrence Russell, Corporal Andy Pennington, and Private Eric Hennie for this trip.

We rolled out of the PRT gate, past the Afghan PRT Police who handle the security on the outer cordon. The patrol destination was in the west end of the city and consisted of a police substation. Kandahar City was jammed with people and vehicles of all types, shapes, and sizes. Jingle trucks, jingle bikes. Elephantine construction equipment. The four G-Wagon patrol weaved in and out of traffic—I cannot give details, because the techniques used by the patrol are designed to save their lives if attacked, and the enemy can adjust *their* tactics to counter ours. Suffice it to say, I was confident, after Sergeant Bradley's briefing, that the possible modes of attack all had responses. My job on contact was to assist the machine gunner if necessary and to assist with first aid if he became a casualty. I was no mere passenger; I also had to watch the right arc of the vehicles for anything suspicious.

The problem was, for the uninitiated, *everything* looked like a possible IED—paint cans, propane cylinders, motorcycles. The list was endless.

"Sir," the driver told me, "you can get tired trying to assess every threat so you have to filter—what is the most likely one today?" The crews had nicknames for key points in the city—Electronic Square, Martyr Circle, Crop Circle—and kept the TOC informed of their progress. If there was an attack, there were various types of responses available, including AH-64 Apache gunships.

Kandahar is known for its bricks, and there were numerous kilns in the west end. Dun-colored bricks were stacked, by hand, by the hundreds and thousands. There was an old man in an old Afghan army uniform. He saluted us grandly as we passed. "He does that every time we drive by," the codriver told me. We reached the first substation, and Bob Hart, wrapped in his gray body armor and carrying a C7 assault rifle, stepped out to contact his Afghan associates. This took about fifteen minutes. One of Sergeant Bradley's crew was a female, a medic, and the local kids thronged to look at her, amazed to see an armed young woman wearing body armor. She waved them back, her hand ready on the C7A1 assault rifle, out of concern that the concentration of people might present a target. The patrol vehicles were in a "defensive crouch" near the collapsed building that was the police station. I was aware of how vulnerable we were—the main east-west artery was next to the station and cars whizzed by. A sniper could have been anywhere in the high ground. The machine-gun crews kept a sharp eye out.

Business was completed. "There isn't a window in that place," exclaimed Bob. "They have two handheld radios and tell us they have to use a taxi to patrol. The commander says his people bring their own weapons to work. A lot more has to be done here."

Sergeant Bradley gave the signal to mount up. We were off to a compound just across the street, where the communications technicians who were with us assisted the Highway Patrol at their station by conducting a quick survey. Then we got back on the road toward the PRT. The PRRs (Personal Radio Receivers) were active. A car of a particular type was shadowing us. The patrol changed routes, but the car stuck to the rear vehicle like glue, albeit at standoff range. It matched the type we had been told the enemy was using as a VBIED. It was unnerving being stalked in a built-up and crowded city like Kandahar—the options to get away from a VBIED decreased in traffic, and escape routes were limited because of narrow alleys that went nowhere. The rear machine gunner was prepared to shoot at the vehicle if it got too close. Indeed, during the first months of PRT operations this year, Canadians engaged and shot up four suspect vehicles on different occasions.

The game continued. Sergeant Bradley employed a number of tactics to confirm that the car was still shadowing us. The uncertainty was palpable, but there was no panic. Calm professionalism reigned. Eventually the car veered off down another route, and we headed for the PRT. Was it a VBIED? Was a suicide bomber behind the wheel? We didn't know for sure. I could not shake the feeling that we had been stalked by some monstrous evil presence.

It was nightfall when we returned to the PRT. A bagpiper waited for the end of the last call to prayer of the night before playing "Scotland the Brave" from the HESCO Bastion walls.

yusuf zoi

I had the privilege of meeting a man who I will call Yusuf Zoi. Yusuf Zoi wishes to keep his real name unknown because of the possibility of violence that may be directed at him for what he has done in the past and what he is doing now on behalf of the Afghan government and the coalition forces. Yusuf Zoi and I had met back in 2003, and it was a pleasure to reencounter him in Kandahar City. We had a number of extremely candid conversations, the details of which I believe represent the views of a significant number of Afghans of a particular generation: people who have seen everything, from the 1960s to the Communist period to the civil war and then the Taliban era. Indeed, Yusuf had worked with the Afghan security forces way, way back in the pre-Soviet days.

Our meetings were always in a relaxed setting, and the level of candor was high. "Yusuf," I asked, "I want to hear what you think the main problems are here in Kandahar province."

"You must keep in mind that this is above all a rural agricultural area. Education is and has always been a problem. Literacy is practically nonexistent in some districts. They are a faithful people but uneducated. The biggest problem we have here is that the people will not accept radical progress. It must be slow. Quick doesn't work here. The Soviets tried that with their programs. The result was the complete destruction of the agricultural system. The people could never forgive the Soviets for that. The revolution was as much against this in the 1980s as anything. Now all Afghans are good fighters. Now there is much outside interference: Iran, Pakistan, particularly, took advantage of the situation in the 1990s. Today's problems are the result of yesterday's circumstances."

"So, " I said, "the people were happy when the Soviets were gone?"

"Oh yes, but peace didn't come to Kandahar. The War of the Commanders destroyed what was left of the economic base. There was lawlessness, torture, hangings from trees. People had their noses cut off. There was male and female rape, outright adultery with both sexes. People no longer supported the mujahideen here. Then Pakistan trained and supported Mullah Omar. He had connections to Rabbani. The Taliban's version of justice was a welcome counter to the lawlessness, at least at the time. But the Taliban closed the schools, they forbade education. They hunted down former police and security officers. I was tortured. Anybody who had investigated or understood the Pakistan-Taliban linkages was targeted by the Taliban. They didn't want the people to know they were working on behalf of the Pakistanis because then they would lose their power base."

"You were tortured?"

"Oh yes," Yusuf said almost matter-of-factly. "I left Afghanistan for Iran. But then the MOIS [Iranian Intelligence Service] wanted me to spy for them and I said no. I even had a turban and a beard in those days; I could have passed for a Taliban." He laughed. "But then the people figured it all out when the Taliban broke relations with almost everybody except Pakistan. The Taliban lost support once people realized they were being used."

"So that's the background. Where are we today?"

"People here are happy with Karzai. There is freedom of speech, there is choice. The constitution, elections, all good. Schools are open. The media is free. But aid promised by the Bonn conference and those programs have been slowly implemented. Those promises have yet to be fulfilled. Now credibility is a problem. That is the first problem. The second problem, naturally, is the Taliban. The enemy has networks that have excellent communications between them; this has been built up over the past few years. But more important, those who cultivate poppy are now working together with the Taliban. The Taliban have sent 'night letters' to people in certain districts that say 'cultivate poppy or we will kill you.' The district chiefs are corrupt. The enemy is using its tribal connections to get at them." Yusuf kicked back and lit a cigarette. He exhaled. I drank some tea.

"The biggest weakness we have is the police and the judiciary. They are not capable of dealing with this combination of traffickers and Taliban. When there is no punishment, there is no credibility." He emphasized his point by repeatedly tapping his finger on the arm of his chair. "Security is everything. Now some people are saying that the Taliban was better at dealing with security issues. This is Taliban I/O [Information Operations]. They are exploiting this, and it is becoming a real problem. The Taliban will now 'protect' poppy growers from the government and therefore transfer the legitimacy of the government to them. The combination of night letters telling parents that if they send their kids to school they will be killed, the fact that schools are all closed in the frontline districts . . . these are serious, serious problems."

"I want to understand Pakistan's role in all of this," I said as I lit a Davidoff and waved out the burning match.

"Pakistan is a *big* problem. We share a language, a border, and a culture. Those suicide bombers are Pakistanis. Mullah Omar is in Pakistan, bin Laden is in Pakistan. The training camps are operating. Quetta is their base. Pakistan is interested in trade routes, We think Pakistan wants to keep Afghanistan dependent on them for trade. Those attacks against the Japanese-supported road engineers west of Kandahar? You have heard of those?"

I nodded. This occurred recently in a district called Zharey and another called Panjwayi. Road building crews had been ambushed with increased frequency. The Gun Devils were investigating.

"We think that is part of a proxy operation designed to interfere with trade between Kandahar and Herat, and onward to Iran. Kandahar is sending a lot of goods west now, much more than before. Some think the Quetta merchants aren't happy with this and are using their connections in the Taliban to interfere. My friend, there are always many layers. Like an onion."

Yusuf gave me another lesson in Afghan economics. "In the Daoud era, we had collective farms and sales. This allowed farmers to afford tractors. It was a good system: several farmers would band together, buy equipment, pool their goods, sell their goods, and split the proceeds. Every three months, government representatives went out and met with the people, like a shura. It was a forum for issues. It demonstrated government interest and support. The farmers paid taxes. There was tax relief if there was a drought. Big projects, like irrigation, were handled by the government. People had a say in what was going on. Produce could be sold at prices that were greater than what poppy would provide. This essentially prevented poppy cultivation. People just weren't interested. There were tangible economic benefits at a low level.

"The Taliban changed all of this. Poppy changed all of this. There were no more cooperatives. This system no longer exists. The Taliban and its allies have more contact with the people than the government. Poppy is more lucrative than the other crops. There is no means to get that produce to market. Now the people have had three years of promises but little has changed. The enemy exploits this."

"But surely this isn't just Pakistan. There must be insiders involved."

Yusuf contemplated something outside the window for a minute.

"There is corruption in Kabul. That is a given, but it affects things here. The international community provides goods and support that is supposed to be delivered to the people via the Kabul government and the Kandahar government. But somewhere between Kabul and the people it gets diverted. The people are now caught between the Taliban and their own government, which is increasingly seen as corrupt. The people are not stupid. You have a phrase: 'cooking the books.' That is what is happening. The army and police numbers are exaggerated, there is not enough training. They are not monitored. The Western training system will not work here."

"Why?"

"In the past we used the military training system to make citizens. Males, who by the way came out of a coeducational system, were conscripted at twenty-two. The soldiers were given basic-needs training, like hygiene. The security forces were not divided by ethnicity. They were not supposed to have allegiance to an ethnic group. The Taliban kept everybody divided. The international community makes the same mistake and should be emphasizing allegiance to the nation. They were taught that they were Afghans, not a collection of tribes. Now the ministries, the ANA, the ANP . . . are all based on tribes. There is a balance of power in the ministries. Who insists on this? It doesn't make sense. When I was growing up in the 1950s and 1960s it was Afghanistan first, tribe second. Where did this tribalism come from?

"You know," he said almost confidentially, "women wore miniskirts here in Kandahar in the 1960s. This burka thing, where did it come from? Anyway, the educational system emphasized an Afghan identity. But now . . . we can't do anything with powder still in our nose and the sound of rockets in our heads. Afghanistan is still a battlefield—the revenge, the tribal violence." He sighed.

"Are we doing the right thing, Canada and the United States?"

"Yes, you freed us from the Taliban. We have to keep working together to solve these other problems. The coalition is happy; it is not selfish. You listen to the people and how to do things in Afghanistan."

At this point I had to attend a briefing, so I arranged another meeting with Yusuf. When we met again, he declared, "We talked about the problems in Kandahar last time; let's talk about solutions. First, government must be in the hands of competent people, not those who are in power because of nepotism and patronage. This mistake was made thirty years ago during the Saur revolution, where power was given to party members and not the people. Now it is the tribal leaders who have power. How do we reduce their power? The DDR process, the DIAG process: these have worked elsewhere, but not in Kandahar or in RC South, especially DIAG. Let us look at the Governor of Helmand." Yusuf offered me a candy. "The ZSU-23 guns have not been taken away from him. He has one thousand armed men who work for him. What is he doing with them? It is not like the north. DDR and HWC are good for heavy weapons but not for the arms he has stockpiled. In Kandahar, Gul Agha initially didn't turn over equipment. Mullah Naqib: same thing. They haven't been 'DIAG'd' because they are being used to fight the enemy. But then there are Ahmad Wali Karzai and Hamid Karzai: they have about a thousand men who are not registered. If we do not have these people registered, they aren't legitimate. If they are not legitimate, they are the moral equivalent of the Taliban."

"So we are back to the problem of the people having to choose between the Taliban, and these guys."

"Yes. The government in Kabul has to tread carefully. It has to change the posts carefully, slowly. Power shift has to be gradual. You have explained to me the 'Chessgame' played by Kabul: exactly! That is the process we need here. Security is better this year than last year, but the norm is fear. The NDS, for example, aren't effective here. Why? I suspect they have become corrupted. There is not enough money. NDS money is being diverted; it is not making it to the 'street' level. We need the NDS to combat subversion. Somebody in Kandahar doesn't want the NDS to be effective. Therefore no money."

Yusuf had put his fingers on a very interesting problem. Was there a possibility that the people would organize and rise up against *both* the Taliban and a corrupt government? Yusuf didn't think the situation had reached that point yet but admitted that it was a possibility. The problem was that the coalition forces would be hit too because they were associated with the government, and the coalition wouldn't be able to distinguish between anticorruption violence and Taliban violence. Yusuf explained that right now there were agitators in the mosques blaming the coalition for all the ills of society. "And you have no one in the mosques to counter this slander," he said.

"OK," I said. "Let me put this all together. We have not one but two fights on our hands. Fight number one is the battle between the Taliban and its ACM supports versus the government and the coalition. Fight number two is the prevention of backlash against the government and the coalition for perceived lack of progress and loss of credibility."

"Yes. We win fight number two by disarming illegally armed groups. We increase the ANA and ANP presence here to establish credibility with the people, which also allows us to work on winning fight number one. It all works together. Then we slowly change who is in power here in the south so that they have allegiance to the government.

"The corruption issue: the tribal focus can blind us, it can contribute to the problem. We need a monitoring system, we need accountability. We must hold people responsible. There must be a means of auditing the provincial government. This doesn't exist today. For example, in Panjwayi, there is a powerful man named Haj Agha Lalai. He takes the benefits of the PRT, but still doctors are killed, clinics and schools in his district are destroyed. Why? The Americans trusted him when they ran the PRT. Why? Who audits Haji Agha Lalai?"

He exhaled. "The provincial government are a bunch of illegitimate donkeys. Let's just buy off the corrupt bastards and put in people who can actually administer the province. But go see for yourself. The government people will flatter you and tell you everything is fine, they have it under control. You must go see for yourself. Go to the districts."

So I did.

east: maruf district patrol

When Andy Bone told me he was going to Maruf, I was excited. The Maruf gig was a long-range patrol that would be conducted over three days in forbidding, enemy-dominated terrain. Maruf was the primary Taliban infiltration point into RC South at this time. Space was made for me on the patrol, which consisted of nine vehicles and about forty people. I awoke early; it was o-dark-thirty, and there was a bit of a chill in the air. I got my kit together and drank a coffee while the CQ smoked away outside the mess tent. There were numerous atmospherics that morning: a sea-can wall, gravel crunching under tan desert boots. Chewing tobacco was spit out into clear empty water bottles or indiscriminately from the cupola of a G-Wagon ("Sorry, Doc!"). Coiled concertina wire on the hoods of the G-Wagons. Gargoyles and ballistic eyewear. A large bald guy going on about "Timmy the Taliban." There was no real tension; it was more "just get on with it." An RCMP officer wearing gray body armor clashing with the arid CADPAT tan of the soldiers from B Company. SAS shemaghs wrapped around throats. The dark copper mountains, with the sun just starting to rise behind them. In the near gloom, a Canadian soldier wearing a black watch cap toque walked up, and I had a flashback to a picture of a Canadian soldier from the Korean War dressed nearly the same way. It was one of those moments where you temporarily move through time and back.

Billy Bolen, the bald guy, used the word "fuck" liberally; he could of course, because he was the Company Sergeant Major and was expected to. He was motivating people toward the front of the column of vehicles that had their engines running. Smiley and a group of Colonel TJ's paramilitaries piled into a Hilux pickup truck. Habib, the terp, was consulting with Matthijs, Niki, and Sanchez. Andy Bone, the patrol commander, was talking with the CQ, confirming that the patrol had enough of what it needed.

I was assigned to a G-Wagon, call sign 21A2. The crew consisted of Master Corporal Keith Porteus, a combat engineer and crew commander; Private Sarah Keller, a medic and our driver; and Private "Dutch" Vandermeulan, a young C9-toting soldier whose "Light Infantry" tattoo on his arm made it clear as to what he did. None were exactly happy with my presence, but what the hell. They didn't know me, I didn't know them, and I could have been the media for all they had been told. Indeed, Keith Porteus had been on one of the patrols that was hit with an IED and didn't like strangers at the best of times asking questions and observing his movements. It's really simple: some people don't want to be judged on their actions by outsiders that, in their view, haven't earned the right to judge. The fact that the soldiers prejudge people defensively is probably a legitimate post-Somalia reflexive action anyway.

I was impressed with Dutch's interest in military history: he was a fan of the Civil War, and he was fascinated by the Arnhem affair in 1944. Sarah and Dutch carried on like brother and sister locked in sibling rivalry, while Keith acted as the older brother of the crew. It had its humorous moments, which are best left unrecorded for privacy reasons, but despite their gruff behavior, I could tell all three were professionals. Sarah explained about the current methods for dealing with traumatically amputated limbs, like the tourniquet the Americans developed so that if your arm was blown off, you put it on yourself with your remaining hand. Slightly built, she had more tattoos than I did. And then there was Keith. He was an unreconstructed Alberta redneck who'd been around. He wanted to blow shit up, not rebuild it. I understood that, given the circumstances. Dutch wanted to engage the enemy and "get some." I understood that too. They did their jobs and did them well, but I found that like a number of guys from Patrol Company, they were completely skeptical about the aid and reconstruction efforts. Some guys resented being put at risk to deliver, as one soldier put it unkindly, "a fat CIMIC guy" into the hinterland to merely talk with the locals. Many of the soldiers wanted to jump in the CH-47s and get "kinetic" on the Taliban's ass, not drive around and do "nonkinetic" stuff. Some even felt deceived: they thought they were coming over here to do what they had done with 3 PPCLI back in 2002. This is a major challenge by leaders in these kinds of environments. Younger soldiers want tangible results, especially when it's *their* hides on the line. The guys were joking about getting Canadian flags tattooed on their lower back "so if we're captured, they'll at least know where we're from."

The Maruf patrol consisted mostly of G-Wagons, some with machine-gun cupolas, some with other equipment, plus a Nyala, Smiley's Hilux, and an ANA Hilux. We learned in the briefing that Maruf was a major transit point for weapons and Taliban infiltrators. This wasn't new; the rugged terrain up there facilitated cross-border movement from Pakistan. The Americans knew that back in 2003 and had conducted a series of raids that uncovered massive weapons caches, with me going along for the ride.

Unlike 2003, however, I would not be taking UH-60s and CH-47s. The PRT patrol would drive from Kandahar City through a contentious district called

Argestan and then into the Maruf district. On the map, it is only one hundred kilometers from the PRT, but it would take nearly a days' worth of driving to get there. "Highway" 627 wasn't paved . . . and then it stopped just outside the district center in Argestan. From there on, it was wadi driving until the remnants of an old road presented itself outside Mohamadazy, which was where we were going. A French SOF forward operating base would function as the patrol base for this operation. The patrol was well planned: there were mission-abort criteria; every possible contingency was covered—"actions on," ambush, separation, mobility kill, IEDs . . . We had fast air on call, the RAF Harriers at KAF, plus AH-64 Apaches if we needed them. The French had assets in the area as well. The CSM, Billy Bolen, appended the briefing: "If the shit hits the fan, step back. We'll do the killing." Oh yeah: intelligence reported that five vehicles of a particular type were now believed to have been modified into suicide IED vehicles, and we could be attacked on our way out of town.

The enemy forces were Taliban and were estimated to number around 150 in the Maruf area. It appeared as though there was a facilitation network in the area that moved men and material, but the French FOB had been hit periodically by Taliban in recent months. Argestan was a separate problem: it was unstable in part because there was a series of blood feuds going on. The Argestan police chief had been assassinated, along with some of his officers. Details were sketchy; the chief's son apparently swore vengeance on whoever did it, but it was not clear. Was it a tribal issue, or did the Taliban do it? Was it both? In any event, we were warned to watch out in Argestan.

The PRT's objectives in Maruf were varied, but essentially they were to assess and possibly expand OGD activity in the district now, and lay the groundwork for expanded coalition operations in the future. These future operations, of course, were kinetic as well as nonkinetic. The main nonkinetic weapons on this patrol were Matthijs and Niki from DFID; Bob Hart from the RCMP; and Sanchez King, who also had some potential projects to support in Maruf. For some reason, we had a British officer from ISAF along for the ride too.

We moved to KAF around 0600 and hooked up with the French SOF liaison. They were mounted in an open jeep that was festooned with scrim and had a comfy chair situated behind the .50-cal machine-gun mount. The bearded French commandos put on their goggles, and we were off down "highway" 627, headed east toward the dusty mountains.

It was a long, slow drive, wadi after wadi after wadi. We moved along a flatter part of the terrain, between two sets of uneven hills, with the higher of the two to the north, or our left, and an equally rugged but stubbier spine to the right. There was ice on what little water there was, but no snow. We drove past two Afghans building a corral out of mud, and it was like going back in time, as if nothing had changed here in hundreds of years, like the G-Wagon had come through some time portal. The builders ignored us, like we were ghosts. The crew was joking about Canadian bureaucracy: every time somebody had a potential medical problem, a CF-98 form had to be filled out. One of the crew wondered if exposure to burning shit particles counted, but another wanted to put down "exposure to an suicide IED" on the form just to see what they would say.

Sitting in the left rear seat, I was keeping an eye out through the increasingly dusty bullet-resistant glass. The sky was blue, no clouds. The hills were various shades of brown below. The remains of houses and compounds broke up the monotony. We watched the ungainly Nyala lumber through the towns; kids gathered in groups and clapped as it made it around corners that looked impossible. People waved. The patrol halted periodically for "health breaks." People didn't just jump off vehicles: the crew would check the ground, dismount, and conduct a drill called "5 and 20s," which amounted to scanning the immediate terrain for ambushers or IEDs, then passengers could dismount and do their business.

In time, we made the Argestan district government compound. Protected by a rusting 23-mm antiaircraft gun, the black and green Afghan flag flew from the wilting pole. We were going to be there for only a limited time, so we ate IMPs (Individual Meal Packs) cold and stretched out. Andy Bone and I had a coffee and got caught up.

We moved off into what Porteus called "dink country": the Maruf-Argestan border area. There were no more friendly waves. The children hid. The tension level increased a little bit. Over the radio, crews reported every possible movement from all quarters. The convoy commander insisted that this be done, but it reached the point where it was overload. I reported "man on hill with a cigarette" in a sarcastic tone from my arc and the crew started mock-reporting completely innocuous things for the next few hours, completely taking the mickey out of the patrol commander. "Brown building on right," "Sheep fucking on ridge," and so on. Like an urban patrol, almost anything could be a threat and alert-fatigue was a real problem.

The chill of the morning now gave way to desert heat. Keller changed the system from heater to air-conditioning, which blew a huge cloud of potentially shit-laced dirt out of the vents. Do I have to submit a CF-98 for that?

It was getting late in the afternoon and the sun was waning. There had been little human contact as we drove through wadis, fording where necessary. One G-Wagon got a flat, which necessitated defensive measures while it was changed.

It was getting dark and there was still no sign of Garang, where the French FOB was located. The hills here looked familiar to me, but I had flown over them from Abu Tow. Then the column stopped. There was babbling on the radio. The French, who were in the lead, were "confused" (i.e., lost). So we sat there, nine vehicles with engines running, in a wadi surrounded with high ground. The decision was made to fire three paraflares so that the French FOB could get a fix on where we were and direct us in. "Yeah, that's the French. Putting the 'special' in special forces!" There were some really pissed off people in the patrol: we're in the Maruf district, enemy territory, the enemy is hiding in the high ground, it is night. We are nowhere near the FOB, and now we're going to fire paraflares, magnesium attached to parachutes that will float down for minutes before extinguishing.

The French jeep then backed up and took off, almost daring the rest of us to follow. It didn't take long before we rolled up to the FOB in the gloom. Night vision is great stuff, and the drivers had shifted over to their helmet-mounted sets. Bounding through the last wadi, we lurched up onto a ridge, and I recognized the fort that the 82nd Airborne raided back in 2003.

The crews were ushered through barbed-wire gates into an outer compound and the vehicles were situated in a laager for all-around defense. The watches were posted, and I joined the OGD reps and Andy Bone in the inner compound, where the French kept their vehicles. It had been an exhausting and mind-numbing day, so almost everybody went to ground. Niki, Matthijs, and I were assigned to a room in the base of the watchtower. The door was covered with a quilt, and inside were three camp beds and a light. I crashed almost immediately.

In the morning I was awakened by a car alarm. It was completely surreal: here we are in the remote mountains six hundred years ago, and a car alarm goes off . . .

I wandered around the FOB. It was very *Beau Geste,* and I expected Gary Cooper to step out from under the mud tower from which a small, frayed tricolor flew next to a 23-mm antiaircraft gun. The Afghan paramilitary waved down at me. It was a very rudimentary place: The shower was in the open and connected to a huge plastic water tank. The shitter was outside the wire in the open between the FOB and enemy-controlled hills. It was a burn pit surrounded with hessian; you had to tell the tower sentry you were going out there or you could be shot as an infiltrator on the way back. At night, they used thermal imagery to keep an eye on whoever was doing their business. I felt sorry for Niki.

The FOB eating room had two guys in it: "Jean-Claude," the FOB commander, and "Henri," his ops guy. They were up early planning a mission. Instead of clearing out, Jean–Claude offered me a coffee.

"So, are you one of us?" he asked gesturing to the beard and civilian clothes.

"Oh no, I'm a historian and I teach War Studies at the Royal Military College of Canada," I explained.

"Do you teach the Algerian war?" Henri inquired.

"*Certainement!*" I exclaimed, and we launched on a discussion of what worked and what didn't back then, how it was applicable now and so on.

"So who are you guys? CPA? First RPIMa?" I named off a bunch of other French SOF units.

"We are mostly 1st RPIMa here," Jean-Claude said with some pride. "You have heard of us?"

"*Absolutemant!*" Although I didn't respect French government policy, I respected France's special operations soldiers. The 1st Regiment Parachutiste d'Infanterie de Marine, or 1st RPIMa, is based in Bayonne, France. It was established in 1962 and is the direct descendent of the first French special operations units set up during World War II to work with the SAS and the SOE (Britain's Special Operations Executive). The 1st RPIMa has taken part in literally every French military operation since then, including every intervention in former French West Africa, to the first Gulf War, the Balkans, and even Rwanda. The smallest grouping is the RAPAS (Recherche et Actions Spéciales) squad of ten men, which is capable of direct action and intelligence collection, but the 1st RPIMa is about the size of a battalion that has all of the usual SOF capabilities.

I was interested in how the French SOF and the PRT got along. Jean-Claude and Henri explained about the transit and weapons cache problems. The FOB's job was to interdict movement when it could, hunt out the weapons caches, and provide a presence in the area. This was a hefty task for a thirty-man FOB, even with the assistance of Afghan paramilitaries. Jean-Claude understood that the support of the people in the Maruf district was critical to the coalition effort here, but, as he explained, they were in three camps: pro-government, pro-Taliban, and the largest bunch was in between. The 1st RPIMa operators also knew that they could be manipulated, if they weren't careful, into acting as proxies in some intertribal conflict. Jean-Claude explained that when they first got on the ground, they were tempted to take an "us versus them" view with the local government and police: French SOF plus government versus the Taliban and its supporters. Henri explained that they backed off and took what he called a "helicopter" view: they stood above it all for a while and saw what was *really* going on first before conducting ops. They were pressured by the higher-ups in the SOF command to "get on with it" but resisted until they could figure out what the game was— and they learned that the police were corrupt or scared to do their job or both. The insurgents had got to the families of some of the police, for example. The population that was in the middle refused to take sides because it was unclear which side would prevail in the Maruf Valley, and they didn't want to side with the loser. Indeed, the government officials in Maruf would appease the Taliban infiltrators because they had no security. Their police were ineffective, the ANA was not present, and this left the foreigners of the SOF. The SOF, however, were not structured or equipped for policing.

It was almost circular. The SOF could not track down and eliminate the Taliban without the population's help; they needed targeting information from the locals since satellites can't see into underground cisterns. The locals would not provide it because they were not secure from the Taliban and feared retaliation. The government couldn't project its authority to protect the people and pressured the SOF to "do something." The enemy from the facilitation network was sortieing out of the hills and coercing the locals in outlying villages that had had a good harvest last year into providing food for them. Transiting Taliban, coming across in groups of about fifty at a time, were terrorizing villages, but gave the FOB a wide berth. The 1st RPIMa could not be everywhere.

Jean-Claude and Henri's solution was a series of incremental projects, done in stages, to gain the trust of the people in the Maruf district. Starting with the area near the FOB, they would try to expand this circle of trust outward until it could reach the outlying villages. They had started a few small projects with the little resources they had, but SOF are not structured for development: their job is to kill. They needed help. They knew the PRT was in the business of nonkinetic attacks and sought a relationship. In anticipation that the PRT would send out a patrol eventually, Henri had put together an appreciation of what he thought would facilitate relationship building in Maruf.

Henri was concerned, however, that indiscriminate development aid dumped into the valley would paradoxically assist the insurgency or be siphoned off by corrupt officials trying to appease the enemy. It therefore had to be controlled and coordinated. At the same time, the reticent local government leadership, which was wavering, could not be isolated from the equation. There had to be buy-in. Jean-Claude and Henri figured that the incremental approach could be leveraged: if the police became more and more motivated by the government leadership, then more aid would be brought in, and so on. There had to be linkage between projects and security. It would be incremental. As Jean-Claude put it, "Westerners are always in a hurry!"

The 1st RPIMa guys wanted to start with medical assistance. Insurgents had burned out a couple of clinics, and they wanted to confront the enemy psychologically on that plane: "The enemy is burning your clinics because he doesn't want you to be healthy. We want you to be healthy." This would lay the ground for other, larger projects. It would act as a stepping-stone. Restoring the clinics would bring a lot of credibility.

But then what? One of the problems the 1st RPIMa noted was that part of the valley was cut off from the other part by a deep wadi. This limited trade between the portions. They reckoned that a small footbridge would facilitate connections between the two sides and increase trade. The government building was inaccessible to a portion of the population; this physical separation produced a psychological separation too.

The medical program and the bridge were the first incremental steps. The 1st RPIMa wanted to consult with the PRT to see what could be done beyond that.

"How does the enemy deal with the FOB?" I asked.

"They see us as an increasing problem. They know why we are here and what we're doing. We have been attacked four times in the past month alone. They use rockets and mortars against the FOB: no head-on assaults or anything like that. The rockets hit the FOB once, but we were able to call in air support and that team was killed. The mortars came from up there." Jean-Claude gestured at the hills in the distance. "They fired at us at night. We used the thermal-imagery equipment to locate them, and then hit them with our own mortar and the 23 mm up in the tower. There were no survivors. Since then it has been rather quiet." He smiled.

Niki was up and we had breakfast. Niki was new at "armed development" and had come in partway through the conversation, so I sketched out what I call my "Niki-gram." Development is represented by a circle; it overlaps with another circle that represents the rule of law and the police. The three smaller circles are the threats to development: essentially the enemy forces. I drew a semicircle between the enemy and the joined circles. This is where OEF and other coalition security forces come in: they shield the development and security process while it is being improved. Development and security cannot be separated in this environment.

Matthijs knew this. He had been working independently on the Maruf problem, in parallel with the French SOF, but now the strands came together. Jean-Claude set up a meeting with the chief of the district. He was a dark-complexioned man who wore a brown and gold skullcap. He also disconcertingly wore jihadi tattoos on his hands. This didn't necessarily mean he was an ACM sympathizer; it could mean that he fought against the Soviets in the past. He thanked us for coming, adding that "since the government in Kabul and Kandahar can't or won't help us, we are glad you are here." It was evident that the French SOF and the PRT had more "street cred" here than the government of Afghanistan. What did he see as the main problem in Maruf? Habib translated: "Security first, then all else will come." Niki looked at me and smiled. The chief explained the complications in dealing with the local population in that there were several *shura* he had to contend with. He wanted to get a "conflict resolution committee" together and bring in all players from all the shura, but he needed something to convince all that they were stakeholders.

Matthijs had the answer. He had had the answer in waiting. The common thing that brought the people together was water. Everybody needed it; it was the basic necessity. And not everybody had it. Matthijs' analysis of Maruf told us a lot. First, the enemy was in fact geographically confined to one area in the hills. The transiting Taliban were a problem but didn't hold ground. The FOB was at the center of the district, and the enemy tended to operate around it as opposed to in it, save for foraging and raids. The "uncommitted" villages tended to be the ones farthest away from the center. Matthijs thought that instead of dropping in four or five large water projects all at once, the effort should be on four series of small water projects. These would be applied incrementally, in keeping with the French SOF's recommendation. This was all good in theory, but Matthijs knew implementation would be a problem.

If workers showed up in the outlying areas to do a big water project, they would attract enemy attention and probably would be attacked, thus forcing the deployment of scarce security resources to that area, where they would be pinned down doing presence operations. It was better to have small local projects: quick in and out. The locals knew what to do with the water; they just needed improved access. I assumed that this could work concurrently with the French SOF idea of medical support or independently from it. Matthijs was concerned that an overt security presence would attract terrorist tactics to scare the locals. He referred to these small projects as "covert development aid": aid would be "infiltrated" and then the government could build trust with the locals before moving on to other stages of development and security.

To get around the problem of providing aid that the enemy could profit from, Matthijs proposed, based on his voting data, that areas of the district that were pro-Karzai in the last election but were at threat on the periphery of the district get the aid first. Not coincidentally, there was a band of villages along the Pakistan border that were pro-Karzai but too far away from the FOB and the government center to tap into resources there (the mountains were part of this problem, as was the lack of roads). Then, Matthijs reasoned, the more uncommitted bands of villages to the north of Maruf and even within the enemy-influenced mountains could see the synergy between water, aid, and security. In addition, there were areas along the border that were depopulated because of the lack of water. Crops could be grown, but there were no people left. Encouraging people to return to these areas would give the government a presence on the border and complicate the enemy's cross-border infiltration.

I would add, from a military perspective, that the more goodwill is built up, the more the locals feel like assisting the security forces. Information would come in like a flood (we saw this in Kosovo) and, when properly filtered, would allow the kinetic use of special operations. In time, the complex of nonkinetic operations protected by the special operations forces would allow greater capacity to be built by local authorities, which would afford better local security, which would result in better information on the enemy, which would lead to better conditions for the people, who would presumably shift their allegiance to the government. In theory. It all had to be explained to the people. And that meant that information operations had to be conducted in the Maruf district to explain what was going on, yet another future project.

We decided to test the theory in a cluster of villages south of the Maruf district center. The patrol drove to Sepalzai, where the French explained that the local people were trying to get irrigation for their crops but lacked the resources. This village was built on a slight hill and consisted of terraced field areas interspersed with a near-pyramid hill as a backdrop. The wadi leading to it had growth in it, indicating that water was present. The vehicles laagered, and solar and hand-cranked radios were given away to the locals who wanted them. The patrol adopted a staged approach: we were nine vehicles, then five held back so we were four, then we were to go on foot after contact. We waited in this flat area; Matthijs though it was better if we waited for the village leadership to come and greet us rather than barging in. A French jeep took up a position opposite the Nyala, and the gunner scanned the horizon.

In time, a cluster of old men carrying staffs arrived, surrounded by what seemed to be about twenty young people. Silver, white, and beige turbans were present, and the men were immediately struck by the presence of Niki, and, when they noticed, our two female medics. After the preliminaries Matthijs, who spoke Pashto fluently and didn't need terps, secured an invite for tea. Andy Bone, Matthijs, Sanchez, Niki, Bob Hart, a French SOF operator, and I proceeded through the winter tree trunks, up a slightly winding path, while the people came out and looked at us.

"*Salaam Alaikum!*" we said, with our right hands over our hearts.

"*Wa Alaikum Salaam!*" the surprised people responded.

We were ushered into a home. From the outside it looked like it belonged on the Tatooine set of a *Star Wars* movie. Inside the main room, which was about ten by twenty feet, there was a window high up on the wall; there were several carpets on the floor (clean carpets) and pillows and cushions, and even wall hangings, which were essentially carpets too. There was an older gent squatting on the carpet; he had a staff, a skullcap, and an extended goatee. Another elder with a gray turban and a long gray beard rocked back and forth gently.

Matthijs ascertained that the village usually had fifty-five families in it, but now there were only thirty-five; the rest had left because of the drought and were dispersed, some working elsewhere. We were joined by three more elders and about five younger men, who were more or less curious observers and gofers for the village leadership. In rapid succession, after much tea, we determined that the main problems here were the lack of a road to the Maruf district building; the lack of a clinic and a school; and the critical need for a dam so the people could get their crops going. They could grow almonds, corn, and wheat; if the water situation was improved, and the road situation was improved, they could be back in production and get the stuff to markets. No water, no crops.

We were making good progress when a disabled guy interrupted and explained his plight. He was a stonecutter who had been seriously injured, and there was nothing resembling disability assistance in this society. He monopolized the situation for some time. The elders clearly were interested in how we would respond to this unanticipated situation and offered no help (i.e., kick the guy out of the meeting). His tale of woe was punctuated with a suicidal plea: he wanted somebody with an AK-47 to put him out of his misery, he said.

We made all manner of sideways glances at each other. It was one of those off-the-wall situations that the U.S. Special Forces encounter on their Q Course.

Matthijs expressed sympathy and gently explained that we were there to help the village as a whole, that our projects were there to benefit everybody generally and we didn't have the resources to deal with this particular case. The man backed off; he'd made his pitch. The elders then diplomatically noted the time and that they had to pray, but please stay for more tea, friends! We want to talk some more.

When the elders returned, it was back to business. As Matthijs and Sanchez were trying to extract more details, I glanced over at the growing number of elders: some men who had been away in the fields heard we were here and dropped in. I remember, very clearly, this one older guy. He was sitting with his legs drawn up, holding on to his staff. One eye had been damaged in a previous war. He had blue robes and a grayish-blue turban. He gave me a half-smile and a wink, letting me know that he knew this game well. I grinned back and he nodded.

The village leadership was asked to compare 2003 with 2005: was it any better? Well, the water situation was a bit better because of melting snow, but the conversation kept coming back to the dam. Then we struck a nerve. Bob Hart asked them about crime. The elders all looked impassively and moved on to another topic. We kept trying to steer the conversation back to security, but it wasn't happening. At a break, I asked Matthijs what was up.

"Well, they don't want to publicly humiliate us."

"How so?"

"They think we're stupid because we don't know about the security situation, but they're too polite to go into details."

We were able to get an entrée when Sanchez asked about the adequacy of the roads. Was travel easier or harder than in the past? Then the elders let slip that there were "thieves" and people were afraid to use the roads. We initially assumed they meant in Argestan, but this was incorrect. They meant in Maruf. It was like pulling hen's teeth. They told us there was no robbery on the roads two years ago, but now there was. Men with guns were shaking people down.

Was it the Taliban passing through? No. Was it the Taliban in the hills near Maruf? No. French SOF? No.

Then we had a collective "aha!" experience. It was the local *police* who were doing the shakedown. The villagers didn't want to insult us because they thought that *we* put the police in place and supported them, we approved of what they were doing! This led to a whole conversation whereby we were able to unravel who was who in the zoo, who controlled the police and so on. It turns out that Bob Hart had met with the police chief the day before at the FOB, and that the chief was part of the problem.

Matthijs adamantly explained that we had nothing to do with the police, and neither did the FOB. What about the Taliban? What did they do? The elders explained that there was no Taliban south of Garang, that *they* took care of the Taliban on their own in the past and were left alone by them. It appeared as if the village could defend itself, but could not project power to secure the road.

Matthijs was winding things up. The gent who was looking at me then asked Matthijs who I was. Matthijs explained what I was doing and wondered if I could ask the elders some questions about the Soviet occupation period.

The older men in the room just lit up like lightbulbs and became animated, talking among themselves. The boss said it was OK, so I asked them what the village had done back then. Had the Soviets come here?

They told me, tripping over each other to fill me in on the details. The Soviets had two headquarters, one in Abu Khalid and another in Hogari. The Soviets never had anything like the PRT or rural development programs at all here. The villages that blocked Soviet maneuvers were destroyed, their people dispersed. There had been many, many engagements in the area. The local men formed a mujahideen unit and rotated through the fields; some fought, others handled the crops. Every so often, the men told me, they would set up a roadblock on the road to Argestan and then ambush Soviet armor.

"Where did you operate from?" I asked and sketched out the area.

"From the same hills the Taliban are holed up in now" was the answer. "We used RPGs and 107-mm rockets against them at the roadblocks from the hills. Then we would fade away and disperse. Those Taliban: they just aren't as good as *we* were!" A forest of heads nodded in agreement.

"So why don't you take care of the Taliban yourselves?" I challenged.

There was much laughter. Then the older man who smiled and winked at me earlier spoke.

"I was the commander in those days. I was a young man. I am now an old man. It is somebody else's turn now, but our young men are no longer here because of the wars and the drought and I'm too damn tired!"

That is how we ended the meeting: it was on a positive note. It is not some cheap cliché to suggest that there was a definite spirit of goodwill established.

We returned to the FOB for the night; it was cold and clear in the mountains. The French, naturally, had wine. And brandy. And coffee. At some point in the evening, information came in that identified where some of the Taliban arms caches in the valley were located. Jean-Claude and Henri assembled a plan to raid them early the next morning before they could be moved or otherwise dispersed. The 1st RPIMa had a number of armed jeeps that looked like they belonged to David Stirling's SAS in the Western Desert: each had two machine guns mounted on them and the symbol from *The Punisher* comic book spray-painted on the hood. A larger, long-bedded Unimog-like truck with an automatic grenade launcher mounted in the rear was part of the collection of *Mad Max*–like vehicles: this was called a VLRA, or light reconnaissance and support vehicle. The 1st RPIMa were bombing up throughout the night. When I awoke in the morning, the compound was clear of French vehicles. They were on a job.

Unfortunately, we had to cut the Maruf patrol short. Matthijs wanted to move to the villages he had identified in the border regions to assess them, but we learned from the French SOF and the locals that roads were nonexistent. It would tax the patrol mechanically to get to the villages the estimate was that it would take fifteen hours. And they were right on the border, which posed security problems. The difficulty in extraction of casualties taken in there with no roads and limited air support finally weighed against it. Matthijs would have to wait for another opportunity.

Our return route to Kandahar City took us through some spectacular territory. Using the principle that you don't take the route out that you took in, the patrol commander had plotted a route that went south of the parallel hills and into the desert. There was more wadi driving, then desert driving, through the tufts of scrub grass that poked up through the soil. We motored along the flat parts in the wide valley, with copper-colored hill ranges in the distance. It took hours and hours. There was little habitation at first, but as we approached the Spin Boldak–Kandahar highway from the east, there were more and more people: nomads with camels; village compounds near water sources; shepherds. There was still the occasional depopulated area with war damage at some crossroads. We looked for the Sarlacc, but it was more and more Sergio Leone territory.

The patrol laagered, the shemagh-muffled gunners observed their arcs, while the orange aerial-recognition panels flapping in the dry wind on the roofs of the G-Wagons. A herd of hairy black camels went by. It must have been like this with the Long Range Desert Group in 1941.

Upon gaining the road, the patrol motored, freed from the grip of wadis and dust. Within an hour we were passing the gates of KAF, which now boasted a freshly painted MiG-21 gate guardian. The "gap" between "No Drug" mountain (so-named because white-painted rocks spelled it out, like Kandahar's equivalent to "Tito Woods" in Bosnia) and the range north of KAF now spilled out into a series of car dealerships, microwave antenna towers, and a new bridge. In 2003 there had been nothing there except an AMF checkpoint. Now there was massive construction, things that would have been unheard of three years ago. Into IED alley: everybody was on guard, even at the end of a tiring patrol. And in no time we were back at the PRT. Just in time for Stephane's prime rib . . .

anton and the kuchi: the reg district

I encountered "Anton the Dutchman" when he came to the PRT to solicit resources for an NGO project in Registan (sometimes just called "Reg"), a desert district west of Spin Boldak bordering Pakistan. I knew from my studies that Registan was dominated by the Kuchi tribe and was considered high risk because of border smuggling. It was also suffering from a long-lasting drought. Anton was fairly strident and abusive: he called all of us at the PRT "naive" and hated Donald Rumsfeld almost personally. I was quite prepared to write him off as an antimilitary, anti-American asshole, *but* . . . two Dutch CIMIC officers arrived in a six-wheeled Patria APC, and he was going to "pitch" them on supporting initiatives in Registan. I decided to watch and learn.

Despite the fact that Anton was overbearing and kept insisting to the Dutch officers that the planned Dutch commitment to the Oruzgan province PRT would be a "second Srebrenica," his insight into Registan was revealing of the complexities that the PRT and the coalition forces in general had to deal with. Especially since water was the key . . .

In Registan the Kuchi tribe is more or less nomadic, and land and water rights tend to be problematic. There are customary "user rights" to wells, passed down on calfskin that have seals from pre-1900s' Baluch and Pashtun kings. These have been photographed and reproduced and function as a "claim."

Well-meaning NGOs, including organs of UNAMA, arrived in Registan to drill wells in the populated areas. The local subtribes or families would tell the drillers, who were Pakistani and subcontracted by the NGOs and who didn't know better, to "drill here," and then they would take control over that particular well and restrict its use. Or the driller would argue that *he* owned the well. This completely threw off the accepted methods by which the Reg residents accessed water. Before, local people dug their own wells. Now, ambitious people, both from Afghanistan and Pakistan, were using the international community to increase their power and prestige at the expense of the traditional system. This situation now became a source of conflict between the tribes in Registan. Violence between subtribes was easily mistaken for Taliban activity.

To make matters worse, the UN decided to "improve" the native wells and brought in trucks loaded with concrete components to be embedded in the ground. This project was a complete failure, and consequently the desert was littered with concrete decaying in the hot sun and had few operational UN-built wells. The Kuchi preferred their own system of digging, which involved lining their wells with wood. They employed their time-honored method of using quicklime and water to produce oxygen in order not to suffocate their digging crews. In time, many of the UN-built wells broke down or dried up. This led to credibility problems with the locals, especially when the Pakistani drillers weren't interested in maintaining the equipment.

Anton then explained the "sheep game." To enhance the survivability of sheep in Registan, a decision was made to initiate a vaccination program and to bring in new sheep to spread out the herds. Rams were imported for procreation purposes and to increase the numbers. But there were not enough rams to go around and only some groups got them; this affected the sheep "balance of power" between the tribal groups, which in turn generated violent friction.

The camel program also ran into problems. Camels are used in Registan to remove water from the wells using a variety of ingenuous methods. Local camel owners lent Anton camels for this purpose and then engaged in a "rent-a-camel" monopoly scheme to rip off the international community. So Anton bought his *own* camels and assigned them to the wells. Anton is now a marked man in Registan.

People ask, "Where *is* that foreigner?" Violence directed against the international community in Registan is driven as much by those who don't want change as it is by the Taliban, who are seeking to stir up trouble.

The Kutchie, who navigate without maps, say the drought started when Pakistan started making "big bangs in the desert." Anton believed that Pakistan was interested in the possibility that cobalt may lie under the desert sands. Suspicion of outsiders was acute, and Anton believed that a military presence would turn off the Kuchi; it would be better to use intermediaries to deal with the Baluchis as well.

"Why, exactly, is this district so important?" I asked. Anton explained that Registan boasted between 2 and 4 million sheep and therefore constituted or could constitute a major portion of the food supply, which spun off benefits for the Afghan national economy as a whole. He told me that Registan had in fact been deliberately depopulated by the Taliban during the drought, that the Taliban used trucks and helicopters to evacuate the survivors. The roots of those people remain in the sands and mountains of Registan and that is why there is gradual repopulation. Full repopulation will require water, and water will facilitate sheepherding. The locals, he said, already know where the water is. The last trip he was on, he noticed that people were planting trees; he believed it was a sign that people wanted to stay.

As I finished up with Anton and the Dutch CIMIC guys in the mess, the large weight-lifting soldier held the door open for me.

"Thanks."

"Roger, confirmed," he said.

IED after IED: the war continues

By the grace of God the Almighty I have brought happiness to Muslims in the Islamic world.

—Osama bin Laden

It was a Sunday, a "make your own omelets" day in the mess: I told the cook this was our opportunity to see how important *they* were. He laughed and explained that he liked to have his staff get at least one morning off. A local guy then walked in with "foot bread," big, flat, spongy Afghan loaves slung over the shoulder. The Canadian cooks wanted to learn from their locally employed cooks how to make Afghan bread. Indeed, the mess had an Afghan night during which various types of Afghan food were available for consumption. I talked to the Afghan cooks about how things were with their families in Kandahar. They told me that a lot of Afghans were coming back from camps in Pakistan, heavily influenced by

Pakistani culture: Pakistani movies and videos, music, and even architecture. The Chinese and Japanese construction engineers were also having an influence on local architecture, and the influx of skilled workers from Pakistan was also having an effect. I asked the cooks if there was any animosity. On previous journeys to Afghanistan, and particularly in Kabul, I noticed a distinct Indian cultural influence. I was told that there were growing problems with more-traditional Afghans, specifically the Mullahs, who viewed these things coming from Pakistan as morally threatening.

The workers pointed to a possible split between the older, Mullah-influenced people and the younger, Pakistani-influenced people. Already there were rampant anti-Pakistan conspiracy theories: everything was Pakistan's fault, Pakistan created the Taliban, and so on. Since the Taliban continued to operate from Pakistan, it really wasn't a theory. The firm belief that Pakistan continued to meddle in internal Afghan affairs really bothered a lot of people. Then there was "ISI panic": Afghans constantly wondered who was in the pay of Inter-Services Intelligence, the Pakistani secret service. It became a running joke in Kandahari society, like "spot the spook" games played by journos. Indeed, some PRT staff had been let go because they were suspected of working for the ISI, apparently.

My friends told me that Gul Agha Sherzai had been a popular and respected Governor, that he was missed. They liked the fact that he had a plan and that he provided security. Reconstruction was actually initiated by Gul Agha and not the PRT, they reminded me. When Gul Agha was replaced with Mullah Nakibullah, Gul Agha's people staged what was called a "Ghost Coup" to stay in power. Nakibullah was replaced with Engineer Yusuf Pashtun, who understood the development plan and was educated. He was made Minister for Housing, and Gul Agha Sherzai was brought back in because Karzai needed a strong guy in Kandahar for the presidential elections. In July 2005, Asadullah Khalid became governor: he had been governor in Ghazni and had a strong security-oriented agenda. He was young and had no tribal links, and both worked against him. The PRT had to navigate through this labyrinthine series of connections.

I was reassessing my research plan and realized I had a gap that could be filled only by getting a certain briefing on Monday, so I went over to the Tactical Operations Centre (TOC) to coordinate with the ops staff. When I got to the inner sanctum, Sergeant Reid and a duty signaler were hovering over the stacked radio sets in the corner of the room. Other TOC staff members were standing by. I moved to a corner of the room to observe.

"What's happening?" I asked Sanchez, who was milling about too.

"An American patrol from the 82nd has just come under attack in the city."

Sergeant Reid was communicating with the 82nd Airborne patrol, trying to get its location, in preparation to sending out the QRF to help.

"It's an IED strike, not a full-blown ambush."

There was another transmission. In military vehicles, there is the vehicle-to-vehicle communications system, and then there is the "i/c," or internal vehicle intercom system, for the crew to talk to each other. The vehicle crew commanders have a switch to move back and forth between the various nets. The American crew commander was transmitting on the net, but thought he was on the i/c. You have to imagine the scene: a jihadi has just detonated himself all over your vehicle; you are unharmed. You are very, very angry . . .

"Is that all you've got, you *fucker*? Is that all you've *got*, motherfucker?" came over the net. Uneasy laughter in the TOC. It was like watching the movie *Pulp Fiction*: it was violent and grisly. *Should* we be laughing?

The American patrol recovered to the PRT; their vehicles were operational. Two uparmored Hummers pulled up and their crews disembarked and started to remove their body armor, which had small chunks of burned flesh splatted all over. The Hummers moved over to the wash rack, and the crews started pressure hosing the remains of the jihadi off the first vehicles. I could see burned chunks all over the hood and gun shield. The American sergeant was pouring water over his head and shaking it off.

"That fucker! *Fuck him!* That's six times, man. Six! *Fuck him!*"

The crews were happy to be alive. In this case, a jihadi using a wheelbarrow or cart that had a large-caliber artillery shell concealed in it had done the deed. Unfortunately for the jihadi, all he succeeded in doing was blowing out the left headlight on the lead Hummer! There was no other damage to the vehicles. Just a blown-out headlight. This man, this Al Qaeda operative, a man who had trained and prayed for the opportunity to kill infidels, killed himself for a Hummer headlight and a few laundry bills. Hell, it was hilarious! It was ludicrous! It was just insane!

I stopped at the mess for a coffee. The large weight-lifting soldier was standing at the dessert counter. He gave me a conspiratorial look.

"Did you know that if you eat bananas before sleeping, the potassium in them gives you fucked-up dreams?'

"Well, uh, no, I didn't . . . "

"Roger, confirmed."

ghorak attack

They revel in stratagems and artifice. They prowl about waiting for their opportunity to pounce down upon small parties moving without due precaution. The straggler and camp follower are their natural prey. They hover on the flanks of the column, fearing to strike but ready to cut off detachments which have gone astray.

—C. E. CALLWELL, *SMALL WARS* (1906)

The dangerous nature of PRT work was driven home on 12 December when Sergeant Jamie Bradley's patrol was attacked with an IED while escorting Phoenix to Ghorak district, a remote rural district to the northwest of Kandahar City. In this attack, a G-Wagon was completely destroyed and two soldiers seriously wounded. It is always interesting to see an incident from many vantage points: I observed the PRT Tactical Operations Centre's reaction to the attack and later discussed the incident with Sergeant Bradley. Taken together, both accounts demonstrate the many layers of complexity that exist in any such incident. Indeed, there were strategic and political ramifications that would generally not be seen by the people on the receiving end, and, at the same time, the emotional milieu of soldiers in contact becomes filtered over the radio.

Phoenix asked me if I wanted to go to Ghorak district with her. She was dealing with a sensitive matter there. A USAID-funded school had been burned, but it wasn't simply a straightforward matter of Taliban arson. There were, it transpired, two separate schools and two separate incidents. The first school had a teacher who received a night letter threatening to kill him. It turned out that a student sent the letter because, he alleged, the teacher beat him. The local police established a guard. To complicate matters, there had been a real night letter a couple of months before. Ghorak was another district that did not boast a coalition presence, so developing an understanding of what was going on there was important.

Phoenix was also dealing with the armed occupation of another school by what were thought to be criminal elements, but the local police would not forcibly remove them. It was unclear why. Even the Deputy Governor lacked the pull to get resources in there to deal with the situation. Phoenix threatened to bring in military force if these men were not removed, and the issue became one of face. I was set to go, but that Monday was the only day I could get a particular briefing from CTF BAYONET at KAF and it had taken forever to set it up, so I declined at the last minute.

"Are you sure you don't want to go? It'll be exciting, I promise! They're probably going to try and kill me this trip." We had a good laugh. Instead, a British reporter took my place on the patrol.

I was trying to use the camp Internet connection to see what was going on back in Canada when it was suddenly shut down. A communications lockdown takes place whenever there is an incident in progress, so I made my way to the

Tactical Operations Centre that morning. At 1058 hours the first report of an IED attack against the patrol came in: there were two Pri 1 (serious, needing evacuation) and two Pri 2 (wounded, but not seriously) casualties. Initially it was reported that my friend Lieutenant Andy Bone, the patrol leader, was one of the Pri 1 casualties. An aerial QRF consisting of American AH-64 Apaches lifted off from KAF, but the ground QRF from Camp Nathan Smith would take time: Ghorak was mountainous and remote. A subsequent report came back that the patrol bagged the "button man," the guy who set up and detonated the IED. There was a lot of discussion about recovering the G-Wagon; the carcass could not be left behind, as it would provide the enemy information and an I/O victory if they could photograph it. Discussions in the TOC revolved around getting an American CH-47 Chinook in to lift it out, but the U.S. EOD unit, TF IED DEFEAT, also had to get in to investigate the site so the brigade headquarters could gain intelligence on the nature of the IED itself. To further complicate matters, there was enemy communications "chatter" in the vicinity of the site, which meant that a secondary attack or ambush could be in the offing against recovery forces.

Sergeant Reid and the TOC staff were very, very professional: there was no panic, nobody was freaking out. I stood out of the way and watched events unfold. An update told us there were three wounded soldiers and a wounded civilian. Did they finally get Phoenix? And who were the wounded guys? The PRT is a small unit; everybody knows everybody. There was a level of unspoken anxiety in the room.

The ops officer, Captain Bob Ritchie, came in. A significant incident report went to National Defence HQ in Ottawa immediately after the attack was reported. They were calling the PRT back. The first thing Ottawa wanted to know wasn't the state of the casualties, or what was being done about them: it was the state of the detainees! The PRT was instructed to contact the patrol, which was still in contact with the enemy, and tell it to make sure that the Geneva Convention was applied. Ottawa wanted confirmation. There were, shall we say, a number of shocked people in the TOC.

There was a debate over the feasibility of slinging the destroyed G-Wagon under a CH-47: this was a sidebar to the other things that were going on, but it affected who would go with the bird, whether the bird would stop at the PRT first, and so on. A UH-60 medevac chopper was now arriving on the scene, but there wasn't enough room for the casualties, so the Pri 1s went first. Then there were reports of a secondary device: TF STORM wouldn't allow its CH-47s to go in until the site was cleared, but the TF IED DEFEAT EOD guys were on the CH-47 . . . A landing zone was declared cleared and the helicopters went in.

The detainees were seen running away from the scene, specifically the trigger point. Two were on a motorcycle, and another was on foot. The patrol had them in custody. The ops officer instructed the patrol not to turn them over to the Afghan police; they should be put on the CH-47 when it arrived and brought back to KAF for interrogation. This is when things started to go haywire. When the CH-47 got to the attack site, the crew from TF STORM refused to take the detainees on board, claiming that they couldn't transport prisoners not taken by American forces. It wasn't clear why, but it most likely had something to do with sensitivity to the Abu Ghraib MP "fraternity prank" and accusations by left-wing human rights critics who were screaming themselves red in the face about the so-called secret CIA torture program.

Simultaneously, Ottawa called the TOC and instructed the PRT not to turn the detainees over to the Americans because, apparently, the sensitive souls in Foreign Affairs didn't want Canada to be accused of being complicit in a KAF version of Abu Ghraib.

It was astounding to see the PRT being forced to expend all this energy to cater to the legalistic bureaucratic mind-set in Ottawa. Nobody in the Ottawa bureaucracy seemed, at the time, to give a shit about our four casualties; the welfare of the detainees seemed to have absolute priority over the welfare of Canadians in the minds and actions of the bureaucrats, if the volume of message traffic was measured and compared. When I went outside the TOC for a break, I saw a couple of NCOs who were beside themselves with rage, with nowhere to vent it. If one of those lawyers or bureaucrats from Ottawa had actually been there, I am convinced he or she would have been physically harmed.

The discussion then revolved around the possibility of using the ground QRF to extract the detainees, but there was no PRT holding facility at Nathan Smith, nor was there a Canadian facility at KAF. Could the detainees be turned over to the coalition special operations people at Ghekho instead? Then the legal adviser (the Canadian version of a JAG officer) got involved: did the detainees commit a hostile act or did they behave with hostile intent? This might determine what to do with them. The situation reached the point where, apparently, the Deputy Chief of the Defence Staff in Ottawa was roused from his bed.

Finally there was a decision from Ottawa: turn the detainees over to the Afghan National Police so that they would not be abused by the Americans.

There is a God after all.

Everybody had a good, ironic, laugh. "They want it, they got it!" one of the TOC personnel gleefully said.

A ground QRF with EOD capability had been launched to a staging place south of the attack site. But now Ottawa, TF AFGHANISTAN, and the PRT had to deal with three issues at once: how to explain all this to the media, how to explain this to the next-of-kin before explaining it to the media, and the detainee issue. There was a deadly synergy here for the bureaucrats: all three had the *potential* to cause political problems and therefore threaten somebody's perceived relative power in Ottawa. It was this potential, as opposed to the actual, that forced the PRT to expend energy and resources to serve Ottawa's political needs, while at the same time the PRT had to deal with the situation on the ground. The real message that should have been conveyed was that this was war, this is a consequence of war, and we are taking the appropriate steps to deal with the incident. I'll explain it later, but the apparent need to feed the media started to loom larger and larger.

Then Ottawa wanted evidence against the detainees. They wanted the motorcycle tested for bomb residue, so now the issue became how the patrol was supposed to get the motorcycle back to Kandahar City. The helicopter crews refused to take it, and it wouldn't fit on a G-Wagon.

"Get Wadleigh. He's with the QRF, he's a biker: he can ride it out" was one suggestion. The prospect of Corporal Wadleigh, with his HD tattoo on his neck, in arid CADPAT with a C7 slung over his back, riding a Honda motorcycle from Ghorak to Kandahar was beyond hilarious. Come to think of it, portions of *Easy Rider* could have been filmed in Ghorak, the terrain was so similar. The rednecks in Ghorak, however, had AKs, not shotguns.

Sergeant Jamie Bradley later explained to me what happened on the Ghorak patrol.

"We had five military vehicles, four G-Wagons and a Nyala, plus a pickup truck with Colonel TJ's guys in it. There were a lot of problems with the terrain: wadis, ravines, lots of rocks, outcroppings. The trail itself, I didn't think even a tractor could get down it. When we got through the village of Shina, it leveled out and was more like desert and flat.

"We never intended to stop in the village itself, but we lost some equipment which was torn off our vehicles by low-hanging trees. We took about five minutes to sort that out and got on our way again. We got some dirty looks from the locals. I was in the second vehicle; it was the fourth vehicle that got hit. We came out of the village and broke out into the open. The first vehicle goes down into this depression into the wadi, no problem. I'm in the second vehicle going in, then the third makes it through. Just as I tipped out of the wadi onto the plateau, there was a loud, muffled explosion. My initial thought was that somebody jumped out of the village and hit us with an RPG. My gunner swung back onto the village. Then the rear vehicle called in and said it was a mine strike. The smoke and dust were settling. My engineers went through their SOPs to clear a lane to the vehicle. I tried to get communications with the hit vehicle but they weren't answering. It took a couple of minutes until they did.

"There were a driver and crew commander in front, with the journalist in the right back, and a turret gunner. The journalist jumped out, he was in a daze, shaken and sore, but he was OK. He should have stayed in the vehicle because of the possibility of a secondary device; we screamed at him to stay in the vehicle. He couldn't hear us. I noticed that the gun turret had been thrown from the top. By the time the engineer got to the vehicle, the driver and crew commander flopped out on the ground too. They were in a great deal of pain. The crew commander was coherent. Our medic, she just wanted to scream down and work on them, but she had to be held back till we cleared the site. It was tough. The engineer found a package of some sort with wires running into the ground, so he got the impression there was a secondary. The gunner, who had been thrown, and the journalist went with the engineer away from the wreck. The gunner had no cuts, no scratches.

"My other guys were rigging an LZ [landing zone], others were preparing stretchers. We asked for medevac, a Nine Liner. There was no fear or panic, everybody was switched on, we had security out. Tor Jan's guys were helping with security. Then I spotted the triggerman. I thought, 'OK, this is a flat area, there has to be a triggerman. Where would he be?' We were a kilometer from the village, so he had to be closer. I could see two to three k's in each direction. I told everybody to look, and it wasn't a minute after I said that than out of the corner of my eye I caught two guys on a motorcycle, in the middle of nowhere. Where did this motorcycle come from? There were driving more erratic and faster than usual. I told TJ's guys to go apprehend them and see what they're doing here. It didn't make sense: if they were 'concerned citizens' coming to check this out, they wouldn't be moving away from us. Even if they weren't the triggermen, it was out of the ordinary and they might know something. Wali caught up with them and said that there was a 99.9 percent chance they were the triggermen.

"As for the Geneva Convention and laws of armed conflict, we couldn't have blown them away because they were suspicious. We had pretty robust ROEs, but unless you actually see them detonate the device, we had no grounds to fire at them. The information they might have is more important anyway. Hopefully it was the right call. Some may beg to differ, but in my mind it was the right call.

"We waited for the chopper to come in. The medic was doing her job. The Americans are an awesome bunch of guys, but they had a considerable distance to fly: they have to warm the chopper up, get the information, and that can take time, in this case forty-five minutes. They were there in fifty minutes. It was a Black Hawk. We loaded up our casualties. Once they were off the X, we still had to maintain security. And we have to deal with the two guys we have. We got word the ANP were deploying to help, They arrived, but we didn't realize they were there to take the detainees. I told them we were OK and didn't need assistance with security, I didn't want to waste their time, you have better things to do. Then they left. What they were supposed to do was take the detainees to the Maiwand district center and hold them. So they got all the way back there and had to turn around and come back to get the detainees.

"Then we had to extract the vehicle by Chinook. And then the TF IED DEFEAT guys showed up to do postblast analysis. The locals were keeping their distance, so something was still going on. It was odd. Usually there would be crowds watching, like honey attracting bees. There was nobody around. It was sketchy. Not one person was stirring in that village. There wasn't anybody moving around. The Chinook then lifted the G-Wagon out of there.

"Wali talked to the detainees. They were more scared than usual. They were stumbling over their words, they wouldn't look Wali in the eye. We loaded them into the back of the Nyala. We then saw dust coming over the plateau and looking through the binocular we saw a police truck. This was the Maiwand police coming back. We got a few pictures of us handing them over to the ANP to cover our ass just in case they showed up dead somewhere on the side of the road.

"There was a third detainee. He was actually a witness; my front gunner saw him digging in the ground, but [he] kept stopping to look at us. It was fishy, so we sent somebody to bring him over to us. As soon as TJ's guys went toward him he bolted. He was a twelve-year-old boy and he was scared shitless. He was actually working a field and had nothing to do with the other two. Wali questioned him, and he gave us perfect descriptions of the other two, right down to their boots and the motorcycle color. He said that thirty minutes before we arrived, they went to the site and fooled around in the wadi for about ten minutes. Then they pushed the motorcycle down the wadi where they hid. He described everything. We gave him water and food and he agreed to stick around. It didn't bother him that we were coalition forces."

The IED detonated under the engine and the blast penetrated the armored compartment via the transmission hump. The driver and co-driver had their legs broken and shattered. The front end was completely destroyed, but the crew compartment survived. "If it had been an Iltis [jeep], we would still be picking up the pieces," Sergeant Bradley told me.

Later on, after the detainees had been given over to the ANP, Ottawa realized it had made a mistake and frantically contacted the PRT, insisting that somebody be sent to assess the status of the detainees and to exert pressure on the ANP to "protect Canadian interests." One of the RCMP officers went with a patrol to inquire into the detainee welfare. Apparently the local police chief greeted him with smiles, whacked a frayed plastic tube onto the table, and inquired whether the Mountie needed to use it. He declined. The detainees were, it turned out, unharmed and quivering with fear but told all without any physical abuse.

I had to stop and reflect after this incident. I was lucky. If I had gone on this patrol, I would have been sitting in the same seat that the British journalist was in when the G-Wagon was blown up. It was pure coincidence that the briefing I needed to attend at KAF was that same day.

the provincial council

If winning hearts and minds is to be successful, it is necessary to demonstrate tangible proof of genuine government concern for the social and economic grievances underlying support for the insurgency. Reforms put into place under pressure of emergency must also be seen to endure long enough to ensure there is no return of insurgency in the long term.

—Ian Beckett, *The Encyclopedia of Guerrilla Warfare*

Another "front" in the PRT's war was the provincial council. Phoenix and Colonel Bowes had business with the council, so I tagged along. After slinging on my body armor, I climbed into the back of a G-Wagon with Regimental Sergeant Major Brown, who prepared his weapons for action in the event of a contact. Phoenix was in the vehicle behind us. It was a bright, coolish day. Our route took us along the river and past the huge Kandahar graveyard. Everything was dun colored. Kids played in the river and waved, while sullen teenagers milled about an intersection. After passing through the old Soviet corps HQ area, which was under ANA control, we bounced off a few speed bumps and swung into the provincial government complex. There were about thirty turbaned men armed with AK-47s, and even some AKS-74U with their brown magazines, lounging about in various stages of relaxation. SUVs were everywhere.

We went through a room with sitting carpets and through some glass doors. The meeting was held in a high-walled room that had several European-style wall-mounted heating units spaced out midway up the four walls. There was no large table; there were numerous plush couches and chairs arranged throughout the room. Phoenix had her shemagh wrapped around her hair like a scarf. There were a number of other women in the room with scarves; there were no burkas. The council consisted of twenty men whom I would estimate to have been in their sixties, but there were a few "young turks" in their forties there too. All were wearing turbans, high-quality ones, with detail in the cloth—gray and brown, black with stripes, even gray on gray—and traditional garb. There were four female members of the council, which surprised me. Ahmad Wali Karzai presided; he had a short, dark beard and was wearing traditional garb.

After the usual greetings, the meeting came to order. Steve Bowes sat up front next to Wali Karzai; this was obviously done to show to the council that the coalition backed him and the government. Steve looked uncomfortable jammed between Wali and a big, big Afghan wearing an American green fatigue jacket on the couch (who I found out later was a man suspected of being the biggest drug dealer in Kandahar). Steve's arid CADPAT clashed with the deep wine red "Corinthian leather." I expected Ricardo Montalban to start intoning any second. The RSM and I sat in one corner near the door; our only interpreter, Habib, was with Steve, so it was difficult to follow. The tone of the meeting was best described as "adamant." The worry beads carried by the older members of council were in constant use.

It was now Phoenix's turn. She had experience with this group, and they knew that USAID wielded some power: there was a level of deference, but you could sense the tension. The discussion was about seed distribution. For some reason, there was a perception in the province that there was some bidding war between USAID and the charity Islamic Relief over the cost of seed. Islamic Relief was, apparently, charging the government 1,300 afghanis for seed, while the going rate for USAID seed was 1,500. Phoenix kept trying to explain that USAID seed didn't cost anything. That somebody was illegally selling USAID seed. That the plan was to give the seed to the government and then the government was supposed to just distribute the seed. Then the conversation veered into other topics. Steve was getting the subtitles from Habib; the RSM and I had to go by tone and volume.

Several times, individual council members excused themselves. I figured they were going to the can. At one point I had to relieve myself, so I left . . . and found a whole bunch of them smoking outside! Wali apparently forbade smoking in the sessions, so these guys were all pacing outside yakking on cell phones and puffing away.

It was interesting watching Phoenix at work. She knew just when to be deferential and when to be adamant. I think the council respected her, but it was for a number of reasons: the respect was based on the power to provide something. This was in complete contrast with another woman from a European NGO.

When Phoenix was done and some petitions were heard by the council, this European woman, who wasn't wearing a headscarf, started to harangue the council members. She went on and on about President Karzai's promise to eradicate child marriages by 2008, that the age of marriage should be raised to sixteen and maybe even eighteen. That fourteen-year-old girls couldn't consent and so on. The council members, including the women, were a bit taken aback by the assault.

"You *must,* absolutely *must,* stop this barbaric practice! It is possible that aid will be cut off if you do not stop it!"

And it went on. The tone was a lecturing one, to grade-five schoolkids or maybe even grade three. Council members started to leave the room in groups of two and three while she was in the middle of the harangue. It was embarrassing. I was concerned that the council might think she was associated with the PRT. Habib assured me later that the council members understood that she wasn't, but that they were upset. There were mutterings about Westerners and their ways. The threat to cut off aid really annoyed some of them, and they had to understand that the PRT and the coalition countries weren't making the threat and that she had no power to actually do so anyway. That took time and effort, time that could have been spent on something more important. And there is no doubt in my mind that this threat, no matter how empty it was to use, was taken to heart by some of the council members.

Habib later told me that the older men leaving the room made several comments in Pashto about what they wanted to do to her, or what should have been done to her when she was fourteen. Her efforts, understandable from a Western standpoint, were completely counterproductive and threatened what the PRT was trying to accomplish. What was more important in Kandahar at this point: security and food, or gender issues? They could not work concurrently. We needed those old men on the council on our side. Alienating them would cause us problems later, especially if the Taliban showed up and propagandized them. "See? The foreigners want to put women in charge of you."

to DIAG or not to DIAG, that is the question

The one who adapts his policy to the times prospers, and likewise . . . the one whose policy clashes with the demands of the times does not.

—Niccolò Machiavelli

The Heavy Weapons Cantonment process had generally been, by late 2005, successful. Tanks, multiple rocket launchers, artillery—these were collected in sites province-wide and were under the positive control of coalition and ANA forces. The main issue now lay with DDR. DDR had significantly reduced the multi-thousand-man "private armies" of leaders like Fahim Khan and Dostum. The Disbandment of Illegal Armed Groups essentially replaced or was a sequel to DDR. DIAG sought to identify and disarm groups that were smaller than the AMF. The intent was to prevent what we saw happen in the Balkans. In Kosovo and Bosnia, we saw the emergence of "security companies" who provided "protection" when the ethnic armies were disarmed. These security companies were heavily armed and were private armies by another name. What was to stop chieftain X from just rebadging his AMF as "police"?

DIAG was supposed to assist with registering any group that carried weapons. In order to be registered, the individuals had to have police training and be certified. In theory, this forced local leaders to send their armed thugs to a police school run by a collection of Western cops. The reality was that the Germans, who were running the police "pillar," were not allowed to leave Kabul. It was too expensive to send every hajji from hither and yon in Afghanistan to Kabul to be trained by the Germans. Few nations wanted to send police to the "hot" areas, like RC South. Canada's two RCMP officers were taxed to the max with police training in Kandahar.

The PRT assisted the provincial government in establishing a weekly DIAG meeting, whose membership included the PRT, ANP, ANA, NDS, UN representatives, a Danish air force adviser, and the Deputy Governor, Dr. Hamiun. Major Sanchez King was the PRT rep, so I accompanied him to one of the meetings to get a feel for what was discussed.

After a hair-raising G-Wagon convoy trip through the city, we were feted at the Governor's Palace. The agenda was unclear. Apparently the meeting would select a "commander" to be "DIAG'd" (a verb) and the appropriate approach formulated.

There was a lengthy reiteration of who may have retained BM-21 multiple rocket launchers, 23-mm antiaircraft guns, and DSKHs, and it occurred to me that there was no baseline of who had what. Sanchez confirmed that the NDS still hadn't put together the comprehensive list of illegally armed groups in the province yet. It was clear the NDS was stalling. With no report, no action could be taken. Essentially the current groups being DIAG'd were names that came from the Governor's office, but this was obviously selective. In many cases the committee seemed to be waiting for "commanders" to show up spontaneously and *ask* to be DIAG'd! It seemed to me, and this may have been the translation, that commanders needed to *apply* to be DIAG'd!

Sanchez quietly explained to me that CTF BAYONET estimated there were twenty commanders from Kandahar province that each had between seventy and three hundred people, and each holding between three hundred and a thousand weapons.

My head whirling, the conversation shifted to a known commander whom the committee wanted to DIAG. He was not on the list. Was it OK to DIAG him? Well, he wanted a certificate to demonstrate that he had done this voluntarily. He wanted a ceremony. Could somebody prominent be there for the ceremony? This might ease his DIAG. It was an about-face.

DAIG posed numerous complications, especially for the PRT. Colonel TJ's people were not on the DIAG list because they intended to take the police Regional Training Centre (RTC) certification course. There was a long lineup, though, and a Kabul-imposed deadline was approaching. Any group not certified by that date would be declared illegal and forcibly disarmed. Another unintended consequence was that former AMF troops, knowing they could not work in the security field without certification, wanted to work for the police. There was not enough capacity to bring these guys into the police training system, so they were hired anyway, given a uniform, and made police. There were untrained police wandering all around the rural areas, many of them under no positive control.

Then there was the Governor and Deputy Governor's Close Protection Party. It hadn't been certified yet because it was so busy. To make matters worse, the USAID security contractor, USPI (United States Protection and Investigations), was also having problems. It was in charge of road-building security west of the city. If it was unable to operate, road construction didn't happen.

In an even more sensitive area, there was FOB Ghecko, the SOF base in Kandahar City. Certain Afghan DIAG committee members were adamant that the coalition SOF groups submit their paramilitaries to the DIAG process, claiming that SOF were not accountable and this ran against the new policies of government accountability. It was thought by some that this was actually an intelligence-gathering exercise against coalition SOF by unfriendly elements in the provincial government who wanted to pass info on SOF to the Taliban and others. It turned out that coalition SOF paramilitaries carried a "get out of jail free" card, which pissed off the local police.

Throughout the meeting, cell phones constantly went off, prompting the committee members, who were all in traditional dress, to flip open their phones to the chimes of Western classical music, space laser gun sounds, and Indian sitars.

A DIAG committee member went on and on and on about Ghekho people driving around in vehicles with tinted windows and how this should be outlawed. It was evident to me that somebody was manipulating the committee for other purposes, and it was being deliberately distracted from its task. It couldn't even put together a comprehensive list of who to target for DIAG. It had a partial list, but a priority couldn't be established. This posed more questions for me: who wanted to protect their private armies and why?

the operational situation: december 2005

On 16 December, the Chief of the Defence Staff, General Rick Hillier, flew in by CH-47 to the PRT for a quick visit. I steered clear of events. He was there to see the troops, after all, and I didn't want to get in the way of the entourage, so I went to the TOC to keep track of what was going on in the province.

It is useful at this point to give a snapshot of what was happening around the province while the PRT representatives were relationship building with the Kandahar power structure. The main coalition bogeyman, Mullah Baqi, was preparing his evil bag of tricks to disrupt what our people were doing. Intelligence from Colonel TJ and other sources warned that more suicide bombers were on the way. An American convoy headed to a security meeting slowed for a speed bump and a suicide bomber detonated next to a Hummer. There was no damage, except to the jihadi. This was the fifth such attack since October.

Mullah Baqi's organization was also engaged in an information-operation campaign: night letters kept showing up at mosques in the Panjwayi and Zharey districts. CTF BAYONET was having problems with how to respond to this sort of behavior. It appeared that its information-operation campaign could deploy leaflets to respond, but the only really effective response was to provide security to the threatened areas. However, BAYONET didn't have the resources to mount a permanent presence there because it had to be everywhere in the province with a single battalion.

Then the Lashkar Gah district center over in Helmand province was attacked by a force of ten land cruisers and about fifty armed men. Six Afghan police were killed and three wounded. All of their vehicles were destroyed. The district center was gutted. This caught everybody by surprise and led to questions as to whether this was drug traffickers attacking the police, who were supporting British-led poppy eradication efforts, or the Taliban. Helmand was practically terra incognita at this point. There had been little coalition penetration in there because Kandahar and Zabol provinces were the main coalition efforts in RC South.

Coalition SOF were at this time tracking a major Taliban leadership target in the northern part of the province, up near Shah Wali Kot. The PRT was instructed to stay out of there for the time being. It sounded like something big was in the offing, but it was difficult to discern because of the security surrounding it.

Steve Borland explained to me how the relationship between CTF BAYONET and the PRT had evolved. The "players" in Kandahar City were numerous. There were the Gun Devils, who passed through going to and from KAF to their operating areas and FOBs up north. There were the special operations people from CJSOTF. The PRT was everywhere. There was little coordination. The PRT worked out an incident agreement whereby the PRT would handle the initial response to incidents within the city: Camp Nathan Smith was closer than KAF in any event, and since PRT patrols were always moving about the city, they could respond faster. In terms of IED attacks, the PRT had its own undeclared IED engineer unit—undeclared in the sense that it was a purely Canadian asset not under coalition control. The Americans had an organization, TF IED DEFEAT, that handled IED matters for the whole CTF BAYONET. They couldn't be everywhere, so the Canadian IED team at the PRT had quick-reaction responsibilities in the city. It also could respond faster than the group at KAF. In the main, the PRT's presence in the city freed up TF GUN DEVIL resources so they could operate elsewhere in the province.

The fact was Camp Nathan Smith's location gave CTF BAYONET a foothold inside the city. It had a helipad, it had medical facilities. It had paramilitaries. It was a valuable organization. The PRT also was responsible for noncombatant evacuation of NGOs in the event of rioting against UNAMA, which had occurred elsewhere. The PRT would assist with extraction, not crowd control.

CTF BAYONET needed as many men as possible in the northern areas. The concept of operations at this point was to covertly insert SOF units as a back-stop and then use the Gun Devils and the ANA to sweep through an area and drive the enemy into the SOF so they could be killed or captured. A number of these operations were conducted northeast and northwest of Kandahar City in December, resulting in one American wounded. The enemy tended to evade the net, possibly because the SOF helicopter insertions were compromised, and the results of these operations were ambiguous at best, at least from the vantage point of the PRT. One operation was considered successful: seven high- or medium-value leadership targets that the OGA considered significant were located, and an airmobile SOF operation was mounted to get them.

"TIC" was a generic term that had come to be used by OEF after 2004 to describe "Troops In Contact." The PRT TOC kept close track of the TICs, as this affected where the PRT deployed patrols. It could be dramatic stuff listening to the radio in the TOC, hearing the play-by-play, anticipating what would happen next. One TIC ran for three days, from 14 to 16 December. It involved one of the Gun Devils' companies. A platoon from this company had an initial encounter with a Taliban force, which became a running battle once a Predator UAV was brought on station and two AH-64s provided support. There was sporadic contact and sporadic firing as the men chased this insurgent group around a mountainous feature near Gumbad called "the Belly Button." Medevac choppers went in to take out casualties; blood trails were followed. The Gun Devils chased the remnants of the group into caves and called in artillery. There wasn't much left.

The Americans had twenty-four killed in action in 2005 throughout Kandahar province. At one platoon house in Gumbad, they had even been harassed by a sniper. This wasn't just some jihadi with an AK-47. It was a trained individual with a long-barreled weapon who knew how to avoid body armor in order to get a kill, generally shooting his victim in the groin area. This individual took out two ANA officers and an American. He then wounded another American moving in to evacuate the wounded. He knew what rank to look for. Apparently two AH-64s were brought in to hunt him down. They essentially leveled the top of a mountain where he was thought to be hiding. A patrol from the 3-319th conducted a sweep, and there was no further sniping at Gumbad.

There had been a number of premature detonations of enemy IEDs in December, but the enemy was evolving too. In one pressure-plate IED attack against the Gun Devils, large rocks had been used to channel vehicle traffic into the strike site. This PPIED was a mine that was detonated by having a vehicle run over two saw blades that, when they made contact, completed the circuit and set off the mine. Ominously, there were reports that the failure of foot-borne suicide bombers between October and December had led the enemy to rethink operations and that there would be more and more suicide vehicle-borne IED attacks in the future. Internal enemy discussions revolved around the need to dramatically increase coalition casualties in order to make up for the foot-borne failures. They feared a loss of face and credibility with their supporters, so more of our people had to die. PRT patrols started to report more and more "templatings" in the city conducted by men who were clean-shaven and had close-cropped hair, which indicated they were jihadis preparing to die. The threat of suicide VBIED was increased to "high" as a result.

The Taliban I/O campaign was also accelerating in the rural areas. A watchman at the school in the Dand district was found lynched. A list of the teachers was found next to the body. Over in Helmand, a teacher at a school for girls was executed right in front of the class. The message was clear: don't go to school or else. Selective assassination was also employed. Mullah Ahmad Shah was assassinated on the steps of his mosque in downtown Kandahar. Shah was outspoken against violence perpetrated by the Taliban. More and more night letters were showing up, this time sent to locals working with the coalition as labor or translators.

Just then the CDS (chief of defence staff) came in, sans entourage, with Steve Bowes.

"Dr. Maloney! How long have you been here?"

"A couple of weeks."

"How long are you staying?"

"Until January."

He looked at Steve Bowes.

"Are you charging him rent?"

west: panjwayi district patrol

> Due to their intensely independent and democratic nature, the powers of
> their headmen, or maliks, were slight. Pathan affairs were deliberated by a
> jirga or council, but the more democratic the tribe or other grouping, the
> larger the jirga with consequent differences of opinions.
>
> —MICHAEL BARTHORP, *AFGHAN WARS*

PRT regularly sent representatives to the Panjwayi district shura. CTF BAYONET
was increasingly interested in this district throughout the fall of 2005 after more
and more enemy activity appeared to be emanating from there. It is important to
understand that there are actually two separate districts: Panjwayi and Zharey, but
the coalition forces and later the media generally called the whole place Panjwayi.
It was unlike any other district in the province in that it was the most fertile since
it was along the Arghandab River. The districts sat astride two major highways:
Highway 1 ran west across the top of Zharey district from Kandahar all the way
to Helmand and Herat. Throughout 2005 there had been a noticeable increase in
ambushes along Highway 1. These started off as IED attacks but escalated to direct
ambushes. The intelligence people immediately looked at Les Grau's books to see
if there was any correlation to the mujahideen efforts from the Soviet period, and
there was. Back then, RPG ambush teams would hit the Soviets on the road and
then fade away into the dense vineyards and compounds in Zharey and Panjwayi.
Another paved highway ran from Highway 1 coming out of Kandahar on a slant
into Panjwayi from the east. The intelligence people believed that there was a "rat
line" into the southwest part of the city through the villages along this highway. A
weapons cache was uncovered by the Gun Devils in November in this area.

Mullah Baqi's organization was operating in both districts, but the only way to
get any information was through local sources—and these were lacking. The best
means to get insight there was through engagement: who were we dealing with
and what did they want? The PRT had engaged the Panjwayi shura on a number of
occasions to establish credibility and relationship-build.

There were other disturbing developments that CTF BAYONET and the PRT
were interested in. A clinic had been burned in a town called Nakhonay, which was
southeast of the town of Panjwayi. There were reports that a group of ten to fifteen
fighters was operating to the west of Nakhonay. At least two IEDs were discovered
in that area by locals before they could be detonated. Some analysts believed that
the Baqi organization possessed a group of fighters that was about a company in
size and that was wintering in the western part of Zharey with an element of it
rotating into Panjwayi and Zharey to get "blooded" against coalition forces.

Sergeant Clayton Schoepp's section conducted the Panjwayi patrol this time. Schoepp, an experienced and quietly confident man, gave the briefing while Master Corporal Mike McCoy provided the patrol with the latest intelligence picture. The patrol was to escort Phoenix, Captain A. J. Lutes, and me to attend the Panjwayi shura. This had multiple purposes. First, there were the social aspects, the "face time" with the Panjwayi leadership. Second, the patrol was to swing through Nakhonay and assess the clinic situation. Third, and most important, the Japanese aid agency, JICA (Japan International Cooperation Agency), was backing off its road construction program in the area because, it claimed, it wasn't safe. The patrol was also to develop information to see if the JICA contractors were bullshitting or not. There were rumors of some intertribal aspects to the JICA contracting that may have aggravated the situation.

We were not to go into Zharey district at this point as it was considered too dangerous. There were ancillary aspects to the patrol, however. There was some concern from elsewhere that the district chief and the district police chief were dirty, but more information was required. The patrol had a specialist with it to take advantage of any opportunities that might arise to gain any additional insight into the state of affairs with these men. Some patrol members would move into the police compound and check it out, ostensibly as part of shura security.

Schoepp's section of G-Wagons roared out the gate in the morning, this time using the rover route past the graveyard. I noticed this time as we inched by a Jingle Truck that there were Christian graves in there with crosses. I found it astounding that they hadn't been interfered with during the Taliban's reign; they didn't appear to be new graves either. We made our way to Highway 1 after negotiating the Crop Circle and made a left turn off Highway 1 onto a newly paved road. As we motored along at a comfortable eighty kilometers per hour, we hit a series of jarring speed bumps. But there were brand-new road signs! We even passed a sign indicating that we were driving past a mosque (similar to the signs in the Gulf region, so you could pull over and pray as necessary). There was a series of high hills to the north and another spine to the south. We were in a valley that had compounds everywhere. We passed a moderately sized refugee camp. This blacktop could have been in Arizona or Utah, out of one of those 1970s road movies like *Electra Glide in Blue* or *Vanishing Point*.

We started to hit tractor traffic and then passed into a market area; everything an Afghan compound dweller needed was on sale. There were bins of produce. Few donkeys; it was all motor traffic, motorcycles, tractors, jingle trucks, Toyota Corollas. It was evident that the paved road to Kandahar had had a tremendous economic effect here. Clearly Panjwayi was well off. So why exactly was the Taliban gaining ground in the district?

I asked AJ what the locals grew here.

"Well, they have five different types of grapes. Some of them are huge, almost like plums. They grow some grain. But for the most part, they dry the grapes in these huge rectangular buildings and make raisins. If they had better storage, they could increase their output." Steve pointed to one of the oblong buildings in the distance.

I had a sneaking suspicion that the locals grew something in addition to grapes, but I kept it to myself.

Sergeant Schoepp led the patrol into the district center compound. The district center shared a wall with the police compound. The section jockeyed its vehicles around so that if we had to get out quick, we could.

The district shura is an important aspect of Afghan politics. In general terms, each cluster of compounds in a district constituted the equivalent of a village, and each sent a representative to the district center on a regular basis to meet, discuss, and hopefully resolve disputes and other problems. The Panjwayi shura, for example, had about thirty representatives in attendance. The district representative to the provincial council would be present, as would the district chief. In the case of Panjwayi, the representative was a man named Haji Agha-Lalai.

Haji Agha-Lalai was a tall man with angular features. He was charismatic, and that charisma crossed the cultural barrier: he didn't speak English. The level of deference afforded to him by the shura members was almost embarrassing. I picked up immediately that Haji Agha-Lalai had something special going on in Panjwayi. In contrast to Maruf, the district had paved roads. In contrast to Maruf, there was commerce. If you asked anybody who the Maruf district representative to the provincial council was, nobody knew. But everybody knew Haji Agha-Lalai. I would have many encounters with him during subsequent trips to Afghanistan.

The pattern of activity in any shura is to introduce guests, discuss business, have lunch, hear petitions from people in the district, then socialize. We sat on mats and cushions on the rectangular porch of the district center. The Panjwayi shura had a lot of interesting characters in attendance. I sat next to Haji Agha-Lalai, but across from me sat four men in traditional dress who were the spitting images of Christopher Lee, Leo McKern, Anthony Quinn, and Peter Ustinov. It was positively surreal. Bird chirps and laser beam sounds emanated from cell phones as delegates excused themselves. Decorated snuff tins were produced and offered to us for use.

Phoenix used the meeting to deal with Haji Agha-Lalai on matters relating to her projects in the poorer areas of Ghorak district, which was to the northwest of Panjwayi/Zharey. Phoenix asked Agha-Lalai through our interpreter, who was wearing a Habs ball cap and a traditional scarf, "How do we help the government help these people?" Agha-Lalai insisted that, yes, there was poverty, yes, there was need, but they needed projects to get the people working, that money should not be just given out, the people needed to be employed so they could help themselves. The main problem was the water projects. Agha-Lalai suggested that irrigation projects could be cooperative projects and employ the local people. The people in Ghorak would be happy when prices for produce went up. And so on. Phoenix explained that USAID had food-for-work as well as cash-for-work programs that could be employed as needed. Phoenix and Agha-Lalai agreed that security was a major problem in Ghorak, that the PRT needed to work through the Ghorak shura and find out exactly what the tribal issues were there first before moving in. Agha-Lalai, through tribal connections, could influence two tribes in critical areas if necessary.

Note that this had nothing to do, ostensibly, with Panjwayi district. The shura served as cover for this and other logrolling-type meetings, just like municipal and provincial politics back home. CTF BAYONET didn't have a lot of visibility in Ghorak. Haji Agha-Lalai could help with that. PRT penetration of Ghorak was problematic from a security standpoint, so some form of standoff aid had to be deployed to help in there. This was how it was done.

This was a side conversation, however. I learned from the shura that most tribal issues in Panjwayi revolved around water access and land division. When we tried to figure out how that connected to the violence in the district, the district police chief insisted that security was good, it was the best, there were no problems. We didn't buy that at all. I noticed he kept clutching one hand over the other, as if he was concealing something. I also noticed that Anthony, Leo, Christopher, and Peter exchanged a lot of glances whenever the police chief said anything.

AJ brought up the problem of attacks against clinics and schools, emphasizing that this was of serious concern to the coalition. The district chief admitted there had been some intimidation, but it wasn't effective. AJ asked him if he had the capability to protect the students and nurses. The chief tried to move the conversation away from the matter, claiming it was a "big issue" and he'd look into it. He counterattacked, telling us about a member of the clerical council who had been killed by the Taliban. People were caught but not punished because the judicial system was flawed. What were *we* going to do about that?

We couldn't tell him that of the eight judges trained by the Italians to work in RC South, most of them claimed refugee status in Italy on completion of their training and stayed there.

AJ worked on the police chief, encouraging him to share information with the NDS to counter the insurgent threat. The police chief told him that he had no NDS here, only a small special team that came and went. He really didn't want

NDS in Panjwayi. He didn't trust them. Haji Agha-Lalai interjected and told AJ that the biggest problem was that there were no night patrols in the district, that there were tribal divisions over the coalition and government presence, and that unity had not yet been achieved on this issue. The troubles in Panjwayi, he told us, really started last year, and it would take time to develop a unified approach to security here. Indeed, in his view, the NDS had to get better. Only with an improved NDS could security improve. And road construction could continue only if security improved. Agha-Lalai, using the usual Afghan "salami tactics," asked AJ if Panjwayi could get an ambulance. AJ told him that security and road building would make the acquisition of an ambulance easier.

After a snack of mango-banana cookies and tea, deliberations continued. The *shura* members readily agreed that their constituents were ready for a polio vaccination campaign: there were positive tests in the district, and this had to be addressed as soon as possible.

Then we hit the real nub of what was going on vis-à-vis road construction and security. USAID had contracted a security company to protect the Japanese-funded road-construction contractors. The section of road that was uncompleted because a mine was found at the site, at a section that Agha-Lalai was nearly frantic to get completed as soon as possible for reasons we couldn't discern, was attacked because the locals from the area the road was going through had not been hired by either the security company or the construction company. Haji Agha-Lalai had presumably made promises to others in the district to get the road done, probably as part of a logrolling exercise, and now that was blocked.

This led to an extended and very animated discussion in Pashto that we couldn't follow effectively. We were watching deep district politics in action. We had no road map. We barely knew the players. Yet what was happening in the district was affecting, in a radiating fashion, surrounding districts, the allocation of aid resources, and the allocation of security resources.

Then a shura member asked for the floor. "Our guests from the coalition should be killing the Taliban and not having to worry or spend time on problems that we can resolve among ourselves." I couldn't have said it better myself.

During a break in the action, Sergeant Schoepp reported to AJ and told him that he sent some men to call on the Panjwayi clinic, which was right next to the police compound. The staff shooed them away, telling them not to come around again because they were afraid of the Taliban. This was odd, given the proximity of the two compounds. The clinic staff had, apparently, lived in fear for the past two months, after a van full of doctors was ambushed and four were killed. The Afghan Health Service and the NGOs working with it were inculcating an unofficial policy of neutralism, and we were a belligerent force to them. It was clear after several conversations later on that this was NGO propaganda promulgated by those who didn't want to work with coalition forces. Whose side were they on? The patrol members also learned that there were cases of what the locals called "blood cancer" among children in a village called Zangabad. The possibility that this could be the long-term effect of Soviet-era defoliation crossed my mind.

The Panjwayi shura gave me insight into the Afghan adjudication process. "Leo McKern" explained to me that fighting between families was an old problem here. Lately two men were killed each and the district center had to mediate between the families. A mullah and a judge were sent in to do the mediation after the funeral to head off a blood feud. It was complicated, "Leo" told me. What was the motive for the murders? *Badal* (revenge)? Was it a cover for something else? He explained that there were still disputes over land problems from the Soviet and Taliban times, that there was payback because the Taliban supported one family over another in a particular dispute and stopped payback against that family when they were in power. Now the family that was prevented from getting payback felt it could go through with the killing because the Taliban was no longer in control. They didn't have enough people to handle all of the cases. In some instances, the chief justice and the mullah were the same person. There was no real oversight.

I had been watching the district police chief throughout all of this, and he kept covering his hand. I was curious. I figured that he had a tattoo that he was con-cealing, and I knew from other trips that jihadis sometimes had themselves inked. During the social part of the *shura*, I asked my new friends "Leo," "Christopher," "Peter," and "Anthony" some general questions about tattooing. Haji Agha-Lalai looked at me with a mixture of feigned impassivity and amusement.

"Oh yes. We have tattoos." "Peter" showed me and the rest of the shura his wrist, which had a series of black-blue dots across it. "I had pain here and the tattoo took the pain away."

Astounding. It was as if he had carpal tunnel syndrome and the procedure relieved the pressure somehow, like acupuncture.

"And I have one too!" "Anthony" proudly rolled up his sleeve to show us something that I couldn't identify. "Do you have these in Canada?" he asked.

"Well, yes." I showed them one of mine, which is an elaborate snowy owl. They oohed and aahed. Phoenix was almost aghast.

"Ah," "Leo" said, "that's just a bird. If you were a real man you'd have a spider or scorpion, something tough. A bird is soft. It flies away."

"Yes, but the owl is a raptor. It hunts at night." I rolled up my pant leg to show him the scorpion piece I had done after my 2003 trip to Afghanistan, to the delight of the shura members who hooted and pointed, crying, "*Laram* [scorpion]!"

I turned to the district police chief and said, "Do you have any tattoos too?"

The others shamed him into displaying a scimitar and crescent moon on the web of his hand. A jihadi tattoo. One of our specialists took note.

Phoenix was cracking right up. "Go, Dr. Maloney, go! It was almost as if you had some secret CIA machine attached to your leg designed to give you the tattoo they wanted to see!"

We had a good laugh. We agreed that Panjwayi needed a tattoo parlor as part of the reconstruction effort—and a winery to take advantage of the amazing grapes. Haji Agha-Lalai tried to maintain his impassive composure throughout. Phoenix told me months afterward that I was still known as "the scorpion guy" at the Panjwayi shura.

We left Panjwayi late in the afternoon and headed south for Nakhonay. Sergeant Schoepp's sections' guard was up, and Wali's pickup truck, loaded with some of Colonel TJ's boys, was in the lead. When we got to Nakhonay, the place was tense. The clinic compound was locked tight, but one could see carbon burns from where the windows used to be. AJ and Sergeant Schoepp used the opportunity to compare notes on what was going on in Panjwayi.

"Well, Wali told us that the cops had been warned we were coming and to put their pot away. There was paraphernalia everywhere. The cops weren't in uniform, for the most part. Wali has a bad vibe about the chief, as we know. A motorcycle that was there has the same plates as one used in a drive-by killing in Kandahar."

"Yeah, there is just something not right with that picture, is there?"

AJ talked with the kids in Nakhonay, since the adults were afraid to speak with the patrol. They explained that one day the police from Panjwayi had come to the village in their white pickup trucks, closed off all the roads, and then burned the clinic.

"Not the Taliban?"

"No, it was the police. They also rob our people."

Curiouser and curiouser. AJ, Phoenix, Sergeant Schoepp, and I discussed the possibilities. First, it could be a tribal issue. The people in Nakhonay may be from a different tribe than the one the police were drawn from. Panjwayi is prosperous and smuggling was probably in progress. Nakhonay may not have been playing the game—that is, not paying off the police—so the Panjwayi cops had come out and burned the clinic in retaliation. Another theory was that the district leadership in Panjwayi was playing the coalition and the Taliban off against each other to survive. A deal may have been cut with the Taliban whereby the Panjwayi cops would burn the clinic as a "pinch-hit" operation; in return, the Taliban would leave the Panjwayi clinic alone. The Panjwayi district chief was old enough to remember how it worked in the 1980s; it is possible that the leadership back then was doing the same thing with the mujahideen and the Soviets. Maybe both theories held and there were overlapping tribal agendas. A further theory was that the people of Nakhonay were slandering the Panjwayi police for their own purposes. Or there were Taliban dressed up as police. Or the police were in fact Taliban. All that was certain was that the people and especially the children of Nakhonay had no access to health care. Who did that benefit?

The police chief was, among other things, found to be selling Afghan National Police uniforms to the Taliban. He was later removed.

north: khakriz district patrol

You think that a wall as solid as the earth separates civilization from barbarism. I tell you the division is a thread, a sheet of glass. A touch here, a push there, and you bring back the reign of Saturn.

—John Buchan (1940)

Khakriz district was a bit of terra incognita northwest of Kandahar City. It was off the beaten path in that it was nowhere near the two main highways, and one had to pass over one mountain range, go through a bit of a desert, and then enter the foothills of another rough area to get there. So why go to Khakriz? A number of requirements came together at the same time. Phoenix had to deal with a reparations issue after an errant B-52 strike had killed the wrong people in a remote village north of Khakriz town. Foreign Affairs wanted visibility on poppy matters, and apparently the UN was keen to have some kind of assessment of the district for its purposes. There had been no survey of any kind conducted by coalition forces, so nobody knew what the attitudes of the population were. What was the enemy up to in Khakriz?

A. J. Lutes lined up what he called the "dancing pandas": Erin Doregan was representing Foreign Affairs on this trip since Glyn Berry was on leave, and Corporal Bob Hart from the RCMP came along to assess the police and provide whatever advice he could to them. Andy Bone was the patrol leader for this one. Once again a convoy of G-Wagons accompanied by an engineer Nyala made its way through Kandahar City. Wali and a group of Colonel TJ's boys led the column. This trip I was once again with Sarah Keller and Keith Porteus, but Dutch Vandermeulan apparently couldn't handle being in the same vehicle with us again so he swapped out to be the cupola gunner in another vehicle. More colder he. The guys were smoking and joking about wearing a "crotchless lobster suit," the problems of using the claws to cock the .50-cal machine gun, and making pincer motions with their gloved hands.[6] "Hey, sir, is there still time to remuster to stunt double?"

We passed the mosque complex and recreation center that sat on the bank of the Arghandab River and went through the ANA checkpoint on the bridge, moving along High-way 1. After passing a gas station, the lead vehicle swung to the right onto what looked like a track and headed north along a rutted road that passed through dormant grape-growing areas. The road went through several village complexes; the sullen looks we got increased in intensity the farther north we went. A lot of people came out to watch. Our gunners waved, and some of the kids waved back, but I was struck with the large number of men in their late teens and early twenties.

We could see the first ridge of hills that paralleled us like a spine to the left. We came to a major ANA checkpoint at a T-junction and headed northwest. I started to get that vibe that not everything was on the up-and-up as we entered the hills. There was yet another ANA checkpoint, this one with a 12.7-mm machine gun in a prepared position. There was a bar across the road, and one distinctly got the impression that government control didn't extend to the other side of it. The convoy came out of the hills, and we were in scrubland that, I found out later, was in fact a huge wheat-growing area in a different season. The terrain was flat, but we could see the hills that marked the location of Khakriz in the distance.

The column passed under the Khakriz "gate," which consisted of three long pieces of what was once a Soviet radio antenna lashed together in an arch. There was an elaborate compound complex on the left that served as a sort of hotel or weekend getaway spot for Kandaharis in the summer. There was a beautiful radiant blue-domed white shrine in the middle of the town, surrounded with brown compounds. Our vehicles laagered in the district center parking lot. As I dismounted, my boots crunched on medical waste, which was lying everywhere. A light brown Japanese pickup truck sat next to the building; it had improvised storage for RPG rounds lashed to the roll bar. Each had several nicked green rockets sticking out of them. Two guys sat on a low wall. One had a PKM machine gun and just stared at us; he wasn't wearing a turban or any form of headdress, which I found unusual. There were armed people milling about, all carried some variant of the AK-47—but they all appeared to be about fifteen years old.

There was a shura scheduled later so that Phoenix could explain how the reparations would be dispensed. I went with Andy and Bob, who were going to see the chief of police. After the tea and cookies came out and the introductions were made, the chief of police, who wore no uniform but had a black beard and skullcap, listened to what Bob had to say.

"We need to have a coordinated vision for all of the police in the province. We'd like to train your police so that they can work better with other police in neighboring districts," Bob said.

"We'd like to do this. But we have found in the past that there is too much information to take on in one day. I explained this to the American female police colonel when she was here," the chief explained through our interpreter. "I'd like our people to have RTC training, it is very good, it will make our people more professional. The most important thing is the RTC certificate: our men can now prove they are professional police. The Americans promised I could send five men to the RTC, but it hasn't happened yet."

It was evident that the chief of police was desperate. He had, he told us, sixty men for the whole district, but fewer then forty-five were armed. More weapons were needed. They worked ten days on and had one day off. Bob asked him what the largest problem was.

"IED placement. We also need mine-clearance training to deal with those." They had no EOD capability at all, of course. "My men aren't scared to fight, but we have enemy everywhere, north, west, and east of here. They come in from the Shah Wali Kot district. My main problem is pay: Chief Wahidi hasn't paid us in some time."

Bob explained that his men all had to register first, then they could attend RTC. Apparently nobody had come up here to register the police in the first place. The chief himself hadn't been paid for over a month. He had put together a payroll, but only enough money for fifteen men came from Wahidi, and even that was intermittent. He also had to pay for two clerks and the district "attorney general." We found out that monthly pay for a policeman was supposed to be 5,000 afghanis, or $96 dollars. The chief was given fuel for his vehicles through a chit system from a government gas station, but he was limited to fifteen liters. He had four marked police vehicles: a Land Cruiser and three pickup trucks. He also had three motorcycles. Bob explained the repair program run by the PRT and the chief expressed interest. He hadn't heard about it before and despaired about maintenance. He had a satellite phone to Wahidi and a radio base station. Communications with Kandahar didn't appear to be a problem, but he had no handheld radios for his officers. Most of the heavy weapons on hand were seized from the Taliban: RPGs and PKMs. His other heavy weapons, like 23-mm antiaircraft guns, he told us, had been turned over as part of the DDR process. In other words, the police in Khakriz were former AMF converted to police. This was essentially a paramilitary organization or a gendarmerie, something distinct from the American or Canadian concept of police.

"I have sixteen prisoners here in jail, but I don't know what to do with them. I can't keep them forever. What is being done about the prison in Kandahar City?" Yet another problem.

"If you arrest a guy laying IEDs, what do you do with him?" Bob asked.

"We hold him, the NDS investigators come here from Kandahar, they build a file and give it to Chief Wahidi, then the prisoner goes to the Kandahar City jail. For regular crime, we establish a shura and determine what to do. The community tends to be supportive. But the Taliban are getting worse here. They assassinated a village elder in a remote village, and there wasn't anything we could do about it. We think the enemy is everywhere to the northern part of the district, but I can't get in there."

Vanilla sponge cake was laid out for us as the discussion continued.

"Chief Wahidi needs to make the rural areas a priority. The enemy is out here, not in the city."

Erin asked if there were school burnings. We had heard about some, but the details were fuzzy.

"There used to be an Islamic school during the Taliban," the chief explained. "We are against radical Islam: the people here, we burned it down on their own initiative. The media did not report this correctly."

The district chief suddenly arrived and took over the conversation. We noted that the police chief, who was fairly gregarious when we were on our own, clammed up completely when the district chief was around. Phoenix took over and explained that she was here to deal with the village that was bombed back in 2001.

"The UN investigated but sat on the paperwork for the past two years. It was only through local contacts that we found out about the situation. I need to meet with the shura and the people who were affected and discuss reparations."

The district chief was intrigued. It wasn't too far a leap to see he was trying to figure out how to profit from this, but Phoenix was already on to him.

"Of course, there will be no *individual* compensation. We will fund projects that will benefit the village as a whole. The people who were hurt by this will determine how the money is spent collectively." Phoenix had another agenda: this reparations program would also be used to get "covert" aid, like in Maruf, into areas that the coalition didn't control, and it would do this in a way that wasn't invasive and obvious. In that way the projects might avoid being attacked. Once trust was built up, further contact could then be made and incremental shifts could take place to get the area on side with the government.

The district chief's face had fallen, but then he perked up and said he needed only three things for Khakriz: roads, roads, and more roads. Phoenix, who was another believer in road building, told the district chief that there had been problems in Shah Wali Kot, that petty disputes within the shura were blocking road development. Could that be avoided here in Khakriz? "No, no, we will cooperate, we will work with you. There will be no harm, no dangers," he exclaimed. Phoenix said she understood and that she would look into road construction in Khakriz, but only if the district chief would ensure that there were no problems with the shura.

Throughout the afternoon we gained more and more insight, like we had in Maruf and in Panjwayi, into how Khakriz (apparently) functioned. The district chief was adamant that the roads were critical, that his people couldn't get produce to market efficiently. He adjusted his gray-black turban. "But we also need irrigation first, to grow our crops before we can get them to market." That was the formula for success apparently, in Khakriz: water, roads, market.

And on it went.

I went outside during a break. Master Corporal Joe Dupuy was eating a banana, looking around warily. He carried a weapon that looked like something Sigourney Weaver carried in *Aliens*. His chest rig was so full he rested the weapon on top of it.

"Roger, confirmed," he muttered.

"Joe, what the hell have you done to that C8?" I asked.

"Well"—he pointed—"this is a 40-mm grenade launcher. That is a laser sight for night work; I can see the dot with my night vision. I have a flashlight here on the left for searching buildings. Oh, and this is a pressel switch for my personal communications system. I Velcroed it on so I can still hold the weapon while I talk." He clicked it to show me.

"How much does all that weigh?"

"About sixty pounds with all the grenade rounds. I have to go sit down now." He moved away.

But there were problems in Khakriz. We all got the feeling that this was all some Potemkin village put on for our benefit. All of us: AJ, Bob, Phoenix, Andy, Erin, me. Members of our protection party kept coming in and whispering about possible enemy movement. When I took a piss break, one of our specialists handed me binoculars and pointed out a two-man observation post (OP) on a hill about a klick away. It wasn't one of ours, and it didn't belong to the police. It was all tranquil on the surface, but something was definitely bubbling beneath Khakriz.

Khakriz was a known transshipment point for opium, which was taken from poppy fields to the north of the town. *Of course,* they wanted irrigation: for the poppies. *Of course,* they wanted roads: to move the product to market. Phoenix knew that the reparations money could be misused, but something had to be done. Any aid coming in here *would* be used to facilitate narcotics production in some way. But to cut the whole place off would only let it fall under Taliban influence.

On the plus side, steps taken to provide aid could be turned to our advantage. If handled properly, they would give the coalition and the government a presence in the district. That presence could be used to penetrate the district in a number of ways, and then that could be exploited later to convert the district to one that would be supportive of the government. But the problem was poppy. And eradication only served to thwart our agenda in that part of the province.

AJ had seen this before in other districts: "It is almost like there is a script going around," he told me when we were safely away from the district leadership. "The script says, 'Thank you for helping us. We will cooperate.' The exact words are used by the leadership in certain districts. And those districts are the ones engaged in poppy production. Word for word," he emphasized.

I found Wali wearing his PRT ball cap and American desert BDUs outside, pacing back and forth, checking the action on his AK-47. He was antsy.

"This is not a good place, Dr. Sean. I feel like I am being watched all the time."

The chief of police told us farmers had been threatened: they were told to grow poppy or they would be killed. There had been night letters sent to schools. A typical night letter would state: "We are the Taliban fighting against coalition forces. Do not cooperate with the Americans. It is on your heads if you do. Shura, teachers, spies, and others whose sons and daughters work for the government: if you don't leave we do not take responsibility for what happens to you. Leave the area, move to Kandahar City, get out now."

The ending was in Arabic: "This jihad is against those against Allah."

The chief of police, when he was alone with us, was furious about the letters. "We found these letters on the doors of all of the mosques. *Our* war is holy! We work for the land and the people of Afghanistan!" he adamantly told us. "It is *Pakistan* that is supporting this."

Our specialists believed that there were no Taliban units per se in the villages in Khakriz district, that the letters were deployed by the Taliban to make people think that there were and to remind them that the Taliban still existed as an entity. Small Taliban units were believed to be in the mountains to the north in Oruzgan province, though not yet in the villages of Khakriz, and they were focused on the access points to Khakriz—Shah Wali Kot, Ghorak—and connected to a "rat line" going all the way west to Helmand province, for example. It was not a coincidence that the Chenar, Lam, and Tambil village complexes, which controlled movement in the Khakriz district, were the enemy target areas for intimidation. They were preparing to come back.

But what was going on in Khakriz? My take was that the local power structure differed from Panjwayi in that the local traffickers had not made an accommodation with the Taliban, that the Taliban were weaker in Khakriz than in other districts, but the traffickers felt vulnerable to the increased Taliban presence and wanted a government shield from them as much as possible. At the same time, they wanted to keep trafficking; therefore, the local power structure was co-opted. The police were in no position to take on the local power structure, but they could focus on the Taliban. Too much policing, however, was bad for the traffickers, so the police were caught in this uneasy state of partial effectiveness. The excuse to avoid effective patrolling in certain areas became "we lack resources," a state of affairs that wasn't difficult to contrive. Indeed, one had to wonder about elements of the police leadership in Kandahar since motivation and pay go together. It was as if they didn't want strong policing in districts like Khakriz.

The chief of police was in an unenviable position. He privately warned us to be careful on the way out. The patrol selected an alternate route back to the ANA checkpoints in the hilly passes. There were some tense minutes while the Nyala crew got a flat and had to fix it. Andy Bone and AJ made a good call.

It turned out the route we came in on was mined after we arrived at the Khakriz district center.

no blood for . . . coal?

During my wanderings around Kandahar Airf Field, I indulged in a hobby of mine, aircraft recognition. KAF was predictable—usually. There were C-17s, C-130 Hercs, ex-Soviet transports like the Il-76, Harrier jump jets. There was even an Mi-26 Halo helicopter with no markings. One bird stuck out, though. It resembled a P-3 Orion maritime patrol aircraft, and it had U.S. Navy markings on it, but as Dr. Noah says in the Bond spoof *Casino Royale,* "it looks like an aspirin, it tastes like an aspirin . . . but it isn't an aspirin." This P-3 had all sorts of weird but discrete bulges and blade antennas.

I know what you're thinking. No, it wasn't a superspook, hypersecret Aries III SIGINT aircraft. It was much more interesting. The aircraft was simply designated the NP-3D, and its product could conceivably alter the future of Afghanistan.

No, I'm serious. Really. Read on.

I was having lunch in the mess at KAF and the guy across from me was wearing a U.S. Navy flight suit. Ensign Mike Kenny, USN, introduced himself, and I asked him if the NP-3D belonged to him. He was taken aback. "You know what an NP-3D looks like?"

"Yeah, but I don't know what it does," I said. The SOF was using an RAF Nimrod maritime patrol aircraft as a surveillance platform over Kandahar. The Nimrod was a modified MPA (Maritime Patrol Aircraft), so I figured that the NP-3D had some SOF support function. After some inquiries, permission was given for me to visit the NP-3D "support facility," which consisted of a couple of run-down shacks that had no external markings. This was getting weird.

The first guy I met had a USGS polo shirt. USGS? Some form of OGA that I hadn't heard of?

"Hi, I'm Jared Abraham. Welcome to the Afghanistan Airborne Geophysical and Remote Sensing Survey."

"You guys are *geologists?*"

"Yep. We study rocks here."

"Come on: you're spooks, right?"

The science geeks—the physically fit science geeks—manning the equipment in the room all started laughing.

In 2001, when Osama bin Laden started releasing videos to the media, somebody noticed that the rocks that his AKS-74U was leaning against had a distinctive pattern. U.S. Geological Survey scientists were seconded to the intelligence effort since there were only so many places in Afghanistan and Pakistan that had that particular kind of limestone deposit. A scientist named Said Mizad, who had been the director of the Afghanistan Geological Survey (AGS) prior to his enforced departure from the country in 1974, was brought in to help out in the effort.

With the collapse of the Taliban regime, USAID started to look at long-term projects to help invigorate the Afghan economy. One planner, looking for an alternative to poppy production, hit on the idea of assessing Afghanistan's mineral wealth as part of a larger economic study. The problem was, where were the records? Who had the data? In early 2004 USAID funded a project to get that data. Conducting a geophysical assessment of Afghanistan was problematic: it was too dangerous to send scientific teams to do ground surveys, so an aerial survey mission was the way to go. Thus the NP-3D.

But why a U.S. Navy aircraft? Why not a civilian survey aircraft? Mike explained that the MANPADS threat was considered too high for a civilian plane. His NP-3D was equipped with defensive systems like any other military aircraft: ECM (electronic countermeasures), flares, chaff. The Naval Research Laboratory, which essentially controls Scientific Development Squadron One (VXS-1), has access to five NP-3Ds based at Patuxent River Naval Air Station in Maryland. Established in 2004, the squadron's planes participated in Project Magnet, which measures the earth's gravitational fields. The crews have experience operating in extreme environments, like Antarctica. The NP-3Ds are also used for a variety of U.S. Navy scientific projects and are made available to other U.S. government departments, like the USGS.

The VXS-1 detachment at KAF needed some additional personnel, like an intelligence officer and a defensive system specialist. "We didn't need those in Antarctica," Mike Kenny joked. The NP-3D brought several sensor systems to the game. The magnetometer and the gravimeter were used to measure subsurface geology, while the photogrammetric camera handled surficial geology and a hyperspectral imaging sensor looked at surficial minerals. Finally, a Synthetic Aperture Radar tracked surficial geology. What it boiled down to was this: the NP-3D flew over Afghanistan on prearranged routes, and all the sensors were turned on to record. The data was sent back to the detachment and integrated with previous data. Out of all of that, a detailed picture emerged, literally, of the geology of Afghanistan. On occasion the NP-3D was assisted by a U.S. Air Force WB-57, a former strategic recce aircraft that carried an AVIRIS (Airborne Visible Infrared Imaging Spectrometer) hyperspectral imaging sensor and a color infrared photogrammetric system. It occurred to me that these systems might have multiple applications.

So? Why was this important? The survey gave probabilities as to what mineral resources lay underneath the surface. Specifically the survey was looking for the probability that Afghanistan possessed coal, iron, gas, and (melodramatic pause) oil.

There were, clearly, multiple political dimensions to this operation. The reason the survey was low-key is obvious. Those enamored with monocausal deterministic interpretations of U.S. foreign policy could have a field day with this: "U.S. military supporting the oil companies by securing Afghanistan from the Taliban" or some such bullshit. Unfortunately, in the Iraq angst gripping the United States and with deluded people like Linda McQuaig writing things like *It's the Crude, Dude,* this bullshit could stick. The fact that the Soviets exploited Afghanistan for its natural gas and oil up north in the 1980s, of course, would not figure into those sorts of "discussions" or "analyses."

In any event, the staff members painfully explained their concern about how what they were working on could be misunderstood or deliberately misinterpreted. One even told me that there were uniformed personnel, coalition and American, who bought into the resource conspiracy theory and some people had been verbally hassled.

The reality of the situation is, as usual, complex. As part of the capacity-building efforts in Kabul, the Afghanistan Geological Survey was revived with the express purpose of helping Afghans help themselves, to wit: "Goal: That Afghanistan leverages its natural resources in order to build a legal, self-sustaining economy." The Afghanistan Geological Survey essentially contracted the USGS and the U.S. Navy to use the NP-3D to collect data, but it was made clear in the contract that the data collected *belonged* to the Afghan government and that it got to exploit the data before anybody else, including the United States. Furthermore, part of the contract stated that none of the data could be given to private companies; data derived from the NP-3D operation could, later on, but not the raw data. Other U.S. government agencies could use the data for "derivative products"; Canada was also involved because some of the data could be used for tactical purposes and was sent to the Mapping and Charting Establishment. The Afghan government, however, was the intended beneficiary. The staff explained that there was little it could do to prevent elements in the Afghan government from cutting side deals with companies in the future.

The Afghan government allowed Australia and ISAF access to the data, again for tactical purposes, but the British and the World Bank fought and fought against this for their own interests, which somehow worked at cross-purposes to the intent of the USAID program. Yes, it was murky. *Syriana*-like, even. There were other interesting spin-offs. To increase the Afghan treasury, which was in poor shape, the Americans permitted the Afghan government to levy "aircraft taxes" and "landing fees" at KAF for the NP-3D, so that whenever the plane landed and took off, the U.S. government forked over a couple of hundred dollars to the treasury.

I saw nothing untoward when I was dealing with the detachment. The intent was clear: we are here to help Afghanistan, and this is one way to do it. The Afghans need revenue, and this is one way to get it. It is an alternative to poppy. It will put people to work. It will increase the country's technological base. Indeed, the detachment was involved with mentoring their counterparts in the AGS, so that capacity could be built in that quarter too. Most Afghan geologists had been trained by the Soviets and were thirty years out of date when it came to techniques and equipment. The Afghan geologists were old; the young needed to be attracted into the trade, and they needed incentives, like money. The aerial survey required a number of GPS base stations; these were manned with a combination of Afghans and Americans.

I looked at the imagery, but I lacked the technical knowledge to interpret it. With some help, I learned that there was some oil, not world class, but every bit would help feed the Chinese and Indian behemoths who were already craving more, with obvious benefit to Afghanistan. The most important mineral was, however, coal. There was a lot of it, and it was high quality, better than European anthracite. It was located in remote areas, however, and roads would have to be built first. No security, no roads, No roads, no coal. You get the picture.

USAID also used the imagery for what they called "Land Use" purposes. This was, I believe, a euphemism for tracking what percentage of agriculture was used for poppy growing, though mapping data from the aircraft was also used for urban planning.

It was evident that the VXS-1/USGS detachment provided a valuable tool for the construction of a new Afghan state, as long as that tool was not misused by those in Kabul. My confidence in that was not high. In time, China was able to bid sucessfully on accessing the largest copper mine in Afghanistan. Who knows how and where money changed hands? Who really did benefit from that transaction? And how will the revenue from that transaction contribute to building a better Afghanistan? For those wrapped up in American "resource war" conspiracies, ask yourself these questions: how many Chinese aircraft conduct altruistic mineral surveys, and would the Chinese government turn over the information to the host government for its benefit?

south: spin boldak patrol

> Mos Eisley spaceport: You will never find a more wretched hive of scum and villainy. We must be cautious.
>
> —STAR WARS (1977)

Right after the Khakriz gig, I assessed where else I needed to go. I had been east to Maruf, west to Panjwayii, and north to Khakriz. It was time to go south, to Spin Boldak. "Spin B" was a typical border town. The main entre pot to southern Afghanistan from Pakistan, it was rife with corruption: border police skimming, payoffs, kick-backs, gambling. You name it, and it went on in Spin B. A lot of people had an interest in ensuring that Spin B remained an economic twilight zone, like Akwasasne in Canada, or the Cayman Islands for the United States, or Ingushetia for the Russians.

CTF Bayonet, however, had only partial visibility in the district. Technically, it was part of the French JSOA ARES. The French special operations forces the PRT worked with in Maruf had their main operating base in Spin B. As I mentioned earlier, the JSOAs under CJSOTF didn't have a robust Civil Affairs or CIMIC capacity, and the PRT did, so the PRT increased its presence in Spin B to gain an appreciation of the situation and make connections with the local power brokers so that the coalition and the government could facilitate assistance to the region.

A PRT assessment patrol was headed for Spin B, so I tagged along. The patrol was going to make contact with the district chief and the head of the Border Police. On the way back, it would stop in at Takrapol, another area the PRT knew little about.* Sergeant Ken Lockie was the patrol commander; Warrant Officer Gavely led the assessment team. Erin would deal with the district chief.

---

* Incidentally, Takrapol was misidentified by me in *Enduring the Freedom* as "Taktapol."

The intelligence staff had more threat data for Spin B than the other areas I visited owing to the fact that the coalition had a near-continuous presence in the district since 2002. The French ran their own HUMINT in the city and could plug into the CJSOTF intelligence stream. They tracked an increasing number of contacts to the east and northeast of Spin B: this was the enemy infiltrating into Maruf district from Pakistan, trying to avoid Spin B. The route from Kandahar City to Spin B was Highway 4, which at this point was paved about two-thirds of the way. There was an active IED cell operating from a village complex called Rabat, which was on this part of the road. That cell attempted to detonate a VBIED but did themselves in.

There was a second IED cell in Spin B itself: the French FOB was frequently targeted with IEDs and mines. Its QRF had been hit on several occasions as it sortied out by radio-controlled IEDs. The Spin B IED cell was also mastering the art of multiple devices to catch first-responders. Another cell in Spin B used motorcycle hit teams to kill individuals: there had been three attacks against the border police in one month. We were told that we would be the most vulnerable visiting the district chief, one Colonel Rezik. He had a reputation as a good commander. His brother had been killed by the Taliban and he was known to be violently anti-Taliban.* The assessment team might be hit collaterally if somebody took at a shot at him.

The trip to Spin B was relatively comfortable and fast compared to the one to Maruf or Khakriz. The patrol had only five vehicles in it. The paved part of the road was rutted and there were the inevitable speed bumps, but traffic was light heading south. Streams of jingle trucks headed north, however, interspersed with min-vans, min-buses, and Japanese compact cars jammed full of people. The road passed over saddles in the hill ranges. It was Tatooine. Black camels owned by Kuchis grazed under a cool, blue sky. I noticed a field of white rocks for what seemed like kilometers as the top gunners in the turrets got down. "Mines from the Soviet period," the G-Wagon co-driver told me. "It's an obvious choke point that they wanted to control, so there were thousands of mines deployed in a radius to keep the mujahideen away from the positions controlling the choke point. We have to get down in case one goes off." I could see de-miners in the distance. Control of all of these saddles would have been critical back then to ensure that the road stayed open. Any would make a perfect ambush point.

The traffic increased the closer we got to Spin B. We passed through Rabat without incident.

Our first call was to the district chief, Colonel Rezik, and the focus was the security situation. I was reminded of Ricardo Montalban by all the crushed velour

---

* Indeed, I found out later that Rezik stood accused of the mass murder of sixteen people that may or may not have had anything to do with the Taliban.

couches in the large, open room. There was no heat and our breath was barely discernable in the cool air. I asked Rezik what he thought were Spin B's main problems.

"It is family, of course. The same families have members on both sides of the border: some are Afghan, some are Pakistan. We cannot completely control the movement of people. As for the IED attacks, we believe this is Pakistan who is behind them. Why? The Pakistanis don't like us. They want Afghanistan weak and disrupted. They are jealous because of our cooperation with you. They attack the schools and bridges. The Pakistani religious parties don't like the schools, while others don't like the bridges because of trade."

Erin asked him if they were getting night letters.

"Rabat keeps getting them up there. The people in Rabat are scared and frightened. This has been going on for three months now there. Again, this Taliban activity is designed to keep Afghanistan weak. There are some improvements, however. Over one-hundred-thirty-one families have returned from refugee camps to Spin Boldak. They see a future here or they would not have come back."

Rezik explained that the facilitating agency was UNHCR, which had a program to assist "internally displaced persons" or IDPs. This program was suspect by the coalition because of its obvious potential to be exploited as cover for Taliban infiltration into Afghanistan from Pakistan as refugees returned home. There were, incidentally, two IDP camps west of Kandahar: one in Zharey district on Highway 1, and another between Panjwayii town and Kandahar City, again situated right next to the highway. It was possible, the chief conceded, that the IDP camp in Spin B was harboring Taliban infiltrators, but he had no specific information.

Rezik was also concerned about increased reports that the Taliban were forcing people in Spin Boldak district to grow poppy against their will. He met with the governor and the police commanders after Karzai decreed that poppy should be eradicated. The responsibility for eradication was placed on the district commissioners by the provincial government, and it was clear Rezik didn't like it one bit. He favored a program that was supposed to give tractors to areas that agreed to adopt other crops, not intrusive and forcible methods. Erin explained that the PRT wasn't interested in supporting the eradication effort and was interested in assisting with alternative livelihood programs, but she needed better information.

"We pass everything we learn to the Frenchmen," Rezik said. "What they do with it, I don't know. What we need is more equipment. We need better police vehicles so we can increase our visibility with the people. They need to know we exist, that we are legitimate. We need credentials that we can show people. At the same time, we need better border control. People need passes and papers, identification. We have had some success at detecting infiltration but identification would improve that. My police need better communications very badly. I am not concerned about medical issues as much as security. We have a clinic here with doctors and nurses; I need to be able to protect them."

It all reminded me of *Miller's Crossing*, when the Italian mobster played by John Polito gives his soliloquy about "running things."

We made our goodbyes. This was a man who was serious. We didn't get the impression we were being bullshitted. He was open and direct. However, at our next stop, it was Potemkin Village–time again.

The patrol pulled into the back of the police compound. There were several rusting Soviet 76 mm guns in a pile. We noticed that there was a six-wheeled stake-bed truck with a tarpaulin covering something in the back: it was a mounted 23 mm antiaircraft gun. The Chief of Border Police was away, so the elderly major domo ushered us past several scruffy men in grey police uniforms to the meeting room full of couches and low tables. There was a map of Afghanistan on the wall. We were regarded with some suspicion, if not hostility.

A man who I took to be the second in command entered the room. He was different: he had a moustache, not a beard. There was no turban or headdress. He was young, most likely in his early 30s, and looked vaguely Indian. The major domo hovered and it was unnerving.

Warrant Gavely started with a list of prepared questions, interpreted by Aktar. The 2IC went, unsurprisingly right to equipment issues and again, it revolved around communications. He needed more iCom radios. The issue was distance for patrols: if they got into trouble they needed to report in, and right now they could not. Only a few of his checkpoints had iComs, though his mobile patrols had more. Most of their operations on the border amounted to tracking operations, he told us. They followed footprints in the sand. This was why the enemy was infiltrating through Maruf, he said, because of the rocky terrain. Tracking didn't work there.

The nature of border operations in Spin B city was different. They intercepted a lot of things at the main border checkpoint and the smugglers started using side roads, so Gavely had to expand his operations laterally. His people found mines, explosives, IEDs hidden in foodstuffs, weapons. He had no EOD capability and wanted one. The 2IC had a list of things he needed: sat phones, night vision and so on. It was the last bit that interested me: he wanted encrypted radios. Not just any radios, he wanted encrypted ones.

"Why do you need these, specifically?" I asked.

"Our opposite numbers in Pakistan are intercepting our communications and passing on the location of our patrols to the Taliban."

We were shocked at such a blunt admission. Indeed, we noticed that Gavely waited for the major domo to leave the room before giving a more detailed explanation.

"The Pakistani Army supports the border police with interception. We have had some of our border observation posts attacked at night. During the day we follow the tracks and they lead to the Pakistani checkpoint stations and observation posts. We think the Pakistani border police in this region are a rogue operation. They are corrupted by the family connections that are on both sides of the border. Then some of these family connections extend to the Taliban. We know these family connections assist with the evacuation of the Taliban wounded and killed by your forces in Afghanistan to Pakistan for medical care or burial."

Gavely's concern was that the higher levels of his government weren't paying enough attention to the border problems. He didn't think his reports were making it past the provincial level. "Pakistan has a history of aggression against Afghanistan. The coalition needs to beware of their tricks."

"Where exactly is the infiltration taking place? Can you show us on the map?" I asked.

"This is a poor map: let me show you a better one." He sent the major domo on some task that would keep him busy and we went to another room. This one had a white sheet hung over the wall. A bearded man in a rough wool uniform who looked about 80 saluted when we came into the room and pulled down the sheet. Underneath was a hand-drawn (Crayon!) map of the border region from Paktia province to Helmand province. I could see the Durand Line. The map minder, who I found out had been a signals officer in the pre-Soviet era Afghan Army, explained through our interpreter Aktar the various symbols. Each checkpoint and observation post was a castle with flags, and the number of "effectives" at each site was noted. The Border Police area of interest wasn't just the border: the saddles in the hills on Highway 4 were also controlled by them. The border posts had some depth and were not all along the Durand Line proper. Clearly, they were also defensive positions.

"Where are the Taliban infiltration routes?"

The operations officer pointed to the Maruf district where it abutted the border and several locations opposite Helmand province. "This is how they are getting in," he said.

"So how does the opium get out?" I asked.

Silence. Time to move on to another topic. Some more tea, perhaps?

It was time to head back to Kandahar City and we departed Spin B. The trip back was not uneventful: we stopped and went into a defensive crouch near Rabat when the lead vehicle saw two young men on a motorcycle stopped near a culvert. It was a false alarm.

We hit Takhtapol in the late afternoon. Takhtapol boasted what amounted to an Afghan strip mall and truck stop on the side of the road opposite the community center. There appeared to be a lot of new construction going on. Takhtapol was a going concern.

We met the local political leadership and were surprised to find out that Takrapol was in fact a provincial district. It wasn't on our maps as such, but apparently the provincial government determined that Takhtapol was a district. The district chief met with us after he finished praying.

"No problems; everything is going smoothly here," he told Aktar, who for some reason was wearing his sunglasses inside. "I need trucks and iComs (of course!). This is the first contact we have had with the new PRT. Some people were here eight months ago and told us that there would be development aid, but we never heard from them again."

Takhtapol had fallen between the cracks: it wasn't in the French JSOA, and CTF Bayonet didn't even know it was a formal district. The fact that it sat astride Highway 4 and was on a major "saddle" made it geographically important. This was also the place where anti-Taliban operations were mounted in 2001. It was Sherzai territory. The district chief was annoyed, however, and he vented to us.

"We were promised tractors. Dand district got tractors and we haven't. I am also responsible for eighty-two villages, each village has one hundred families. We need schools here, but I have no teachers, no tables, not even chalk. I want my police to attend the RTC." And so on. Water was a big problem: there were thirty-five empty wells, he told us, that were drilled by Pakistani contractors who didn't do the job properly. "We need water for the crops," he said. "We do have a clinic."

He then surprised us with a frank discussion about Takhtapol economics. "Takhtapol people grew poppy and we were quite prosperous here," he said as he waved his arm and indicated the strip mall market and the construction. "The people heard what the new rules were, what Karzai said. They stopped poppy production and wanted to grow wheat. But then the fuel price went up with the fuel tax. The provincial government promised us tractors if we would stop poppy production. So we stop growing poppy, but no tractors showed up. Our people are getting desperate. Some wheat has been grown, but not enough to make money from."

The implication was that this district was aligned with the previous governor and his extended family. When the new governor took over the Sherzais were out of favor, so the people of Takhtapol had no leverage at "court," so to speak, and the bureaucracy still hadn't adjusted to the fact that the new district existed. The chief explained that there was no security problem in Takhtapol . . . but there might be if things didn't get sorted out. Soon.

conclusion: repatriation

As the eyes of the world focus elsewhere, we should not forget that the
experience of Afghanistan is a proving ground for whether the international
community can stay the course beside a fragile country as it builds
itself up from the aftermath of conflict.

—James Wolfensohn, President of the World Bank, 2003

made my way home from Kandahar via Camp Mirage in early January 2006. I
was still processing the details of my third Afghan experience when I went back
to work at Royal Military College and prepared a lecture on PRT and SAT-A
operations. I had dropped in to talk with a staff member.

"Did you see the news this morning? A Canadian civilian from the PRT was
just killed in an IED attack," he informed me.

I felt like I'd been body-slammed. I immediately did a calculation. Erin came
out on the same Herc as me, as she was going on leave. That left either Michael
Callan or Glyn Berry. The images of both men went through my mind. And, of
course, there would be guys from B Company escorting whoever was hit. I'd have
met some of them too at one point or another. Did the Thomb Raider finally get
it? Or Sarah, Dutch, or Keith?

Sketchy details emerged, and then the media reported that Glyn had been
killed in a suicide VBIED attack in Kandahar City. Pictures showing an overturned,
ripped-open G-Wagon were on every media outlet, followed by details of the heroic
efforts of one of the medics, Corporal Paul Franklin, who helped the wounded live
even though his legs were shattered (and later had to be amputated). I had met
Paul on one of the patrols I was on in December.

I immediately returned home and wrote an article explaining what Glyn was
doing and that his death had not been in vain, knowing full well that there would

be questions in the media as to what we were doing in Afghanistan and why it was important. I used the word "assassination" in the article, and I still use the word, even though investigators suggested that it was a random SVBIED and that Glyn couldn't have been deliberately targeted.[1] Mike Capstick gave me the gears in an e-mail after he read the article, but the dictionary defines "assassination" as a killing for political purposes. The convoy was attacked by people who are using violence to change the political direction of Afghanistan. Glyn was killed by this violence. He was killed for political purposes. Therefore, he was assassinated. Enough semantics.

Glyn's assassination had significant effects on the PRT and consequently the coalition effort in Kandahar. The psychological shock in the already jittery Canadian aid departments was profound. The elements in CIDA and FAC who really didn't want Canada engaged in Afghanistan demanded greater security measures that they would have to approve—and they took their time approving them. Michael went on extended personal leave, probably at the behest of CIDA. Erin did not return to Kandahar. The projects that Erin and Glyn were working on ceased, or at the very least went into suspended animation. Michael's Confidence in Government program ground to a halt and would not resume for months—and when it did, it was in a different form. Momentum was not completely lost, however, by the RCMP, the DFID, or USAID, but new security measures had to be implemented, and everything became just a bit more inefficient. An investigation was initiated into possible ISI penetration of the PRT. Could the ISI or elements in it have assisted the Taliban with targeting the PRT? It was entirely possible in that environment. Glyn's assassination was a real coup for the Taliban, let alone the aftereffects it had on the PRT's activities. He was of ambassadorial rank, a high-value target.

One can only speculate what impact the killing had on our Afghan partners in the provincial government. Some of the interpreters started getting night letters. Habib eventually quit working for the PRT when he couldn't get life insurance. That was a real loss, as Habib was one of the best. Another PRT worker found a grenade attached to the door of his house. The Taliban were bold enough to even attack Colonel Tor Jan's compound next door with a drive-by shooting, and a VBIED was found and defused down the street from the PRT gate. There are some who insist that there is no evidence that the PRT was being singled out for enemy action any more than other coalition forces in Kandahar City, that the enemy views all coalition forces as one, that we can't make any conclusions. I disagree. I respect the enemy's analytical capabilities, and I believe that somewhere in their planning cells in Quetta or in Kandahar they recognized the PRT's activities as a threat to them and that someone took steps to degrade its capability.

The PRT would not be back on track for nearly six months. During that time, in the spring and summer of 2006, Regional Command South, and particularly Kandahar province, experienced the greatest level of insurgent violence since 2001. Our own media then indulged in an orgy of criticism, slamming the effort for using "too much violence" and not "doing enough development" and claiming that we were "losing Afghanistan." There were some other detrimental changes unconnected to Glyn's killing. Matthijs Toot would leave DFID and join the Dutch effort in Oruzgan province. The French special operations forces would precipitously pull out of Maruf and head north to Nangarhar and Kunar provinces. American CERP (Commander's Emergency Response Program) money would dry up for a time once the transition was made from the American-led Combined Task Force BAYONET to the multinational CTF AEGIS. I would never find out why Master Corporal Joe Dupuy said, "Roger, confirmed," all the time.

On the plus side, the PRT played an important part in paving the way for the deployment of CTF AEGIS. The information it collected was voluminous, and the penetration it gained in the more remote districts and into the political and social soul of Kandahar province was sizable.

The DDR and HWC programs were major successes and contributed significantly to stabilizing Afghanistan in the uncertain years. The Chessgame, played behind the scenes and coupled with DDR and HWC, was also successful at laying the groundwork so that the 2004 and 2005 elections could take place. The fact that the 2004 national and 2005 provincial elections were held at all, and the fact that there was a large turnout for them, were major successes. Without the Constitutional Loya Jirga and the elections, the international community's tasks in the provinces would have been even more difficult.

The Canadians in SAT-A successfully mentored the Afghan government through the International Monetary Fund (IMF) and World Bank processes, and the Afghanistan Compact was signed in January 2006. This permitted the first tranches of a $10 billion (yes, with a "b") aid package to start flowing for development, though this would be a slow and laborious process with many obstacles at the federal and provincial level. There remains the possibility that the suicide attack campaign in Kandahar conducted in the fall of 2005 was designed in part to influence the IMF and the World Bank not to invest in Afghanistan. If so, that effort failed. The situation in RC North, where the German PRTs were operating, remained stable and continued to be so in 2008.

After some finagling, the Netherlands agreed to deploy to RC South in 2006, despite a stepped-up Taliban terrorism campaign that may have been designed to influence the Dutch parliament and convince it to stay out. Australian and British troop commitments to RC South, made around the same time frame, plus Canadian and American diplomatic efforts, were instrumental in getting the Dutch to join the effort. CTF AEGIS would assist with this deployment using information and insights provided by the PRT.

In 2006 the Taliban and its allies mounted the most significant attack yet on the emergent institutions of Afghanistan and its people. I would return that summer and accompany Task Force ORION and Combined Task Force AEGIS as they took on the insurgents and held the thin red line in RC South. The fight for Afghanistan was on.

Security and development go hand in hand. You can't have one without the other.

notes

part one. the war in afghanistan, 2003–4

1. Jean-Charles Brisard, *Zarqawi: The New Face of Al Qaeda* (New York: Other Press, 2005).
2. Confidential interviews.
3. For the details of the command relationship between CJTF-180 and CTF DEVIL, see Sean M Maloney, *Enduring the Freedom: A Rogue Historian in Afghanistan* (Washington, D.C.: Potomac Books, 2005).
4. Diego A. Ruiz Palmer, "The Road to Kabul," *NATO Review* (Summer 2003): 9–12.
5. Confidential interview.
6. Ibid.
7. For a collection of media articles examining the problems in Bosnia and Kosovo between France and the United States, see http://mprofaca.cro.net/ frspynato.html, specifically Thomas Sancton and Gilles Delaphon, "The Hunt for Karadic," *Time,* 10 August 1998; Charles Truehart, "France Denies Foiling Plans to Arrest Bosnian Serb War-Crimes Suspect Radovan Karadic," *Washington Post,* 24 April 1998.
8. This section is based on a series of in-camera discussions with Canadian and NATO personnel, and on access granted to the author to view certain planning materials.
9. The ISTAR squadron combined electronic warfare, signals intelligence, and Coyote reconaissance assets in one subunit.
10. Interview with Lieutenant General Andrew Leslie, Ottawa, 14 March 2007.
11. Ibid.
12. On matters relating to the Tier I SOF organizations, I have assembled this and the next paragraph from a number of sources, some of which include Headquarters U.S. Marine Corps Intelligence Department, "Mobilization-Current Vacancies," www.hqinet001.hqmc.usmc.mil; DCIPS/IPMO Update

No. 2005-5, "Support to Army's Civilian Human Resource Support Plan," www.dami.army.pentagon.mil; Flynt Leverett, "Events Leading to Iraq Invasion," www.cooperativeresearch.org; exmi.blogspot.com, entry dated 11 November 2005 dealing with the "Sand Pit" facility in Kabul, TF-5, and the OGA; Jim Maceda, "US Downplays al-Qaida Manhunt," 19 April 2004, www. msnbc.com.

13. Ibid.

14. See Anonymous, *Hunting al Qaeda: A Take-No-Prisoners Account of Terror, Adventure, and Disillusionment* (St. Paul, Minn.: Zenith Press, 2005).

15. Interview with MSG Michael Threatt, 20 September 2006, conducted by the Combat Studies Institute Operational Leadership Experiences Program.

16. "Special Operations Medics Respond to Afghanistan School Bombing," Armed Forces Press Service, 30 August 2004.

17. Threatt interview.

18. Briefing to author, CJTF-76, Kabul, December 2004.

19. Pervez Musharraf, *In the Line of Fire: A Memoir* (New York: Free Press, 2006), chap. 25. See also Happymon Jacob, "US-Pakistan Military Operations in Pak-Afghan Border," *Issue Brief* 1, no. 3 (March 2004), www.observerindia. com; Greg Bearup, "US Directing Operations in Pakistan Border Battle," 22 March 2004, www.smh.com.au.

20. Norwegian Refugee Council Internal Displacement Monitoring Centre, *Pakistan: A Profile of the Internal Displacement Situation,* 10 October 2006.

21. Afzai Khan, "Pakistan's Hunt for Al Qaeda in South Waziristan," *Terrorism Monitor* 2, no. 8 (23 April 2004).

22. Confidential interview.

23. Ibid.

24. Ibid.

25. Kenneth Katzman, *CRS Report for Congress: Afghanistan Presidential and Parliamentary Elections,* 8 April 2005.

26. Joint Electoral Management Body fact sheet, "Wolesi Jirga and Provincial Council Elections, Afghanistan, 2005."

27. Katzman, *CRS Report for Congress;* "Afghan Voter Registration Site Attacked," RFE/RL, 6 July 2004; "Taliban Targets Election Workers," RFE/RL, 26 June 2004; "Taliban Targeting Would-be Afghan Voters," RFE/RL, 27 June 2004.

28. Keith A. Milks, "22nd MEU (SOC) Arrives in Afghanistan," *Marine Corps News,* 14 April 2004.

29. Keith A. Milks, "22nd MEU Afghanistan, Recap," *Marine Corps News,* 3 September 2004; Kenneth F. Mackenzie et al., "Marines Deliver in Mountain Storm," *Proceedings,* November 2004.

30. Interview with Major Deitra Koranado conducted by the Combat Studies Institute Operational Leadership Experiences Program.

31. ISAF Briefing, "Afghanistan: Support to Presidential Elections."

32. Katzman, *CRS Report for Congress.*

33. Ibid.

34. The substantial maneuvering vis-à-vis the other presidential contenders is beyond the scope of this study, but it is important. The Chessgame, as discussed later in this section, was an integral part of this process and was designed to keep the Northern Alliance's potential for military intimidation out of the picture as much as possible.

part two. NATO ISAF: kabul, 2004

1. Armored recce squadrons used to have armored soldiers trained for demolition and close-recce tasks. In reorganizations, the "plug-and-play" approach argued that assault troops were not needed and that infantry could do this. This disrupts the integrity of the squadron, according to the Strathconas I talked to, and both the infantry and armored sides resented the enforced situation.

2. I call it that because when we compare what Ms. England and her MP friends did with detainees with what Saddam's Mukhabarat did to their detainees, it is radically different in quality and quantity. Naked humiliation with a bag over your head, or being slowly lowered into an acid tank or wood chipper? You decide which is worse.

3. Edward R. Smith, *Effects Based Operations: Applying Network Centric Warfare in Peace, Crisis, and War* (Washington, D.C.: Department of Defense, 2002), xiv.

4. Indeed, some of the Task Force DEVIL leadership from the 504th Parachute Infantry Regiment and the 82nd Airborne units that I visited in 2003 were transferred to the 25th Infantry Division after its headquarters returned to Hawaii from Afghanistan, presumably to improve things in certain quarters.

5. For more information, see Lieutenant Colonel Exterkate, "NATO's ISR Challenge during ISAF VIII," *Journal of the JAPCC* 3 at www.Japcc.de. According to Exterkate, "Although the LUNA actually never identified any imminent rocket launches, it was generally accepted within the ISAF VIII community that its presence had a deterrent effect." Duncan Campbell believes that the Cold War–era German SIGINT station in China is still active. See "Attack on America," *Guardian,* 15 September 2001.

6. Note that this skittishness started to drop away when the new Chief of Defence Staff took over in 2005. As with everything, it is a leadership issue.

part four. the war in afghanistan, 2005

1. See http://www.setaf.army.mil.
2. Ibid; James F. Gebhardt, *Eyes Behind the Lines: IS Army Long-Range Reconnaissance and Surveillance Units*, Global War on Terrorism Occasional Paper 10, Combat Studies Institute Press.
3. Rich Mattingly, "Marines Track Down Insurgents in Afghan Valley," Armed Forces Press Service, 3 January 2005.
4. Rick Scavetta, "Marines Return to Tora Bora for Operation CELTICS," Armed Forces Press Service, 31 May 2005; Rich Mattingly, "Operation MAVERICKS Captures Suspected Terrorists," *Defend America News*, 5 April 2005; Rich Mattingly "Operation SPURS," *Defend America News*, 7 February 2005.
5. Stephanie L. Carl, "Operation ENDGAME," *Defend America News*, 1 April 2005.
6. "SOCCENT Warrior: Leading the Fight in the Hot Spots: Iraq, Afghanistan, and the Horn of Africa," *Special Operations Technology* 4, no. 2 (2006), online edition.
7. "Letter Shares Fate of Destroyed SEAL Team in Afghanistan," 23 August 2005, www.military.com.
8. Tony Allen-Mills, "Downed US SEALS May Have Got Too Close to Bin Laden," *Sunday Times*, 10 July 2005.
9. "SAS's $100m Mission to Fight Extremists," (AAP) *Sydney Morning Herald*, 13 July 2005.
10. Transcript, "SOCAUST Media Briefing Post-Op SLIPPER," 27 September 2006.
11. Ibid.
12. Netherlands Ministry of Defence study, *Evaluatie: Nederlandse Special Forces Taakgroep in Operatie Enduring Freedom April 2005-April 2006* (n.d.).
13. KSK stands for Kommando Spezialkräfte, or "Special Operations Command," but the virulent German left, protesting German involvement in Afghanistan, called them "Kommando SpetzialKillers."
14. The KSK, apparently, was drinking too much for the likes of the 25th ID commander, who politely told them in a letter that their services were no longer required.
15. Charlie Coon, "Special Forces Soldier Receives German Medal," *Stars and Stripes*, 14 September 2006.
16. Deryk Cheng, "NZ SAS Eyed for Afghan Mission," *New Zealand Herald*, 16 November 2005, NZHerald.co.nz.
17. Interview with SFC Donald Grambusch, 25 July 2006, conducted by the Combat Studies Institute Operational Leadership Experiences Program.

18. CTF BAYONET briefing to the author, Kandahar, December 2005.

19. In-camera discussions with CTF BAYONET personnel, Kandahar, December 2005.

20. Jon H. Arguello, "Paratroopers Deal Blow to Taliban in Remote Valley," *Defend America News,* 10 May 2005.

21. CTF BAYONET briefing.

22. Jon Arguello, "New Hospital Symbolizes Afghan Progress in South," American Forces Press Service, 26 January 2006; "US Soldiers, Afghans Complete Road Project," CFC-A Public Affairs, 10 January 2006.

23. CTF BAYONET briefing.

24. Jacob Caldwell, "Operation DIABLO REACH BACK Targets Militia," *Defend America News,* 28 June 2005; Jacob Caldwell, "DIABLO REACH BACK," CTF BAYONET Public Affairs, 18 July 2005; Jacob Caldwell, "Fighting Afghanistan's Taliban," *Soldiers Magazine,* October 2005.

25. "3-319 AFAR TF GUN DEVILS: Providing FA Fires for Afghanistan and Maneuvering on the Enemy," *FA Journal,* 1 September 2006.

26. Elaine Hunnicutt, "Coalition Delivers Aid to Ghor Province," *Defend America News,* 28 February 2005.

27. "Letter Shares Fate of Destroyed SEAL Team in Afghanistan," 23 August 2005, www.military.com.

28. This section is based on a series of in-camera discussions with Canadian and NATO personnel, and on access granted to the author to view certain written planning materials.

29. *Joint Election Management Body Final Report-Afghan Elections 2005,* 1–2.

30. *Freedom Watch,* 10 October 2005.

31. ISAF News Release, 3 April 2005 and 12 July 2005.

32. ISAF News Release, 8 August 2005.

33. *Romanian Military Newsletter,* 26 January, 2006, http://www.mapn.ro/newsletter.

34. Mike Pryor, "82nd Airborne Unit to Bolster Election Security," *Defend America News,* 8 August 2005; Mike Pryor, "Red Falcons Ensure Violence-Free Election."

35. Strategic Advisory Team–Afghanistan, "An Assessment of the 18 September Election Results," 3 November 2005.

36. Ibid.

part five. the strategic advisory team–afghanistan: kabul, 2005

1. NDHQ, like Canada, is a no-smoking country.

2. Elizabeth castigated me for referring to her in this fashion in an article. I'm making amends.

3. On the origins of CJCMOTF, see Sean M. Maloney, *Enduring the Freedom: A Rogue Historian in Afghanistan* (Washington, D.C.: Potomac Books, 2005).

4. Sam the Eagle was a character on *The Muppet Show*. Yes, I'm serious.

part six. the canadian PRT: kandahar, 2005

1. See Sean M. Maloney, *Enduring the Freedom: A Rogue Historian in Afghanistan* (Washington, D.C.: Potomac Books, 2005).

2. Roto 0 is the first unit to deploy on a Canadian operation: following rotations are called Roto 1, Roto 2, etc.

3. See Maloney, *Enduring the Freedom*.

4. A tip of the hat to author Clive Cussler's descriptions of his character Al Giordino.

5. The categorization of injuries is Priority 1 through 3, 1 being the worst.

6. This is a reference to their body armor, which is restrictive and can make it difficult to move around in the cupola of the G-Wagon.

conclusion: repatriation

1. I disagree with this conclusion, by the way.

index

about the author

Dr. Sean M. Maloney is the Historical Advisor to the Chief of the Land Staff and is an Associate Professor of History at Royal Military College of Canada. He served in Germany as the historian for 4 Canadian Mechanized Brigade, Canada's Cold War NATO commitment in Europe. The author of nine books—including the controversial *Canada and UN Peacekeeping: Cold War by Other Means* and *Learning to Love the Bomb: Canadian Nuclear Weapons and the Cold War*—Dr. Maloney also has extensive research experience in the Balkans, Middle East, and particularly in Afghanistan, where he has observed counterinsurgency operations in the field since 2003.